UNITED
AND
UNITING

UNITED
AND
UNITING

The Meaning of an
Ecclesial Journey

Louis H. Gunnemann

UNITED CHURCH PRESS
CLEVELAND, OHIO

Scripture quotations are from the *Revised Standard Version of the
Bible,* copyright 1946, 1952, and © 1971, 1973 by the Division of
Christian Education, National Council of Churches, and are used by
permission.

Library of Congress Cataloging-in-Publication Data

Gunnemann, Louis H.
  United and uniting.

  Bibliography: p. 186.
  Includes index.
  1. United Church of Christ—Relations.   2. United
churches—United States—Relations.   3. Ecumenical
movement—United Church of Christ.   I. Title.
BX9885.G86   1987   285.8′34   87-14718
ISBN 0-8298-0757-8 (pbk.)

United Church Press, Cleveland, Ohio 44115

————— To the Members of the United Church of Christ, —————
Who Cherish the Gift of Unity in Christ and
Give Themselves to the Ministry of Reconciliation

CONTENTS

PREFACE

The plan for this book had its inception in the convergence of three sets of circumstances. With the approach of the thirtieth anniversary in 1987 of the birth of the United Church of Christ, an opportunity seemed to be presented for completing some work I had begun several years ago on matters of polity and organization. Of greater significance, however, was the growing awareness that the third decade of UCC life and mission stands in marked contrast to the first two decades, which I had sought to interpret in *The Shaping of the United Church of Christ* in 1977. The interaction of organizational development and radical social change had dominated the first two decades. How were third decade developments to be understood? That question led me, then, to begin an assessment of the meaning of the whole UCC ecclesial journey, but with special reference to the formative influence of the ecumenical movement exhibited in the ecumenical events of the 1980s.

In late 1984 these concerns and reflections were brought into a new focus by a request from the UCC/EKU Working Group. This group, sponsored by the United Church Board for World Ministries, had been involved in the development of the "Full Communion" covenant between the United Church of Christ and the Evangelical Church of the Union (EKU) of the German Democratic Republic and the Federal Republic of Germany. The Working Group, recognizing the special aspects of UCC history related to the "full communion" relationship voted in 1981 by General Synod XIII, asked me to give assistance in recording and interpreting the story. As I began research into that relationship it became clear that the story was a most significant aspect of the UCC ecclesial journey in its ecumenical context. Placing it in that context allowed me to bring together in this account the reflections and concerns about the UCC as it moves beyond the first three decades of its mission.

As I write these words the import of the critical world events of the past two years underlines my own sense of the urgent tasks before the United Church of Christ. Setting our house in order for a more faithful and vigorous sharing of responsibility in the whole ecumenical community for the cause of justice, peace, and reconciliation is the immediate and pressing task I want to encourage.

Although I take responsibility for the content of this book, it will surely be clear to any reader that many persons have contributed significantly. I am deeply indebted to Frederick Herzog, M. Douglas Meeks, Max L. Stackhouse, and Frederick R. Trost, who served as reader-consultants throughout the project and without whose wisdom and encouragement much would have been omitted, and that indebtedness extends to my son Jon P. Gunnemann, and to Virginia H. Child for their reviews of the manuscript. Interviews with Ruben H. Huenemann, Peter J. Meister, Howard Schomer, and Harold Wilke were especially helpful in the work on the UCC/EKU relationship. In this connection it is gratifying to acknowledge the support given by the United Church Board for World Ministries, through Kenneth R. Ziebell, as an expression of its ecumenical commitment. President Avery D. Post gave extensive time in interviews and made available especially important documents and records.

Every writer depends heavily on libraries and their staff. I wish especially to express gratitude to Ms. Florence Bricker, archivist, and Ms. Elizabeth K. Sanders, researcher/cataloger, of the Lancaster Central Archives, Lancaster, Pennsylvania; Dr. Harold Worthley of the Congregational Library in Boston; Dr. Lowell H. Zuck, archivist for the Evangelical Synod records at Eden Theological Seminary, St. Louis, Missouri; and Dr. Arthur L. Merrill, Director of Library Services, and Ms. Sue Ebbers, librarian, at United Theological Seminary, New Brighton, Minnesota.

It is not possible to name all those throughout the United Church of Christ who have encouraged me in this project. Their interest and support is gratefully acknowledged.

As in other cases, it has been a special privilege to work with Ms. Marion M. Meyer, senior editor of United Church Press/The Pilgrim Press. Her skill and counsel are reflected throughout the book.

For many years and on many projects my wife, Johanna Menke Gunnemann, and I have worked as a team. Her skill at the typewriter is eclipsed for me by her understanding of the faith and her insights concerning the church. Together we have "breathed and lived" this book. It could not have been written without her love, commitment, and understanding.

"Historians generally illustrate rather than correct the ideas of the communities in which they live and work."[1] This perceptive comment by historian-philosopher Arnold J. Toynbee serves as an appropriate description of what I am seeking to do in this book. The community of faith that was named the United Church of Christ in 1957 has exhibited from the very beginning some singularly formative ecclesial ideas, expressed in the intention to be a *united* and *uniting church*. In their original form and meaning those foundational ideas may need no correction. From time to time, however, they need to be *illustrated* in the context of their ongoing expression and development. The task of the historian, then, is to identify and interpret—to illustrate—the historical context in ways that call for and encourage a recovery of the original vision. In that experience there can be a self-corrective process, providing subsequent generations with a vision both tested and clarified.

This book is an invitation to readers to join in a recovery of the vision and, at the same time, to allow it to correct, through historical perspective, their own understanding of the United Church of Christ. There is, of course, no single history of any community or institution that is self-explanatory. *It is the thesis of this book that the needed perspectives for a fresh and renewed understanding of the vision that created the United Church of Christ are framed by the history of the modern ecumenical movement.*

The urgency of such renewed understanding is apparent at every level of the church's life. A persistent thread of self-questioning (who are we?) runs through many discussions and publications of the past decade of UCC history.[2] In every assembly of the General Synod, as well as in many Conference annual meetings, the same self-questioning underlies debates and decisions. To some extent this may be due to the fact that the UCC organizational structure has features quite unlike those prevailing generally in Protestantism. As a community of faith seeking to be a new form of the church for a new time, we entered uncharted territory in ecclesial understanding and organization. As others have acknowledged, the UCC "represents a special development in church history."[3] This has required new learnings all along the way.

However, some of the questioning reflects a widespread malaise about the church, particularly in its denominational form. Publications from almost all "mainline" churches exhibit similar uncertainties and questionings about the church's future.[4] "Who are we?" is a question arising not only from confusion and uncertainty, which is characteristic of unsettled times, but also, especially in the United Church of Christ, from the absence of a common language of faith by which the community of faith is identified as church.* That deficiency is a heavy burden in a community where diversity, although often cherished, is too easily offered as an excuse for avoiding common theological language or definitive confessions of faith. The condition reflects the pluralism of the culture, of course. But we have been slow in learning the painful lesson that "as the church loses its common theological tongue, it loses its ability not only to speak as a church but to *understand itself as church*."[5]

The negative influence of pluralism on the language of faith and theology, however, is exacerbated in the United Church of Christ by another condition, also shared by other church bodies but rooted in the special circumstances of our spiritual and cultural ancestry. The reality that the UCC has never developed a common language of faith and theology derives, in part at least, from what many observers have noted as the tendency toward "historical amnesia" in the church and the culture generally. Historical amnesia essentially destroys the ability to "own one's history" in a way that gives depth to present existence. As many have noted, "The sense of historical discontinuity is the blight of our society."[6] The effects of that blight are heightened by a tendency to be highly selective in any reference to history, choosing only that which supports certain values. The tendency is encouraged by the daunting complexity of the diverse

---

*A common language of faith can serve as a means of identity only when it is "catholic" (universal) in its derivation and expression. This will be discussed at length in the concluding chapters of this book.

strands of UCC history. To the extent that historical selectivity prevails, the foundations of a common language of faith are eroded. Historical amnesia destroys both communication and community, making the question, "who are we?" a plaintive and bewildered cry.

Self-questioning, confusion, and the absence of a common language of faith gives rise to the parallel question addressed to us by others: "Who are you?" The question of identity is disconcerting on two levels. In what might crassly be called "the marketplace of religion" where, unfortunately, the average church member is forced to locate, church identity has social as well as religious importance. The need at this time, however, is not primarily social; it is essentially a matter of faith identity. It has existential significance; and to those whose concern it is to be faithful it is necessary to be able to identify individual faith confession in relation to the church in its apostolic, evangelical, and catholic traditions.[7] "Who are you?" is a referential question, implying the need for witnesses, those given only in community. Its reality rests on a corporate, not a private or individual, confession of faith. Corporate confession of ecclesial identity requires a common language of faith, clearly consonant with the gospel.

In quite another context, and at this stage in the church's life equally critical, the question "who are you?" can be embarrassing as well as disconcerting. In ecumenical circles the question is seriously raised: Is the United Church of Christ really a church?[8] Here again, the absence of a common language of faith, especially that which relates to the gospel in unequivocal terms, to the sacraments, and to the ministry, is a heavy liability. *In ecumenical relationships historical amnesia is seen as more than a human failing of memory; it is regarded, justifiably or not, as a lapse in faithfulness to the gospel.* In any case, what is at stake is the credibility of the United Church of Christ as church.

That, in turn, has raised the question of accountability to a new level of urgency. To whom are we accountable in the claim to be a united and uniting church? Certainly first to Christ, the head, as the apostle Paul makes clear in 1 Corinthians 12 and Ephesians 4. It is clear, however, that in both lines of his argument the apostle correlates accountability to Christ with accountability to other members of the body that is the church. The UCC cannot avoid its responsibility to the "one church" that is Christ's risen body in the world.

5

It is more than a matter of being charitable to say that no one is intentionally being irresponsible in this matter; it is, rather, a matter of *acknowledging that learning to be accountable to Christ and Christ's body requires a radical transformation for which many of us may not be ready.* For that reason, recovering and reclaiming the original vision is of utmost importance. Placing that vision in the frame of ecumenical history leads to critical clarity about its claims on us today.

The interweaving of that history with the United Church of Christ experience in being a united church requires attention to details easily overlooked. Four quite obvious points can be made in support of this thesis.

First, recovery of the vision is inevitably accompanied by a new appreciation *of foundations that are not of our own making but upon which we have been privileged to build.* Ecumenical developments of the past two decades in particular have expanded our understanding of the distinctive aspects of the UCC ecumenical vocation. Appreciation of these aspects is a counterforce to the persistent malaise experienced by many in the more difficult periods of the past thirty years.

Second, *the need to be understood as well as to understand ourselves as Christ's church requires that we acknowledge and accept that history* with gratitude and critical honesty. Such honesty is needed simply because history is always a "construct" that enables the grasp of reality. To own one's history is to engage in the repentance from which gratitude springs. When the experience of owning one's history generates gratitude, we can more fully appreciate that "history is never simply 'back there,' it is the depth dimension of our present . . . , a venture in self-understanding."[9]

Third, the historical context provided by the ecumenical movement *keeps our perspectives of understanding in a universal, wholistic framework* that counters the new parochialism in American church life. Parochialism in church life has always been a persistent distortion, exhibited in exclusivistic congregationalism* and denominationalism. Its resurgence in this time is in large part a

---

*This term is used as formulated by the Consultation on Church Union to identify the attitude that the church is defined only in enclaves of local gatherings. It does not refer to a polity system.

6

reaction to the confusion and rootlessness of religious pluralism, and parallels an increasing tribalism in society. When security is sought by substituting loyalties to "lesser lords"—whether in persons, ideologies, or value systems—loyalty to Christ is undercut. By offering cultic intimacy and an immediate private experience of belonging, exclusivistic congregationalism isolates persons from the totality of human experience. In so doing it destroys accountability. Ecumenical vision and commitment provide the countervailing energies to that distortion.

Fourth, the framework of understanding gained from the modern ecumenical movement yields *critically important perspectives on the place of the church in the fulfillment of God's mission in the world.* The ecumenical era marks radical changes in ecclesial self-understanding in which the accents fall on the divine intention for the church rather than upon definitions of the "true" church. Although the call for a new orientation of ecclesial self-understanding has been the focus of much of the ecumenical effort, change has come slowly. As will be shown in the development of the theme of this book, the formation of the United Church of Christ was an explicit attempt to give expression to that new orientation. In that respect, the UCC represents a testing of the vision, and its experience reveals the problems and pitfalls, the failures and deficiencies, the struggles and defeats in any such effort. Overcoming the centuries-old habits of ecclesial differentiation while at the same time confronting the challenges of an increasingly hostile society, became an all-consuming enterprise which, because of its complexity, is little understood among us.

To see the vision in the grandeur of its promise is one thing. To accept the claims thereby made on us is another. The vision and the claim require an honest facing of the question: Have we been, and are we now being, responsible? What is at stake is not the existence of the United Church of Christ, that is its survival, but faithfulness. In the *Basis of Union,* by which we were brought into being, we declared a readiness "to die, if need be, as a denomination" for the sake of *the church* in its oneness. That readiness includes the willingness to be claimed and empowered for God's reconciling mission in the world, for living in God's *oikumene.*

1

Introduction to a Journey Undertaken

The story of the United Church of Christ represents the undertaking of a journey in ecclesial formation. That journey had its inception in the rising ecumenical concerns of Western Christendom in the mid-twentieth century. The first three decades of UCC history, from 1957 to 1987, are intimately interwoven with the course of modern ecumenical development. This may be claimed in some degree, of course, for all church bodies involved in ecumenical concerns. At the same time, this perspective is definitive for the United Church of Christ, for the union that produced it has its major sources in the common ecumenical tradition which is the mark of twentieth-century Christianity. In 1963, six years after the union, one observer claimed: "[The] ecumenical spirit remains the *major force,* the center of attention, that makes the United Church cohere, that directs its future."[1] Can the same claim be made now, thirty years later?

To employ the ecumenical heritage as a primary means of interpreting the meaning of UCC history is to be responsible to the original vision that gave birth to this church body. That vision, as set forth in the *Basis of Union* and interpreted in the Constitution and Bylaws, has been summarized frequently in the phrase "united and uniting." Those words are expressive of *being* and of *purpose,* of something achieved and something always to be sought. In the briefest possible fashion they tell us who we are and what we are about. They express both identity and vocation. At the same time, the brevity and terseness of the phrases require interpretation. *United* as identity, and *uniting* as vocation have meaning that derives from two major sources: first, the imperative and character of Christian unity as interpreted in the New Testament; and, second, the story of modern ecumenism in which the imperative of Christian unity has gained new significance in a fragmented world.

In the following pages I shall draw on both sources to discover and interpret the meaning of the ecclesial journey that began in 1957. For the Evangelical and Reformed and the Congregational Christian people, the union of their church bodies was understood as a faith response to the prayer of the Christ "that all may be one." As a people of the biblical tradition, that faith response was to God's call to leave the security of time-tested understandings and habits of church life and to venture into uncharted territory.[2] It was a call to be united and uniting with a clear conviction that church union was a crucially important step toward the realization of Christian unity. It was a call to a journey in which the requisite organizational form of the church would in itself become an instrument of growing unity. Ecclesial formation—that is, the shaping of the visible form of the church—was a fundamental aim of the journey, requiring a continual commitment to look beyond organizational formation to the unity of the spirit that is God's gift to the church. Ecclesial formation became, then, the ecumenical vocation of the new United Church of Christ, a calling with requirements and claims beyond the experience of those who had been claimed by the vision. Those requirements and claims unfolded steadily throughout the journey.

The realization that union achieved is not in itself unity, however, comes slowly and somewhat painfully as the church seeks to respond in faithfulness to God's call. At the same time, union consummated and unity sought in hope and trust have provided essential elements of vision and courage for the journey. A people on a journey live "between memory and hope," as Charles Shelby Rooks once so helpfully expressed it.[3] As in all meaningful journeys, memory and hope are among the resources from which continuity and purpose may be drawn for travelers of succeeding generations. Memory and hope are the source of renewal and strength that God gives the community of faith for difficult times on the journey.

In the case of the United Church of Christ, memory and hope characterize the special heritage received from the mothers and fathers of the Congregational Christian and Evangelical and Reformed communions. For those church bodies had long histories of journeys, with beginnings in England and on the Continent of Europe dating back to the sixteenth century. In their journeys the memory of the graciousness and faithfulness of God, who had led

10

them to the new world, gave them hope for the continuing journey of faith. Those journeys merged in the mid-twentieth century, despite diverse beginnings and radically different experiences, not by human design but by the dominant and ever-present conviction that the unity of the church is God's instrument for the unity of humankind. In the brightness of the ecumenical vision of that time, differences were subordinated to the joyful and reassuring discovery of a common tradition. That tradition had emerged in fuller vigor as the church's responsibility for healing and reconciliation in a fragmented world became clear.

It was characteristic, then, for these two communions to be caught up in the growing ecumenical activity of the period from 1910 to 1960. As ecumenical fervor and vision increased they were at the forefront, giving leadership that eventuated in the founding of the World Council of Churches in 1948.[4] In that movement a venture in ecclesial formation was a time of learning and testing, not only for the UCC but also for other churches seeking ways to realize the ecumenical vision. Clarity of vision is one thing; finding ways to respond to it is another. As on any journey, every purposeful step opens new vistas and introduces new conditions. For the UCC the new vistas and new conditions included not only an inspiring and ever-expanding ecumenical consciousness, but also painful and traumatic experiences in societal responsibilities. Moreover, it soon became a time of wrestling with the meaning of the gospel of God in a world radically different from the biblical world in which the models of the faith are so memorably exhibited. For that reason every turn in the journey was challenging and demanding; new learnings had to be matched by new commitments.

For the United Church of Christ the matching of new learnings with new commitments was complicated by the gradual realization that church union is a limited way of expressing unity. Christian unity was indeed a powerful vision, and church union was seen as a means of realizing the vision. In the first decades of the ecumenical movement, that seemed for many to be a settled matter. Moreover, it appeared to be confirmed by the relatively impressive number of unions accomplished in the first half of this century. By the end of the 1960s the UCC was only one of more than two dozen unions of denominational bodies in the United States. Worldwide, there were equally as many formations of union or united churches. In many respects all these drew their vision and energy from the efforts of the Life and Work and the Faith and Order Conferences which, in the first half of this century, gave the ecumenical movement its substance and strength. However, by the time of the founding of the UCC in 1957, the ecumenical vision had undergone considerable change, gaining new perspectives on the requirements of Christian unity. These looked beyond the uniting of separate organizations. The overwhelming sense of endangered human existence that emerged from two World Wars and other disastrous conflicts raised many existential questions for the worldwide Christian community. Church unions, important as they might be in many circumstances, seemed to have little to offer the increasingly fragmented world in its growing despair.

Within the first decade of the United Church of Christ's ecclesial journey this reality brought about a shift in the focus of attention and the expenditure of energy, as the church in the late '60s sought to be responsible to the claims of a disrupted and despairing society.[5] New conditions called for a regrouping of the company of travelers. The ecumenical spirit, to which Robert Spike referred, appeared to give way to what seemed to many to be a new center of attention, a new major force in ecclesial formation. But was it new? As will be shown later in this book, the shift of attention and energies was away from being united and uniting, to *service* in God's *oikumene* as an expression of the ecumenical vocation. What, then, was happening to the ecclesial journey undertaken so courageously in 1957?

By the early 1970s being *united* was no longer the compelling identity for many UCC people, and serving as a *uniting* church seemed to some to lack relevance as a vocation in a despairing world whose victims of hopelessness were at the very doorsteps of the church. In such circumstances, how does one "explain" the United Church of Christ? That became a question not only when seeking to interpret the church to outsiders; it was an even more compelling question for those who had long been deeply involved in its life. For the latter group it was not simply a matter of *identity* but of *authenticity* as church. Indeed, identity and authenticity are the interrelated aspects of the self-understanding that is the very essence of the shared bonds of the community of faith. Paul S. Minear has underlined the cruciality of self-understanding in *Images of the Church in the New Testament,* where he writes:

The Church's self-understanding, its inner cohesion, its esprit de corps, derive from a dominant image of itself, even though that image remains inarticulately imbedded in subconscious strata. If an inauthentic image dominates its consciousness, there will first be subtle signs of malaise, followed by more overt tokens of deterioration. If an authentic image is recognized at the verbal level, but denied in practice, there will also follow sure disintegration of the ligaments of corporate life.[6]

Those who were deeply involved in the church's life in the '70s can attest to the "subtle signs of malaise" and even to some "disintegration of the ligaments of corporate life." It was a time of intensive questioning and soul-searching, and for some a time of fearful doubt. The realization that unity involved much more than the combining of two venerable church traditions required re-evaluation. The social crises of the 1960s exposed the reality of divisive social problems in the life of the church itself. Injustice and oppression of persons of other races, of minorities, of either sex— expressed in both overt and covert forms in the church's life—could not be denied. Disunity in the church was as much a result of social divisions as of theological differences. In every General Synod from 1969 through at least 1979 debates tended to be heated as groups and individuals sought ways to come to terms with new and trying circumstances. The unity celebrated in faith and hope in the first decade of the UCC seemed illusory to some, while for others the ecumenical vision lost its brilliance.[7] A learning as profound as frightening, which came to many in that time, is that from a human standpoint the life of the church is exceedingly fragile.

As trying as such times may be they are also, by God's grace, often salutary. From the perspective available at the end of the third decade of this ecclesial journey, it is certainly possible to point to the beginnings of new and revised perceptions of the original vision at the very time when "subtle signs of malaise" were becoming more visible. The turning point in the journey came at General Synod IX, meeting in St. Louis, June 22–26, 1973. In the records of that meeting there is remarkable evidence of the recapturing of the original vision even while literally burdened with the responsibilities thrust upon the church by tumultuous social change.

In all respects the tone of that Synod's deliberations was set by President Robert V. Moss in his opening address, "A Message for the Pilgrims." To a community of people on an ecclesial journey, that message served to link the current burdening tasks and responsibilities of a pilgrim people of the Reformed tradition with a new perception of both the beginnings of the journey and its goal in Christian unity. That message prepared the way for Synod action on a resolution submitted initially by the Commission on Christian Unity and Ecumenical Study and Service, titled "The Ecumenical Stance of the United Church of Christ."[8]

This affirmation of the church's ecumenical stance gave clarification to the meaning of the vocation of the United Church of Christ in the context of new ecumenical circumstances and developments. Acknowledging the cost, the affirmation claimed: "Ecumenicity is not an option for us; rather it is a mandate that prohibits a restrictive view that would separate mission from unity, or unity from mission. . . . The goal is the union of the church and the union of creation, and mission and unity are processes to be followed."[9]

Stating the church's ecumenical stance in this way had the effect of focusing attention on the original vision and vocation. It was a salutary occasion in every way, engendering a new sense of responsibility not only in ecumenical matters but with respect to the church's self-understanding in mission as well. Signs of renewal were made visible. Memories of fractious debates, of misunderstandings and of dissatisfactions were mellowed in the experience of a renewed sense of vocation. Such renewal did not come without struggle. It involved not only the effort to press on into new discoveries but also a continual reassessment of old images and new perceptions. In that process the journey between memory and hope often required painful honesty. Only then was it possible to distinguish between authentic and inauthentic images for the sake of making necessary new commitments.

Renewal of ecumenical vision did not, however, reach deeply into the work and mission of local churches. The major changes were reflected in greater clarity about the intentions of the UCC for those with specific responsibilities in ecumenical relationships. Some structural changes seemed to be required for more intentional implementation of the ecumenical stance. The Commission on Christian Unity and Ecumenical Study and Service had urged this strongly in its 1973 report to the General Synod. It was a crucial time in UCC involvement in the Consultation on Church Union, requiring input far beyond the limited resources available to the Commission.* In consequence of the newly articulated ecumenical stance and of the Commission's concern for effective implementation of the same, General Synod X, in 1975, established the Council for Ecumenism to "serve in advisory capacity to the President (as chief ecumenical officer of the church) . . . and assist in preparing ecumenical policies . . . [and] in keeping the commitment of the United Church of Christ as a united and uniting church before its membership and its fellow denominations."[10] This step, which eliminated the Commission on Christian Unity and Ecumenical Study and Service, was designed to give the UCC greater organizational effectiveness in ecumenical matters. All this was part of a significant "turning the corner" in the fulfillment of the ecumenical vocation of the UCC on its ecclesial journey.

To experience unity in spirit as well as in body became an increasing concern. As a company of God's people on a journey, a sense of unity, of being truly united, is of major importance. For many persons the substance of the image of unity is rarely expressed in classic faith terms, such as "oneness in Christ." Rather, unity is imaged for them in experiential terms that express shared memories and hopes, disappointments, and achievements. For some persons that meant the experience of stable procedures, time-tested organization, confident reliance upon precedent, and goals identified and accomplished. For others the experience of unity is more an affective matter, a sense of community, and a sense of the power of the Spirit overcoming differences. These two approaches to the experience of unity were tested repeatedly in the '70s and '80s. At every turn in the journey there inevitably were different responses. The experience of being *united* was often in tension with the calling to be a *uniting* church. For many persons, to be united in community and organization required a settledness of understandings and uniform practices. If, at the same time, the church seeks to be involved in ongoing efforts to unite with others—to be uniting—settledness and community are threatened. Hence the tension that subtly inhibits the extension of the forms of unity.

---

*David G. Colwell, who served as chairperson of the Commission, also chaired the Consultation on Church Union for one term.

As partners who had pledged themselves to be "one body" on the journey of unity, Congregational Christian and Evangelical and Reformed people brought with them habits and attitudes, practices and assumptions which, in the first decades, provided essential self-understanding in the common enterprise. Continuity in self-understanding, in local congregations especially, is dependent on respect for the traditions in which they have been nurtured. Article IV, paragraph 11, of the Constitution clearly affirmed and assured such respect: "Congregational Christian churches and the Evangelical and Reformed Church unite in the United Church of Christ without break in their respective historic continuities and traditions." The maintenance of such continuities in local churches, of course, is rarely a problem except in highly transient communities. In fact, it is in the local church that the experience of being *united* and *uniting* has been remote and somewhat unreal. In the absence of opportunity and intentional effort, that experience has been denied in many local churches that continue to be identified solely by their original Congregational Christian or Evangelical and Reformed name. A persistent and subtle parochialism easily enshrines old habits and perspectives, extending their influence into succeeding generations.

The problem of continuity appears in a quite different and more critical form in the organization and functioning of Associations, Conferences, the General Synod, and some national-level bodies. In all these, to be *united* and *uniting* is both the responsibility and the objective for which the Constitution and Bylaws were designed and adopted. That instrument serves as the "covenant" by which the United Church of Christ knows itself and is guided on its ecclesial journey as a united and uniting people. Assurance and commitment to continuity are at the heart of this instrumental covenant—"without break in their respective historic continuities and traditions." This has been an exceptionally difficult obligation to meet within the structures by which local churches are incorporated into the UCC.

One of the important, and sometimes discouraging, learnings on that journey has been that unexamined attitudes and assumptions can become burdensome and encumbering "baggage." The periodic abandonment of unnecessary baggage is as important for God's people on their ecclesial journey as it is for any traveler who has long distances to cover. The impedimenta of ecclesiastical habits add disproportionate and often destructive weight to otherwise meaningful and important traditions. Unexamined assumptions and habits of thought and action often lead to paralyzing idolatry or to evasive rationalization. In principle, the discarding of unnecessary and inhibiting ecclesiastical impedimenta would be expected as new generations emerge. But here, too, old habits and perspectives may be enshrined and regarded as inviolable. They become impedimenta, not because they are invalid or even unusable, but because they are so easily inappropriately used. A people on a journey cannot afford baggage that is inappropriate to the conditions of travel.[11]

At the same time, new habits and new perspectives appropriate for the journey are dependent on the "historic continuities and traditions" in ways that are not only important but also potentially enriching. The task of learning how to use them requires time and attention, which are often at a premium on a journey. Giving new content to traditional words and phrases cannot be left to mere circumstance. Intentional and critical reflection is needed, for example, to make such cherished terms as freedom, order, autonomy, confessions, and liturgy, appropriate to the emerging new circumstances of the journey.

At the close of the third decade of this journey it is possible to say that a critical assessment of old images and new perspectives has begun to engage the attention of increasing numbers of concerned persons. In that, there is a promise of significant renewal. The dimming of the original vision was countered in the mid-1980s, by a recovery of concern for the faith of the founders. In the early '80s, partly in consequence of fundamental theological issues raised in General Synod debates over human sexuality, minority rights, inclusive language, and so forth, there was deepening concern to examine in depth the faith professed by the church. Theological questions arising from these emotionally conditioned issues merged with those which, for many persons, had remained unanswered with reference to the nature of the church's responsibility in the world. The existential aspects of faith take on major importance when the private, personal faith securities, into which persons often retreat in times of unsettled societal conditions, are exposed to the "acids of modernity."[12] In meeting after meeting

17

throughout the UCC, speakers gave increasing attention to issues of authority for faith (biblical, creedal, experiential), the nature of the church, and other related questions of fundamental theological substance.

Not surprisingly, the closing years of the third decade became known as a period of theological "ferment."[13] In time that may be seen as the dominant internal characteristic of the third decade. An impressive list of events, movements, and documents makes this period stand out in marked contrast to the first two decades, when the new church's attention and energy were concentrated on organization and mission.[14] There was a growing awareness of a disturbing theological vacuum in the church. For those persons not so immediately affected by the existential questions discussed above, the sources of the ferment were considered in somewhat broader terms. Identity questions had been persistent in many parts of the church. Others were touched more acutely by an increasing spiritual exhaustion and malaise following years of strenuous efforts to deal with the needs of society. Still others could agree with President Robert V. Moss who, in an address at the 1975 General Synod, claimed that the church had reached a new level of maturity. For these persons a recovery of theological concern and activity was indeed a mark of ecclesial maturity.

In the mid-1970s the Office for Church Life and Leadership convened a theological seminar that was asked to reflect on aspects of "the faith and ministry of the United Church of Christ in these times."[15] The seminar report, titled: *Toward the Task of Sound Teaching in the United Church of Christ,* was distributed widely to all clergy, accompanied by suggestions for use in local churches.[16] In its accent on sound teaching, the seminar report underlined three "core dimensions: confessions of faith, polity in process, collegiality for accountability." This was the earliest widely disseminated document touching on the central issues of the faith in the church's theological self-understanding. Ironically, it did not receive significant attention until nearly seven years later when theological discussion had become more intense and focused.[17]

In 1977, the year of the release of the seminar report, Charles Shelby Rooks wrote:

> It is . . . true . . . that as a denomination we have made little conscious effort to unravel the web of our beliefs and construct new

18

thought appropriate to the conditions of *this* century. . . . For tw
years we have tried to be a denomination in process of *becomii.*
primarily by being a denomination engaged in *doing.* The task of the
next twenty years is to be in process of *understanding* and *believing.*[18]

Writing in the same issue of *New Conversations,* Theodore H.
Erickson warned of the danger in "addressing issues of the world
from a perspective that assumes commitment without the experience of faith." He went on to call for an intensity of dialogue lest
*"we fail our ancestors in the faith, and we deny the imaginations of
those who first believed in the possibilities of a United Church."*[19]

It would be inaccurate to imply that the spiritual exhaustion and
malaise prevailing in the United Church of Christ by the end of the
second decade was unique to its own experience because of its
newness. Newness was partly responsible for some aspects of a
theological and spiritual vacuum in the UCC, but all of Christendom, in the West especially, exhibited similar internal conditions.
Martin Marty, citing the uncertainty of the future of mainline Protestantism as seen in the late '70s, claimed that the UCC people
"will have to become more aware than before of their tradition and
what will have to be retrieved from it. *They will have to complement
their secular engagement with more intense devotion to the core
beliefs of Christianity than before."*[20] Marty's reference to the
uncertain future of mainline Protestantism reflects, of course, the
ever-increasing awareness of declining church membership in most
denominations, including the UCC. Even more, however, it reflects
the widespread amorphousness of theological and doctrinal standards that was increasingly the characteristic of those church
bodies once known for their Reformation heritage. This condition,
however explained, had resulted in debilitating ambivalence in most
denominations when, facing the pressing demands of *survival* as
denominations, they also had to respond to new perceptions of the
church's nature and task.[21]

For the UCC this ambivalence was, and continues to be, compounded by the somewhat unusual interweaving of the theological
strands brought together in the 1957 union. "Calvinian, Lutheran,
Wesleyan, Zwinglian and left-wing theological perspectives are not
only indicated in the historical development of these [strands] but
are clearly identifiable in the congregations of the United Church

en Rooks remarked that "we have made little con-
o unravel the web of our beliefs" he was referring not
nished task but to a reluctance to undertake the task.
something formidable and threatening in such an
those diverse traditions of the faith, each with its
story of loyalty and devotion as well as its misunderstandings
and idolatrizations.

Nevertheless, since the end of the '70s especially, a deep-felt
need has come to the surface—the need to "complement their
secular engagement with more intense devotion to the core beliefs
of Christianity." While some may prefer to avoid the task, especially because of anxiety caused by the ever-present and ever-
intensifying polarization between the so-called conservatives and
liberals, the time of intense and disciplined theological effort has
come for the UCC.

That effort involves "owning" the history of the faith traditions
that produced the UCC. To do this requires not simply a reclaiming
and reaffirming of original faith traditions, but also a serious and
disciplined application of the "Protestant principle." This use of a
self-critical method (reformed and always reforming) takes the faith
foundations in the traditions seriously, but *always under the con-
straint of covenant responsibility.* In such an enterprise, being
responsible to God for one another as God has covenanted in
responsibility for the church, is to enter into the "process of understanding and believing" that liberates from the idolatries and ideologies that destroy community. It can and does lead to the self-
understanding that strengthens the ligaments of the church's corporate life.[23]

A most helpful illustration of the range and depth of theological
ferment during the third decade of the UCC's life may be seen in
five documents that were widely disseminated between 1983 and
1986: "A Most Difficult and Urgent Time," issued by thirty-nine
UCC seminary faculty persons; "The Craigville Colloquy Letter"
from the voluntary gathering of nearly one hundred and fifty UCC
people in 1984 to mark the fiftieth anniversary of the Barmen
Declaration and to assess its meaning for the church today; the
Dubuque Declaration issued in 1983 by the Biblical Witness Fellowship; "The Prophet Speaks to Our Times" from Christians for
Justice Action; and a second Craigville Colloquy message in late
1985, "Scripture/Word in the United Church of Christ."[24]

An additional exhibit of this period of theological ferment may be seen in the series of consultations sponsored by what came to be known as the Biblical, Theological, Liturgical Group. Since 1978 this informal group has gathered persons periodically for discussion of scholarly papers on subjects of importance to United Church of Christ self-understanding, particularly in relation to the sacraments and to the issue of authority for faith.[25] This group initiated the Craigville Colloquy series, which has given a "grass roots" character to current theological discussion.

The common characteristic of these documents is their implicit and, in most cases, avowed intention to "recall the United Church of Christ" to its vocation, purpose, roots, and traditions. The appeal of each is *ad fontes*—to the *source,* although the source itself is identified in differing ways. What emerges from a review of these documents is not a satisfying and conclusive consensus but a helpful portrayal of the dimensions of the struggle to articulate faithfully how the United Church of Christ understands itself as church. Equally important is the reality that these efforts at theological self-understanding exhibit a level of covenantal responsibility which, in a variety of ways, can be identified as a primary characteristic of the UCC's ecclesial journey. The principle of covenantal responsibility underlines the journey metaphor with the all-important characteristic of continuity.

That continuity lies first and foremost in God's promises as witnessed in the biblical record, not simply in confessional statements and creeds—the latter serving as instruments shaped by pilgrims of earlier generations as they struggled to articulate the faith in their times. This in no way detracts from the importance of those instruments for the journey of succeeding generations, but it does subordinate them to God's decisive Word/Act in Jesus Christ, the singular "confessional authority" by which the church lives. Both in the context of its own special history and of the emerging ecumenical consensus concerning confessional authority, the UCC has much to learn (and, perhaps, to unlearn!) along every step of the pilgrim way. The *biases for and against* confessional instruments in the life of the church are deeply embedded in the several traditions incorporated therein. For that reason, the learning and unlearning will be an important part of the journey at all times. Moreover, it is of the essence of theological and spiritual renewal, so much desired and needed as the church faces new tasks. Theological renewal, however, cannot be understood as a concern and development only of the UCC on its journey. The context of that renewal is the experience of the worldwide community of faith on its journey, as made evident in ecumenical relationships and responsibilities. It is to these that we turn for clarity of understanding concerning the meaning of the UCC's ecclesial journey.

In the next two chapters, therefore, attention is given to an assessment of the significance of changes in the ecumenical movement for the UCC as it seeks to fulfill its vocation to be united and uniting. Three chapters are then devoted to specific ecumenical relationships. In those relationships the commitment to be united and uniting is tested; the dimensions of the task can be more clearly discerned. Taken in the order of their beginning in UCC experience they are: (a) the relationship with the Evangelical Church of the Union in both the German Democratic Republic and the Federal Republic of Germany, publicly symbolized in the 1981 General Synod vote on "full communion" with those bodies[26]; (b) the ongoing conversations with the Christian Church (Disciples of Christ); and (c) continuous involvement from the beginning in the Consultation on Church Union.

As will be shown, the selection of these three examples is not arbitrary. They are relationships deeply interwoven with the major strands of UCC history. They exhibit those aspects of the response to the imperative of Christian unity that are rooted in the traditions represented in the parent bodies, and are of the very essence of the UCC. They also reflect in concrete rather than abstract ways its experience in its commitment to be united and uniting.

At the same time, it is important to acknowledge that the UCC ecumenical experience and involvement is not limited to these three sets of relationships. The broader, and in some ways less focused, relationships are equally important: those related to the World Council of Churches, to the world communions (both as part of the World Alliance of Reformed Churches and as participants in interconfessional dialogue), to national and regional councils of churches, and to ecumenical partnerships developed in UCC world mission programs. Where appropriate, references to these are included in the effort to evaluate and understand the range of ecumenical commitment and involvement.

2

The Context of the Journey: Ecclesial Questions

In its journey as a united and uniting church, the United Church of Christ has had to engage in the critical ecclesial questions that have characterized the ecumenical era. The mandate of Christian unity, underlined by a new emerging consensus in biblical scholarship and by the desperate circumstances of humanity in the twentieth century, has made the church a primary focus of concern: its nature, its visible form, and its place and task in God's *oikumene*.

Age-old questions about the church have taken on a new urgency. Not since the sixteenth-century Reformation have these questions received such intensive review. From the seventeenth through the nineteenth centuries the issues of faith in Western Christendom were centered upon the individual believer and the eschatological hope for the "kingdom of God." While that habit of thinking and believing is still dominant, the primary focus of attention in this century's ecumenical circles is the church and its task. As is well known, the church as a theological problem emerged in the early part of this century as a particular concern in the mission fields. Concern about the nature of the church and its task at the World Missionary Conference at Edinburgh in 1910 gave rise to the Faith and Order Movement, in which ecclesial questions in relation to the faith were the focus of attention. The urgency of the problem was compounded by the worldwide crises of humanity that unfolded in the following decades. *The quest for a form of the visible church that would be a faithful response to the claims of Christian unity began to dominate the theological enterprise of the ecumenical movement.*[1]

Critical ecclesial questions, then, became the special context of the United Church of Christ ecclesial journey. In this chapter I shall give attention to two sets of events and influences that became determinative as this community of faith sought to shape itself in obedient and faithful response to the vision by which it was created: (1) the immediate ecumenical context (the period of 1910–48) of the vision to be a united and uniting church as this related to the particular characteristics of the uniting bodies; (2) the reality of shifting ecclesiological perspectives as the ecumenical movement matured theologically in response to changing social, intellectual, and religious currents.

In a journey of more than forty-five years, counting the all-important pre-union experiences of the uniting communions, UCC people became uncomfortably aware of a mounting "ecclesiological deficit."[2] That awareness became a key factor in developments of the third decade of the journey, leading specifically to an intentional search for self-understanding as church.

THE ECUMENICAL CONTEXT OF
THE VISION TO BE
UNITED AND UNITING

Church historians in future years are likely to comment on an unusual feature of the birth of the United Church of Christ: In its concern to be a united and uniting church, the focus of attention was almost exclusively on the form of organization (that is, polity) rather than on the essential nature of the church (that is, ecclesiology or the doctrine of the church). The dominant questions, in other words, did not focus upon the nature of the church but upon the need to devise a viable form of the visible church that would express the unity of God's people. The reasons were twofold. On the one hand, questions of order (form) and government (polity and organization) are the *given* questions in a voluntaristic society where organizational initiative rests with the church itself. On the other hand, the questions about the form of the church must also be seen as a response, first, to the dominant ecumenical issues of the first half of the twentieth century and, second, to the particular ecclesial experiences of the uniting bodies as they are traced farther back into their histories.

The character of ecumenical discussions between 1925 and 1948 provides clues for understanding the ecclesial concerns of those who were negotiating the union of the Evangelical and Reformed Church and the Congregational Christian Churches. In fact, it is fair to say that these ecumenical discussions, and their concurrent developments, were *foundational* to those that produced the *Basis of Union,* adopted in 1948–49. Most influential were those that took place within what is known as the Life and Work Movement, which organized world conferences at Stockholm in 1925 and Oxford in 1937.[3]

Emphasizing "ecumenical fellowship through worship and service," this movement aimed to express organic Christian unity by "bringing Christians and churches together in works of love and mercy and in a developing atmosphere of mutual understanding and trust."[4] From such mutual understanding and trust the needed consensus in matters of doctrine, worship, and polity could be confidently expected. Underlying that confidence, of course, was the central conviction of the ecumenical faith; namely, that the One Church (*Una Sancta*) of Christ is at work in and through all churches of Christian confession, giving commonality and focus to their witness in the world.

Nils Ehrenstrom has characterized the moving force of the Life and Work Movement as *socio-moral ecumenicity.*[5] There is no question that it had immense influence in the Western world, even as it did on the mission fields where the spectacle of a "divided church" gave little hope to a divided world. Those engaged in ecumenical service in the 1920s were acutely aware of the fear and anxiety generated by a devastating World War and the persistent threat of another, by the collapse in deep cynicism of efforts to establish justice and hope in the foundation of a peaceful world, and by the growing specter of totalitarianism. The response of the Life and Work Movement was an ever-increasing commitment to the cause of Christian unity as expressed in the concern for an "undivided church." That commitment carried the concerns of the Life and Work Movement into lines converging with the Faith and Order Movement, in which the theological questions concerning the nature of the church were primary. Nevertheless, the Life and

Work Movement's focus on church unity as both an aim and a consequence of "ecumenical fellowship in worship and service"[6] made its mark on all who were involved in the ecumenical enterprise.*

The significance of these influences for the *Basis of Union,* upon which the United Church of Christ was founded, lies in the subordination of doctrinal differences to the goal of unity. That goal was defined by the imperative need for an undivided church. The substance of the faith was assumed, as was the nature of the church. Most important was the task of defining the undivided church and declaring commitment to it as a faithful expression of obedience to the will of Christ. The preamble of the *Basis of Union* illustrates this:

> We, the regularly constituted representatives of the Congregational Christian Churches and of the Evangelical and Reformed Church, *moved by the conviction that we are united in spirit and purpose and are in agreement on the substance of the Christian faith and the essential character of the Christian life;*

> Affirming our devotion to one God, the Father of our Lord Jesus Christ, and our membership in the holy catholic Church, which is greater than any single Church and than all the Churches together;

> Believing that denominations exist not for themselves but as parts of that Church, within which each denomination is to live and labor and, if need be, die; and

> *Confronting the divisions and hostilities of our world, and hearing with a deepened sense of responsibility the prayer of our Lord "that they all may be one";*

---

*It is important to recognize that the concept of socio-moral ecumenicity, although grounded in the ethos of the Life and Work Movement, was not in any sense theologically bereft or shallow. Faith and order questions were of critical importance to all who, under the influence of Life and Work ecumenism, worked for unity. But such questions were considered to be *continuing* questions and not preconditions for the united church as unity was given expression. The concurrent influence of the Faith and Order Movement, which had its inception in the results of the World Missionary Conference in Edinburgh in 1910, must also be recognized. It is noteworthy that this is exhibited in the UCC ancestry by one of its architects especially, George W. Richards, who was also deeply involved in the Faith and Order Movement as chairperson of the American Theological Committee of that movement.

Do now declare ourselves to be one body, and do set forth the following articles of agreement as the basis of our life, fellowship, witness, and proclamation of the Gospel to all nations. [Italics added]

Seeing obedient response to the prayer of our Lord "that they all may be one" as a way of modeling reconciliation in a divided and hostile world was the dominant motivation in the pre-union days as negotiations were extended throughout the 1940s. It was socio-moral ecumenicity moving from vision to reality. Affirming agreement "on the substance of the Christian faith and the essential character of the Christian life," and assuming the word church to mean the *Una Sancta,* the one holy catholic church, the uniting bodies found no impediment to the goal of Christian unity. In the act of union, Christ's will and the believer's duty coalesce. This had two important consequences in the foundational self-understanding of the United Church of Christ as it began its ecclesial journey; both consequences have deep roots in specific aspects of the historical development of the two united bodies.

The first consequence of the subordination of doctrinal differences to the goal of Christian unity through church union was an all-pervasive tendency during the first two decades of UCC history to neglect, and perhaps even avoid, ecclesiological questions. Although such questions arose repeatedly they were rarely addressed. And perhaps they were not fully understood; for, as we shall elaborate on this matter later, both uniting bodies had more than two hundred years of experience in concentrating on issues of personal and individual faith but *relatively little occasion to question the nature of the church.*[7]

It is, further, of no small significance that the deliberate downplaying of doctrinal concerns as well as ecclesiological questions was recognized and warmly approved by observers from other churches in both Europe and America, thus exhibiting the dominance of socio-moral ecumenicity.[8] A successful union of diverse traditions and polities was considered a turning point in American Protestantism, thus illustrating the prevalence of high expectations in ecumenical circles. Was the euphoria warranted? Even thirty years later it may be impossible to give an unqualified answer. Critical reflection about accomplishments of any kind tends to come slowly and with lengthy hindsight. But especially for those who have taken part in three decades of this ecclesial journey, the growing awareness of an "ecclesiological deficit" began to raise questions.

The second consequence of the practice of subordinating doctrinal differences was the increasing dominance of a social activism that often lacked clearly articulated theological grounding and consistent development. A frequent criticism of General Synod actions alluded to "ad hoc theology" and "theological rationalization." The absence of theological perspectives, reflecting in a consistent way the traditions that had united, seemed to many a flagrant denial of the constitutional provision: "Congregational Christian Churches and the Evangelical and Reformed Church unite in the United Church of Christ without break in their respective continuities and traditions."[9] Neither the means nor the occasion seemed to be available to those who were concerned to understand the faith foundations, theologically identified, of the social responsibility they so devotedly espoused. In a world where technological development increases the pace of social change in quantum leaps (and therefore increases social pain and need), the church is often overwhelmed with tasks and comes up short of vision, time, and energy for sustained theological reflection.

These consequences of a then prevailing ecumenical emphasis on union with minimal concern for ecclesiological questions were compounded significantly for the new United Church of Christ by some little-recognized aspects of Congregational Christian and Evangelical and Reformed history.[10] One of the most perceptive discussions of these was provided by Hanns Peter Keiling in 1969 in a German doctoral dissertation: *Die Entstehung der "United Church of Christ."*[11] Although little known because it is unavailable in English translation, Keiling's book underlines important ecclesiological issues in the two uniting bodies that were determinative of the outcome as exhibited in the *Basis of Union*.

For the purpose of discussion here, attention must be given to a point of critical importance made by Keiling: that in the union negotiations "a fundamental ecclesiological dialogue did not take place." Two major reasons were given. First, on the Congregational side, congregational polity was already in a state of confusion as exhibited in strains that developed especially from 1871 onward, when Congregational churches began moving toward a denominational form of organization. The issue was of polity—the relationship between the local church and other churches, as well as to national bodies. Two views of that relationship were in tension: the "independist" and the "conciliarist." The movement toward a conciliar position, which would make a union possible, engendered lengthy debate and, unfortunately, some division within the Congregational fellowship. At the same time, that movement led to the conception of a new approach to church order, voiced by both union partners but especially by the Evangelical and Reformed Church.

The second reason for the absence of fundamental ecclesiological dialogue was traced by Keiling to the relativizing of doctrinal commitment on the part of the Reformed Church in the United States when it united with the Evangelical Synod of North America in 1934. In that process, the Reformed Church, which by tradition was explicitly confessional, moved under the pervasive influence of Pietism toward the "unionist" tradition, in which confessional standards tended to become subordinate to scripture and freedom of conscience. The Evangelical Synod, which had brought the "unionist" tradition from Germany in the nineteenth century, had been deeply influenced also by Pietism. The Reformed Church held solely to the *Heidelberg Catechism* as its defining confession, while the Evangelical Synod churches affirmed not only the *Heidelberg Catechism* but also *Luther's Small Catechism* and the *Augsburg Confession*. The latter position was adopted by the new Evangelical and Reformed Church.

It is clear, then that neither the Congregational Christian Churches nor the Evangelical and Reformed Church was *at that time* predisposed to any extensive consideration of doctrinal, and especially ecclesiological, matters. The pressing practical questions, if the goal of unity was to be achieved through church union, were of polity, the form of government in the new organization. On matters of polity, of course, the Evangelical and Reformed people were inclined to be flexible, whereas their Congregational Christian colleagues in the union endeavor found polity to be the critical point on which all other matters turned. As a tradition with a strong "independist" spirit, confirmed in nearly three centuries of experience but never fully worked into a *denominational* form of organization, the Congregational Christian Churches found flexibility both difficult and threatening.

The commitment to Christian unity and the will to unite with other Christians had long been a major tenet of Congregationalism.* That tenet was expressed clearly in the Burial Hill Declaration in Boston in 1865 at the first national-level gathering of Congregational Churches. It was reaffirmed more explicitly in the "Declaration on the Unity of the Church" by the newly formed National Council in 1871 in Chicago; and in Kansas City in 1913 the theme of the unity of the church was linked to the specific polity accent of Congregationalism on freedom and fellowship.[12] This increasing self-consciousness about congregational polity as the churches became more aware of denominational identity eventually became the major hurdle in the effort to unite with the Evangelical and Reformed Church. It is clear that, throughout the period from 1871 to 1938, the commitment to unity was on a collision course with the central polity accents of Congregationalism. The tension between the two strains of self-understanding, the *independist* and the *conciliarist,* was increased by the difficulty of reaching a common understanding about the requirements of the deeply cherished ideals of freedom and fellowship. As Keiling pointed out, church union could come about only when these accents moved from an independist to a conciliarist basis. For this reason, the fulfillment of a calling to Christian unity meant a painful journey to a new self-understanding and a new era of church organization.

In contrast, the Evangelical and Reformed Church, with an equal commitment to unity and union, experienced no such internal struggle toward self-understanding. Here again the historical experience illustrates the reasons. Coming from the continent of Europe, where churches were defined either creedally or confessionally but organized under civil authority, the Evangelical and Reformed people had not known the need to define themselves as

---

*It is more than a footnote in ecumenical history that in 1910 the National Council of Congregational Churches was one of the three American denominations (besides the Disciples of Christ and the Episcopal Church) to respond enthusiastically to the invitation of Episcopal Bishop Charles Brent that led to the Faith and Order Movement. See R. Rouse and S. Neill, eds.: *A History of the Ecumenical Movement* (London: SPCK, 1948), p. 408.

church in terms of polity. George W. Richards, in writing about the Evangelical and Reformed Church, pointed out that "its polity is an adiaphoron, not a matter of indifference, but of preference."[13] The starting point of this understanding of polity, according to Richards, is the doctrine of the church where it is defined as "the body of Christ, the fellowship of the redeemed, created by the eternal Word of God; . . . *it is not primarily an organization or an institution but an organism and a fellowship, a new mode of God's presence.*"[14] With that presupposition about the nature of the church, the question of polity is not predetermined, nor is it *jure divino.* When the church is "a new mode of God's presence" its form may be designed on functional rather than theoretical principles. Church union, then, for the Evangelical and Reformed Church meant an opportunity to be responsive to the leading of the Spirit by designing a new polity and a new mode of organization for a new age.

Many persons within the Congregational Christian fellowship shared the concern for a new approach to organization and government without abandoning the deeply cherished principles belonging to their history. The consequent move toward a conciliarist position through years of difficult debate and negotiation can be understood as the birth pangs of a new understanding of the form of the church, and thus, as Keiling characterized it, "a qualitatively new church order for the United Church of Christ." On the Evangelical and Reformed side the experience of waiting while Congregational Christian friends worked through their critically important debate was sometimes frustrating and puzzling. That frustration rose to anxiety in 1948 when a set of "Interpretations" was added to the *Basis of Union* to satisfy special concerns among the Congregational Christian Churches. It prompted a resolution from the Evangelical and Reformed General Council expressing "the hope that . . . the new church not merely develop a compromise of the two former polities but may bring a new polity and plan of organization to the United Church."[15] President Louis W. Goebel, writing on behalf of the Evangelical and Reformed Church to Douglas Horton, General Secretary and Minister of the General Council of Congregational Christian Churches, emphasized that the Evangelical and Reformed Church had "no other purpose than to protect the freedom of the United Church to evolve its own polity."[16]

In view of all the above it would have been reasonable to expect a "fundamental ecclesiological dialogue" between the uniting bodies. Such a dialogue undoubtedly would have contributed to an intentional effort to devise a new polity and plan of organization, thus fulfilling the hopes so frequently expressed. But the hope for the "new" seemed to be foreclosed in large part by the "Interpretations" that were added to the *Basis of Union*. The compromises contained therein became inhibiting, creating uncertainty and tentativeness in the new United Church of Christ. Although the absence of such dialogue at that time was apparently of minimal concern because of the prevailing ecumenical concentration on nontheological matters, it is clear it had important consequences. Such dialogue would have given greater depth to the debate within the Congregational Christian fellowship. Moreover, it would have been equally beneficial to the Evangelical and Reformed Church people, among whom there were relatively few who had faced up to the difficult questions of order and polity as these began to emerge with increasing urgency in the mid-twentieth century for all Protestant churches. Certainly for the UCC it was the beginning of an ecclesiological deficit that grew in the succeeding years of its ecclesial journey.

CHANGING ECCLESIOLOGICAL PERSPECTIVES ON THE ECUMENICAL SCENE

Our further consideration of the ecumenical context of the birth and formation of the United Church of Christ must take into account the far-reaching changes in ecclesiological perspectives in the period between 1948 and 1978. Tracing these changes can be helpful in our understanding of the ecclesial journey that began with the adoption of the *Basis of Union* in 1949 and was set on its course in 1957 when the union was consummated.

By the late 1970s many of these changes were viewed negatively by some observers, as evidence of the demise of the ecumenical movement.[17] It is a fact that the decade of the '70s was a time of some confusion and a weakening of ecumenical fervor. Radical changes in the theological climate of the '60s seemed to many to have eroded the theological bases of the ecumenical vision of the post-World War II period. The influence of neoorthodoxy, which had set much of the tone and direction at the Amsterdam Assembly in 1948, seemed to diminish in the face of theological fads that accompanied the increasing privatization of religious faith. Negative assessment of the ecumenical scene, however, proved to be somewhat shortsighted. By the end of the decade there were already signs of a reinvigoration that issued in significant ecumenical advance in the following years. The power of neoorthodoxy reasserted itself in a focus on the nature of the church, aided by intense concern for the biblical message and for liturgical renewal in Protestant bodies that had long neglected such matters. All this became evident in the changes on the ecumenical scene.

Of special importance to the United Church of Christ are those theological developments that have provided new ecclesiological perspectives for its ecclesial journey. The self-understanding formed by socio-moral ecumenicity at the time of its birth gave way to a new sense of ecumenical responsibility grounded in the radical nature of the gospel. Ecclesiology derived from the nature of the faith, instead of from the moral claims on the Christian conscience, gave to the church not only a new ethic but a new self-image in which the visible form of the church takes its shape from its essential nature.

The dimensions of these changes become clear in a brief review of the period from 1948 to the present. This is the era of the World Council of Churches, which had its birth in Amsterdam that year. Defining itself as "a fellowship of churches which accept the Lord Jesus Christ as God and Saviour," the World Council claimed the singular aim "to call the churches to the goal of visible unity in one faith and in one eucharistic fellowship expressed in worship and in common life in Christ, and to advance towards that unity in order that the world may believe." The christological formula at the heart of this definition and theme gave clear direction to the ecumenical movement as a whole, and specifically to the emerging ecclesiological understandings of the following years.

Three important changes in ecclesiological perspectives developed between 1948 and 1968, that is, between the founding of the World Council of Churches at Amsterdam and the Fourth Assembly at Uppsala. Colin W. Williams has identified these three changes in terms of a radical shift in focus.[18] That shift was from "self-conscious ecclesiology," in which the question of the nature of the church is addressed directly, to the "question of God's mission in the world," in which the nature of the church is addressed indirectly.[19]

The first change, as Williams noted, took place between 1948 and the Assembly at Evanston in 1954. This can be characterized as a move from comparative ecclesiological discussions—explaining commonalities and differences[20]—to a concentration on images of the church drawn from the new biblical scholarship of the early decades of this century.[21] This emphasis had a normative role in the implicit ecclesiological assumptions of the United Church of Christ *Basis of Union* (1949) and the Statement of Faith prepared and approved in 1959. The congruence of this emphasis with the theological temper of both the Evangelical and Reformed Church and the Congregational Christian Churches in this period is noteworthy: a strong emphasis upon the biblical norms for the church even as confessional norms were relativized; and the growing influence of neoorthodoxy, at least in its early Barthian mode, which can be traced in both traditions.[22]

The second change came in the period between the World Council of Churches Assembly at Evanston in 1954 and at New Delhi in 1961. In this case the essential character of the church, as exhibited especially in the biblical categories, began to give way to the accentuating of "mission" as the definitive mark of the church. Important as may be the continuities of the church from its biblical roots, it was seen to be equally important for the church's self-understanding to regard itself as the creation of God's purpose for humanity. This accent grew out of the deliberate decision of the Faith and Order Commission to consider the doctrine of the church in relation to the work of Christ and of the Holy Spirit. The significance of this change of emphasis lies in seeing the church in dynamic rather than static institutional terms, that is, in terms of its *being* as a living response to God's call in Christ. More than anything else, this accent is the major theme of the 1959 *Statement of Faith* of the United Church of Christ. Its influence in UCC theology in subsequent years can be easily identified.

The third change in ecumenical ecclesiological perspectives became prominent in the period from 1961 to the Assembly at Uppsala in 1968. It was most helpfully characterized in the report of the World Council's study of "The Missionary Structure of the Congregation," titled *The Church for Others.*[23] This report reflected in many ways the natural development of the concept of the church as God's mission. In particular, it was a development of a major emphasis in the Barthian ecclesiology of the earlier period, where the accent was placed on obedience to the living Christ as the mark of the church's presence in the world.[24] The logical consequence of that emphasis for many was the disconcerting realization that the focus of attention must be on the world rather than on the church. Out of this emphasis came the well-known slogan: "The world sets the agenda for the church." The shift here was away from the church as an institution marked by its primary role as God's mission in the world, to God's struggle with the world through Christ's humanizing and liberating work. In this model, interpreted most radically by J. C. Hoekendijk,[25] the visible church as structure and institution is diminished in significance. What is important is participation in Christ's struggle with the powers that are antithetical and hostile to God's purpose for the world.

This was, in many respects, the most radical change in the theological temper of the ecumenical era. It introduced "worldly theology," placing the work of God in the world through Christ ahead of the church as an institution. The effect on the churches was dramatic, for it called into question almost all previous thinking about the visible church. It moved the church to a watershed point of self-understanding. When linked with the experience of the profound and traumatic societal changes of the same period, it introduced a sense of insecurity, aimlessness, and anomie into the ecclesiastical establishments. It undercut the institutional loyalties of church members. For the United Church of Christ on its ecclesial journey, barely two decades along the way, the vision, once so inspiring and energizing, began to dim.

Was the original ecumenical identity of the UCC out of step with these trends, as some claimed?[26] Did this contribute to a lessening of ecumenical commitment? Clearly, the times called for adjustments in ecclesial self-understanding. How to be a united and a uniting church in such times required a rethinking of the ecumenical vocation. That was especially difficult in times that were against any focus of attention on institutions. Anti-institutional attitudes, so rampant and extreme in many segments of Western culture, simply added to the theological biases toward traditional ecclesiastical structures. "Worldly theology" in the '60s and '70s had little or no vision of institutional forms of church life. At the same time, "worldly theology" was—by its emphasis on the church as the "sign of God's kingdom" and as the "new community of God" in the world—already posing the question of a new form of the church for a new style of participation in God's work in the world.[27] That question returned with compelling force to give the UCC a renewed challenge to understand and articulate the meaning of its original vision and the journey it has undertaken.

The renewed challenge to ecclesial self-understanding is, of course, an outgrowth of the striking ecclesiological perspectives developed in the period between 1961 and 1968. From 1968 through the mid-'80s the key to further development of these perspectives is to be seen in the focus of attention on the nature of God's activity in the world through Christ. To learn what God intends and is doing in the world requires a reconsideration of the gospel of God in Jesus Christ. From this perspective, ecclesial self-understanding is to be derived from the person and activity of Jesus Christ, not from any institutional concerns and activity, not from any sociocultural concepts of the place of religion in human life, but solely from Jesus Christ. Jurgen Moltmann interpreted it in his book *The Church in the Power of the Spirit:*

> The lordship of Christ is the church's sole, and hence all-embracing, determining factor. . . . If for the church of Christ, Christ is the "subject" of the church, then in the doctrine of the church christology will become the dominant theme of ecclesiology. Every statement about the church will be a statement about Christ.[28]

The intensifying accent on an ecclesiology formed in christological terms produced a dynamic, in place of a static, ecclesial self-understanding for the churches influenced by the ecumenical movement. The form of the church in the world conforms to Christ, who as "servant" was and is the "messiah" for the world. In this form the church is always concerned with obedience to Christ, not with self-establishment or permanence or security. The compelling concern is to live and act in every circumstance of the world's need as Jesus Christ acts in the fulfillment of his mission.

Attention to Christology, then, became the distinguishing mark of ecumenical ecclesiology in the third quarter of the present century. But this focus on Christology is easily misunderstood if it is removed from the context of God's mission in the world. As the history of the church shows, christological interest has long been confined to individual and privatist religious pursuits. Learning Christology in a new mode has subtle inhibiting habits of mind and spirit to overcome: the habit of seeking to know Christ more intimately by withdrawal from the world; the habit of limiting concern for the world to the advantages of one's own social and political loyalties; and the habit of defining God's kingdom in terms that guard individual and group securities. Christology in the new mode requires ecclesial learnings that call for continual and critical reassessment of human inclinations to mold the form of the church in the service of parochial and provincial interests. At the same time, it calls for the obedience that Christ learned and exemplified.

Major contributions to this ever-widening and ever-deepening comprehension of these christological emphases came from many sources in the worldwide Christian community. Some of the contributions from the "young churches" of the Third World became radical challenges to the traditional ways of "doing theology" in the long-established churches of the Western world.[29] Jurgen Moltmann's work, cited above, illustrates a response to those challenges as understood from a European context. In the North American church community Frederick Herzog, among others, has interpreted the radical rethinking needed as a response to the new christological studies.

In his *Liberation Theology,* in which the issues raised by the racial struggle of the late '60s are addressed, Herzog argued that "Christ is the question."[30] In so doing he sought to move the theological task of the church from its long-time focus on questions arising from human self-awareness and concern (Descartes, Schleiermacher, Ogden, Dewart, and others) to the task of learning what God is doing in and through Jesus Christ. In that effort he was especially concerned to show the distinction between *liberation* theology and *liberal* theology. In a later volume, *Justice Church,* Herzog has taken up the concomitant ecclesial questions, identifying the "new function of the church in North American Christianity."[31] He claimed that these new learnings do not come easily: "Only gradually is it dawning on us that the struggle over the nature

37

of the church is over *the church immersed in history versus the church separate from history.*"[32]

How the church can be immersed in history and what that means for the articulation of its faith became the chief focus of attention in the 1980s. Christological questions had to be examined from within conditions that reflected the new kind of world in which the church must serve. The ever-changing character of human history was setting new scenes in which the relevance of the church's faith was being tested.

ECUMENICAL TESTING AT THE END OF THE THIRD DECADE

The foregoing survey of changing ecclesiological perspectives on the ecumenical scene simply underlines the correlative character of questions concerning the nature of the church and of the faith confessed and declared. What was at stake then in the concern for Christian unity was not simply a resolution of differing understandings of the nature of the church, but a clarification of the faith that the ecclesial body exhibits. This was the point being made by the concentration on christological questions in the ecumenical enterprise from 1952 onward, as Geoffrey Wainwright had argued when he wrote:

> At stake . . . is precisely the identity of the church and therewith the nature and substance of truth and the condition of its authoritative expression. To seek and confess the ecclesiological location of one's community is an act of discerning and proclaiming the gospel itself. There is no preaching and living of the gospel without at least an implicit ecclesiological claim being made.[33]

For the UCC the crucial question emerged: What was the "implicit ecclesiological claim" made in the union achieved in 1957? That is, what is the ecclesiological location of a "united and uniting" church? What was and is the faith declared and lived by the United Church of Christ as an ecclesial body?

In a significant way these questions provided an ecumenical framework for the somewhat diverse discussions characterizing the

38

"theological ferment" of the UCC that began in the late 1970s.* The focus of the ecumenical discussions of this period gained universal attention in 1982 when the Faith and Order Commission of the World Council of Churches released a report on *Baptism, Eucharist and Ministry*.[34] This report, the result of five decades of study and discussion, presented a consensus on the sacraments and the ministry that effectively enables every Christian communion to find and confess its "ecclesiological location."

The singular importance of this document for the United Church of Christ was underlined in the opportunity it gave for intensive participation in the ongoing task of Christian unity exploration. By inviting official responses from the churches, the Faith and Order Commission emphasized the intimate linkage between "local church union and the search for universal consensus."[35] That was an acknowledgment of the importance of the "changes taking place within the life of the churches themselves." The UCC and other united churches were being challenged to ask "how their understandings and practices of baptism, eucharist and ministry relate to their mission in and for the renewal of human community as they seek to promote justice, peace and reconciliation."

The UCC response to the *Baptism, Eucharist and Ministry* paper was initiated by the Council on Ecumenism, and officially approved by the 1985 General Synod.[36] In preparing the response the Council on Ecumenism sought assistance from Conferences, Instrumentalities, seminaries, and local churches. Acknowledging that "although the document speaks to us diversely, it speaks powerfully. . . . Within the United Church of Christ, as well as in our ecumenical relationships, *Baptism, Eucharist and Ministry* holds great promise as a signpost on our pilgrim way toward a deeper understanding and a more faithful embodiment of the one Church of Jesus Christ that is sent to the one humanity that is made in the image and likeness of God."[37]

---

*See the discussion in chapter 1. The "Sound Teaching" document; the papers on the sacraments from the Biblical, Theological, Liturgical Group; *The Dubuque Declaration* of the Biblical Witness Fellowship; the themes of the Craigville Colloquies—all reflect the concern to clarify and restate the faith that the church declares and demonstrates.

Although the text of the UCC response is of utmost importance in the continuing discussions in both ecumenical circles and local churches, of equal importance are reflections on the response and the BEM document itself, which appeared subsequently.[38] All these represent UCC involvement in the process of finding and acknowledging its ecclesiological location. In many respects this set of discussions, when taken together with the products of the theological ferment that began in the '70s, represents an important effort to overcome the deleterious effects of the ecclesiological deficit inherited from the pre-union period. Of equal promise are the ensuing discussions in which the *Baptism, Eucharist and Ministry* text is related to the long-range research project of the Faith and Order Commission, "Towards the Common Expression of the Apostolic Faith Today."[39]

Ecumenical discussions of the substance of the faith, as they relate to the United Church of Christ self-understanding as church, inevitably become a time of testing and learning. As a people on an ecclesial journey we are challenged at every turn, not to justify ourselves but to clarify vision and to be clear about the requirements of the ecumenical vocation we have claimed. To be a "united and uniting church" requires special diligence lest too much or too little is claimed. What, for example, is the meaning of the phenomenon of a "united church" in relation to the changing ecclesiological perspectives traced in this chapter? That question requires intensive consideration as the conditions of the ecclesial journey are assessed.

Christian Unity and Church Union: Models and Directions for the Journey

In its journey as a *united* and *uniting* church the United Church of Christ has had many companions. Although the concept of church union can be dated from the early decades of the nineteenth century, it did not flourish until energized by the twentieth-century ecumenical movement. Since 1925, for example, more than sixty church unions have been formed worldwide, with at least one third of them being transconfessional. By the 1970s *united* churches represented an ever-broadening expression of church unity.

Not all church unions have been motivated by the goal of Christian unity. The union of one or more church bodies to achieve organizational unity is often the result of external sociocultural pressures. Political and economic factors can be identified in many cases. The Church of the Prussian Union, for example, was formed in 1817 by imperial edict, with quite explicit intentions to enhance national unity. Other such instances, in western Europe especially, could be cited. In North America some of the earliest church union proposals predate the emergence of significant ecumenical influence.* In large part they reflect the economic, political, and social idealism—undergirded by Christian convictions about Divine Sovereignty and Benevolence—which characterized the expansion and

---

*Three examples of proposed unions, motivated by external as well as internal concerns in North America, are: (1) The 1801 Plan of Union between Presbyterians and Congregationalists; (2) The Philadelphia Plan of 1918, proposing a federal union of nineteen denominations to form "The United Churches of Christ in America"; (3) The formation of the United Church of Canada in 1925—the only one of these that succeeded.

development of church life in America. Socio-moral ecumenicity, discussed in the previous chapter, therefore found itself at home in North America. The end of World War I gave rise to new hope and vision for common action to overcome all forms of human social division and animosity. It was accompanied by a wave of church union proposals. The aftermath of World War II, marked by wrenching political, economic, and social changes, extended the church union movement dramatically throughout the world.

THE UNITED CHURCH MODEL OF ORGANIC UNITY

As a worldwide phenomenon, *united* churches have become a dominant model of Christian unity. Their place within the ecumenical movement—since many developed before the post-World War II period, parallel with and often independently of the ecumenical enterprise—has been a matter of debate and some tension.[1] Ambivalence about the need and form of church structure to express Christian unity has been characteristic of the ecumenical fellowship from the nineteenth century to the present. The World Council of Churches remains clearly neutral with respect to a required form of visible unity. At the same time, *united* churches, by their growth and influence, have become the most visible form. In that respect they represent a concrete response to the World Council's declared purpose: "To call the churches to the goal of visible unity in one faith and in one eucharistic fellowship expressed in worship and in common life in Christ, and to advance towards that unity in order that the world might believe."[2]

The very prominence of *united* churches in worldwide Christianity, therefore, has called for critical reflection on their strengths and weaknesses, their role in ecumenical responsibility and work, and their relationships to other Christian bodies—especially the World Communions (sometimes called Confessional Families). These matters have been addressed in a series of international Consultations of United Churches, beginning at Bossey, Switzerland in 1967.[3] They were encouraged and assisted by the World Council's Faith and Order Commission. The reports of these consultations show not only the complexity and difficulties in-

42

volved in being *united* and *uniting*, but also the high expectations and goals that motivate them. In addition, they provide definitions and guidelines for understanding the character of united churches and their place in the concern for Christian unity. Although there is no singular model for united church structure, the objective is corporate or organic union. This is one of the primary guidelines derived from united church consultations. Thus the Limuru Consultation stated the conditions that belong to organic union: "A common basis of faith; a common name; full commitment to one another, including the readiness to give up separate identity; the possibility of making decisions together, and of carrying out the missionary task as circumstances require."[4]

Such qualifications leave open the matter of organizational style, with the consequence that united churches have adopted quite diverse forms of government. As would be expected, many have simply combined features of the standard congregational, presbyterial, and episcopal polities. The results have often been less than satisfactory, exhibiting the provisional nature of organizational structures of churches "on the way." As in the case of the United Church of Christ, such combinations, even on a minimal level, have been achieved at the neglect of fundamental ecclesiological discussions.[5]

Nevertheless, the specified conditions of organic union, as quoted above, clearly indicate the sine qua non elements of Christian unity: foundational faith, covenanted commitment, a shared identity and the death of former identities, and openness to a new life together "that the world might believe." To what extent does the UCC as a united church exhibit these conditions of organic union? Although these conditions give no absolute guidelines, they do suggest general categories of essential elements offering opportunity for self-assessment, and thus exhibit some of the limitations of the union model of unity.

1. *A foundational faith,* that is, "a common basis of faith." For the UCC this faith foundation is clearly identified and affirmed in Article II of the *Basis of Union* and in the Preamble of the Constitution and Bylaws. By their votes adopting these documents, the Evangelical and Reformed Church and the Congregational Christian Churches took the definitive step toward *organic union*. Subse-

43

quent voting by local churches as they sought and received membership in the UCC made the same affirmation.

The importance of this clear affirmation has not been fully understood and appreciated in succeeding years. Roger L. Shinn has helpfully described the ambivalence, for example, that many UCC people feel about confessions of faith.[6] In fact, for many persons Article IV, paragraph 15 of the Constitution seems to cancel the key role of the faith affirmation in the Preamble by asserting the right of the local church "to formulate its own covenants and confessions of faith." Is paragraph 15 a license, or is it a charge of responsibility, with which no other person or body may interfere, to develop its own confessions and covenants in a manner congruent with the Constitution? Debate about this will not cease. For those who interpret "autonomy" as "right," that paragraph becomes a license to declare freedom from any common expression of the faith, or any common action. Is that construction of its meaning congruent with the Preamble and with paragraphs 8 and 14 in Article IV, both of which are directed toward establishing the "oneness" of the United Church of Christ? Its very identity as a *united* church is at stake here.[7]

In its ecclesial journey of three decades the UCC has suffered from popular misconstructions of these basic documents. Internal indecisiveness has resulted and that, in turn, has presented a confusing public picture. Intensive and continuing internal dialogue about the foundational faith has been needed for clarified self-understanding. "It is essential that united churches continue after union to struggle with questions of faith and order."[8] In the UCC such struggle often has been of an ad hoc and somewhat haphazard character, as I have shown earlier. Although there are many internal reasons for urgency about foundational faith matters, there are equally many external reasons, particularly as a matter of accountability in the family of united churches.

The manner of affirming the United Church of Christ foundational faith in the Constitution and Bylaws in itself provides a charge of responsibility that is reiterated in paragraph 15:

It claims as its own the faith of the historic church expressed in the ancient creeds and reclaimed in the basic insights of the Protestant

Reformers. *It affirms the responsibility of the church in each* ╱ *tion to make this faith its own* in reality of worship, in ho⸝ thought and expression, and in purity of heart before God. ι_ added]

That responsibility, of course, belongs to each local church as well as to the United Church of Christ as organized regionally and nationally. On a denominational level, the formal assignment of that responsibility as it relates to the internal life of the church was given to the Office for Church Life and Leadership in 1973.[9] Projects on sound teaching, worship, theology, polity, and the publication of a book of worship illustrate that office's handling of the assignment. In external relationships, this responsibility for the faith foundations of the UCC is officially implemented through the Council on Ecumenism.[10] Involvements in the faith and order projects of the several ecumenical bodies of which the UCC is a part provide channels for contributions to and learnings from the wider ecumenical fellowship.[11]

As in many united churches, particularly where a variety of traditions and practices prevail, the establishment of linkages between denominational, regional, and local church levels has been difficult to achieve. In fulfillment of its responsibility to its "sister" united churches, as well as to itself, the UCC has before it an unfinished task. Making the "historic faith its own" is a consequence only if each generation is involved in "unraveling the web of our beliefs." Only then can the continuity and unity of the church be experienced in such ways that "new thought appropriate to the conditions" of the age be constructed. Affirming a common basis of faith is a critical first step in the responsibility to "seek and confess the ecclesiological location" of the United Church of Christ.

2. *A covenanted commitment*—"full commitment to one another." To speak of full commitment to one another in a united church as *covenanted* commitment is to underline "the intrinsic mandate of Christianity," which is *"to share the claims of the other."*[12] To live in covenant is to live *for the sake of the other* in a relationship where commitment is defined in the Christocentric terms of trust, love, and obedience. In that relationship, mutual

accountability is the modus vivendi of authentic unity and community, the unerring mark of the community as *church*. In this way accountability is not judgmental and exclusionist but reconciling and healing in the manner of Christ.

The place of mutual accountability as the "manner of being" in the community of faith is not simply an in-house issue. It has crucial importance for both internal and external relationships. Internally, it touches on the fundamental aspects of being a *united* church, that is, an authentic community in which reconciliation and wholeness are the experience of being the Body of Christ. Mutual accountability as the mode of being of the church is the way of testing its faithfulness, not only to a common basis of faith rooted in the historic faith, but also in the ongoing responsibility of making the faith its own for a new time as well. The fulfillment of mutual accountability internally is like the process described by Paul S. Minear, who wrote that "discovering and rediscovering an authentic self-image will involve the whole community not only in clear-headed conceptual thinking and disciplined speech, but also in a rebirth of its images and imaginations, and in the absorption of those images in the interstices of communal activities of every sort."[13]

Externally, full commitment to one another as mutual accountability relates to the recognition given to a united church as *church*. It is one thing to describe the community of faith as *church;* it is another matter for that community to be so acknowledged. This is to say the obvious, of course: that organizational merger does not produce organic union, nor does it result in a united church. In the family of united churches, the authenticity of the United Church of Christ as *church* rests on mutual accountability in reference to the *fides qua creditur.*

The exercise of mutual accountability as an experience of covenanted commitment in the UCC has been inhibited by a historically limited and partial view of covenant community; and a constitutional provision that, although unintentional, effectively limits accountability in the structures of our church.

The concept of the church as a covenant community is rooted, of course, in the biblical account of God's relationship with Israel.[14] That covenant of grace, fully expressed in the Christ-event, is the ground of both human freedom and accountability. The "welfare of

46

[handwritten at top: covenant is comm...]

the other," conceived in Christocentric terms, exhibi[ts] [po]tialities of that freedom, and sets its limits. The m[e] possibilities of this covenant relationship engages [in] every new setting and every generation. Rarely, ho[w] church explored the radical possibilities of the cov[enant] set forth, for example, by Walter Brueggemann in his [...] a Subversive Paradigm,"[15] in which he identifies the marks of the covenant community as a community of God's "freeing" Torah; of "solidarity about the knowledge of God" that is "attentive to the needs of brothers and sisters"; and of a community that "knows about, experiences and practices forgiveness." Acknowledging that "these marks of the covenant community are not new," Brueggemann makes the crucial point that

> they characterize a *subversive ecclesiology* in deep conflict with our conventions. It is important to see how extensively our usual notions of community are refuted here—notions which are either of communities of *fate* (into which we are locked without choice) or of *convenience* (in which we have no serious or abiding stake). Against both of these, we are to have a *called* community—not a voluntary association, but a people addressed and bound in a concrete and abiding loyalty.[16]

[handwritten: That practice forgiveness]

The ecclesiastical institutionalization (or domestication!) of the covenant paradigm has inevitably muted its radical potentiality. That has been its religious distortion. At the same time, the secularized covenant concept of the Enlightenment, especially under Thomas Hobbes and John Locke in the late seventeenth century, appeared as a social contract, subtly altering the church's understanding of covenant. The shift was from obligation for the "welfare of the other" to "mutual self-advantage and limited liability." Only when the covenant is an expression of radical grace can there be radical freedom from self-advantage and a corresponding acceptance of liability (obligation) as the gift of freedom.*

Closely related to the above is a second inhibiting factor in the exercise of mutual accountability in covenant: the inclusion of a

---

*The implications of this and the following arguments are developed more fully in the final chapters of this book.

[handwritten: freedom with accountability]

[handwritten: covenant — as concern about the "welfare of the other"]

titutional provision that effectively limits accountability in the CC. The language employed in Article IV, paragraph 15 interprets *autonomy* primarily as "rights." This interpretation of autonomy substitutes the rule of contract for the rule of covenant. The paragraph, as the historical record shows, was intended to protect the local church in the determination of its own life without interference from any ecclesiastical unit. Concern about such interference was rooted in the experience of the church through many centuries.

The question not fully faced and addressed in the UCC in the years of its journey is: What is the function of such a historically-conditioned definition of autonomy in a *united* church in which the covenant modus vivendi is mutual accountability expressed in *concern for the other?* In covenantal terms, autonomy is responsibility for self-rule, that is, a responsibility that makes mutual accountability supportive. The UCC ecclesial journey as a *united* church is hampered by avoidance of "clear-headed, conceptual thinking and disciplined speech" in reconsideration of this constitutional provision. The process need not be adversarial; in fact it will not be, if undertaken in covenanted commitment. *But it is the process required by mutual accountability.*

3. *A shared identity*—which is accompanied by the "readiness to give up separate identities." Organic unity raises the question of identity to existential levels. Bishop Stephen Neill, in discussing obstacles to unity through church union, has said: "The final and terrible difficulty is that churches cannot unite unless they are willing to die."[17] The death of which Neill speaks is that of Christian identity tied to a particular community and/or organization, and that is true for most individuals. The UCC *Basis of Union* clearly acknowledged that the faith communities known as Congregational Christian and Evangelical and Reformed would have to die in order that Jesus' prayer could be fulfilled, "that all may be one."*

The surrender of an identity is a subtle and complex process not only for individuals but also for organized communities. Among the aspects of identity with which a united church must deal are those

---

*The Preamble reads: "Believing that denominations exist not for themselves but as parts of that church, within which each denomination must labor and, if need be, die. . . ."

that, although often treasured for the quality of diversity, easily become occasions for division. But "unity in Christ leaves no room for any autonomy of tradition, culture, ethnicity, race, class, sex, politics (or anything else that we call 'Christian pluralism') by which we justify our divisions."[18] It is, then, the *autonomy* of diverse elements of identity that must be challenged and surrendered in a united church.

For the UCC this aspect of identity poses problems deeply rooted in history. Diversity is one of its most, perhaps *the* most, remarked identifying characteristics. The reasons are well known. As many have shown, we have an unusual number of diverse elements, corresponding to those listed in the above quotation.[19] And yet, other denominations can make similar claims. In a mobile society, diversity is a pervasive feature.

But what is the implication of the UCC claim to diversity as an identifying characteristic? Does it signify the autonomy of individual freedom and private judgment? Or is it an acknowledgment of gifts from the Creator for which the church has a special responsibility? The validity of the claim to be a united and uniting church hinges on the answer. Absolutizing (asserting autonomy) of individual freedom and private judgment may elevate diversity but preclude the possibility of exhibiting the unity of the Body of Christ. The apostle Paul's clear statements about this in 1 Corinthians and in his letter to the Ephesians draw the lines of limitation around the place of diversity. Acknowledging that we have been "called into the church" requires accepting these limitations. There is "one Lord, one faith, one baptism, one God." The experience of that oneness may be diverse, but the identifying mark is *oneness*, not diversity.

Absolutized diversity easily surrenders to a dogmatic pluralism that has become a distinguishing feature of our so-called postmodern culture. As a "prescriptive belief system"[20] pluralism effectively denies the reality of the unity of God's *oikumene*. Diversity as a cherished gift of God may contribute to the fullness of the experience of unity. It is for this reason that the issue of diversity is so critical for the question of identity in uniting church bodies. Organic union can subsume diverse identities in its structural expression only when those identities are surrendered. *"The former identity need not be entirely discarded. . . .* The churches cannot

49

enter union without risking this identity, but they need not neces-
sarily lose it."[21] To surrender an identity is not to discard it but to
*subordinate it in the service of a new and larger identity.** Unless
that is done, a united church has neither an identity with which to
strengthen "the ligaments of its corporate life" nor an identity that
demonstrates its authenticity as church.

4. *An openness to new life*—"sharing decision-making" for the
sake of the mission. Openness to new life as a characteristic of the
organic union that constitutes a united church clearly suggests that
reform and renewal should be expected as a continuing experience.
Unity expressed through organic union has only the objective "that
the world may believe." Church union, therefore, is always a confession that the divisions healed in the uniting of two or more
church bodies had their roots in human proclivities that make it
difficult if not impossible for the world to believe. Overcoming the
divisions through union is then both a confession and a commitment: commitment to be open to new insights, new responsibilities,
new ways of living—all in response to the leading of the Holy Spirit.

The urgency behind this feature of organic union lies in the ever-
changing conditions of the world in which the church must live and
fulfill its mission. However, the problem faced in maintaining a
spirit of openness after accomplishing union stems from the difficulty of overcoming old habits of thought and action. New vision
requires new styles of decision-making and action for which few are
prepared. The inevitable conflicts arising from the tension between
old and new are frequently exacerbated by the excitement of inno-
vation that grips new generations. This often accounts for the
"structure" problems that seem to dominate the union experience
even decades after a united church is created.

"Where is the renewal and reform, if it is guaranteed in advance
that each denomination can go along as it has in the past? The call
is to new and radical obedience."[22] Organic union cannot exist if
openness is ruled out in advance. Sometimes, in union negotiations, resistance and anxiety are met by assurances that not many

---

*This is the point expressed in ecumenical discussions by use of the words "inte-
grated diversity," a formulation designed to overcome the intimated compromise in
the words "reconciled diversity."

changes will be needed.[23] In the United Church of Christ there has been ambivalence about openness, particularly on the local church level in communities little affected by membership mobility. At the same time, the very structure of the denomination, regionally and nationally, has given opportunity for openness and creativity in mission. Reform and renewal cannot be enforced, nor can openness in habit and thought be imposed. This spirit results only from the commitment to one another that organic union implies.

The openness of the community of faith needs careful definition. It is grounded not in a spirit of irresponsibility where "anything goes," but in the faith conviction that the church is the province of the Holy Spirit. A tradition that cherishes John Robinson's oft-quoted words,"The Lord has yet more light and truth to break forth from his holy Word," and which confesses that the Holy Spirit is "creating and renewing the church of Jesus Christ," receives openness as a gift that is a mandate. To cherish this gift and to explore its potential obediently and expectantly is the mark of a united church.

FURTHER QUESTIONS FOR UNITED CHURCHES

The foregoing assessment of the United Church of Christ as an example of the organic union model of unity prevailing in the family of united churches, serves as an illustration of some of the risks and problems. However, for those on this ecclesial journey, both the positive and negative experiences would lead them to affirm Bishop Stephen Neill's comment:

> Time has shown many imperfections in their [united churches] work, and much revision of the original ideas of union has had to be carried through. But those who have had experience of life in these united churches are almost unanimous in affirming that, though union may have brought loss in certain directions and though some hopes may have been unfulfilled, it is impossible that they should ever consider going back to their earlier state of division.[24]

At the same time, the united church model has not been without its critics. The ever-increasing number of church unions since the 1960s has been paralleled by increasing activity among the World

Confessional Communions. That phenomenon has heightened the concerns of critics and brought an intensified effort among the united churches to examine and assess the model of organic union. This was reflected in these lines from a recent international gathering of united churches:

> Our reflections about the one ecumenical movement convince us, first, that united and uniting churches have a unique perspective on catholicity and reconciliation to share with others, and, second, that dynamic links need to be established between "local," multilateral church unions and other approaches to visible unity (e.g. councils of churches and bilateral conversations carried out through Christian World Communions). We have much to gain by teaching each other in the common search for visible unity shaped by our confessing the one apostolic faith and sharing one eucharistic fellowship. Conversely, we have much to lose whenever these different approaches and models are viewed as alternatives, whenever a "competitive ecumenism" polarizes the search for unity.[25]

In many respects the passage above is descriptive of the United Church of Christ's attitude and involvement in further church union, particularly through the third decade of its ecclesial journey. It represents a maturing of the church union concept in its own experience, in which both the potentialities and the limitations of the church union model are recognized. The result has been deliberate and restrained participation in further union plans, accompanied by expanded engagement in interconfessional dialogue and a more extensive utilization of the ongoing faith and order explorations under the World Council of Churches.

Our response to further church union proposals will be discussed in succeeding chapters. It is important here, however, to refer to the interconfessional dialogues and Faith and Order discussions that have occupied attention in the past ten years alongside church union interests.

Bilateral discussions between confessional communions were accelerated after Vatican II, when Roman Catholic initiatives gave them considerable impetus. Such discussions represent the rising concern in the ecumenical movement not only for visible organizational unity but doctrinal and confessional agreement as well. Although World Confessional Communions have existed for many years, the vigorous ecumenical thrust of the 1960s and '70s tended to make them more self-conscious. As church unions increased across confessional lines, questions about the identity and role of particular confessional traditions were heightened.[26]

As a full member of one of the oldest and largest of these confessional communions—the World Alliance of Reformed Churches[27]—the United Church of Christ has become a regular participant in bilateral conversations. The chief example is the Lutheran-Reformed dialogue which, following a productive period of activity among European churches, has produced three series of dialogues in America. The concluding report of this series[28] asked the participating member churches to take action on four major recommendations:

a. Recognize one another as churches in which the gospel is proclaimed and the sacraments administered according to the ordinance of Christ.

b. Recognize as both valid and effective one another's ordained ministries, which announce the gospel of Christ and administer the sacraments of faith as their chief responsibility.

c. Recognize one another's celebrations of the Lord's Supper as a means of grace in which Christ grants communion with himself, assures us of the forgiveness of sins, and pledges life eternal.

d. Enter into a process of reception of this report so that it may become a part of the faith and life of each church at the deepest level. . . . [Then follow eleven steps in the recommended process.][29]

Interconfessional dialogues of this kind provide another perspective with which to evaluate the church union experience. For the UCC especially, this becomes a helpful way to address the "ecclesiological deficit" that it has carried throughout its journey. Although united churches do not possess a distinctive ecclesiology or doctrine of the church, engagement in interconfessional dialogue requires consideration of the entire doctrinal corpus of their confessional traditions, including ecclesiology. In the case of the Lutheran-Reformed dialogue, the Reformation doctrinal tradition of the UCC, encompassing both Lutheran and Reformed elements, sets out for consideration a much-needed historical context as its doctrine of the church is explored.*

A similar opportunity and process became available to the United Church of Christ when the Faith and Order report on *Baptism, Eucharist and Ministry* was received following the 1982 Lima Consultation. The issues addressed in this report had been under discussion in various ways for nearly fifty years. They were brought to a focus in relation to unity when, in 1961, the New Delhi Assembly of the World Council of Churches defined the goal of unity in this oft-quoted statement:

> We believe that the unity which is both God's will and his gift to his church is being made visible as all in each place who are baptized into Jesus Christ and confess him as Lord and Saviour are brought by the Holy Spirit into one fully committed fellowship, holding the one apostolic faith, preaching the one Gospel, breaking the one bread, joining in common prayer, and having a corporate life reaching out in witness and service to all and who at the same time are united with the whole Christian fellowship in all places and all ages in such wise that ministry and members are accepted by all, and that all can act and speak together as occasion requires for the tasks to which God calls his people.[30]

In the interval between 1961 and 1982, work intensified on questions of baptism, eucharist, and ministry, yielding finally a remarkable consensus document. The process of reception, discussion, and reporting to the Faith and Order Commission ensured full participation of the member churches of the World Council. For the UCC this involved a procedure set up by the Council on Ecumenism, which required study and responses from selected Conferences (and through them, local churches), Instrumentalities, and

---

*Examples of both Lutheran and Reformed doctrinal traditions can be traced not only in the Evangelical and Reformed history but also in that of the Evangelical Protestant Church and in the German Congregational Churches, which became a part of the National Council of Congregational Churches in 1925 and 1927 respectively.

seminaries. The final response, prepared by the Council, was then submitted to General Synod XV in 1985. The approving action of the General Synod included these words:

> The Fifteenth General Synod of the United Church of Christ . . . covenants with the Faith and Order Commission to continue the study of Baptism, Eucharist and Ministry, in partnership with other churches, and *receives it* into our life as a church for the guidance we can take from the text for our worship, educational, ethical, and spiritual witness; [and] recommits itself, in response to Baptism, Eucharist and Ministry to be a "united and uniting church" that intends to share responsibly in the quest of the churches for the faithful manifestation of the unity of Christ's one church.[31]

In this case, as in the Lutheran-Reformed dialogue, the UCC's ecumenical engagement in matters pertaining to the "faith that unites" is given the widest possible context. The mandate of Christian unity and the commitment to be a united and uniting church are held in necessary and fruitful tension.

It is clear, too, that the networks of ecumenical involvements exhibited in the preceding discussion bespeak a dynamic rather than a static set of relationships. They provide, therefore, a worldwide sharing of expanding vision, creative discovery, and new opportunities for ecclesial self-understanding among all participating bodies. They are especially important, therefore, for united churches whose experience in organic union needs to be tested in the larger sphere of ecumenical possibilities under the mandate of unity. There is one further development in these relationships, which will serve to bring this chapter to a close.

THE CONCILIAR MODE OF UNITY

The New Delhi (1961) definition of Christian unity, to which I have referred, generated concentrated effort to find *models* of unity that would be genuinely expressive of the dynamic character of the church and as free as possible of organizational limitations. From these efforts of the Faith and Order Commission, and dating from the Fourth Assembly at Uppsala in 1968, there emerged an emphasis on "the church as conciliar fellowship." The following description of conciliar fellowship was formulated by the Commission in 1973.

> The one Church is to be envisioned as a conciliar fellowship of local churches which are themselves truly united. In this conciliar fellowship, each local church possesses, in communion with the others, the fulness of catholicity, witnesses to the same apostolic faith, and, therefore, recognizes the others as belonging to the same Church of Christ and guided by the same spirit. As the New Delhi Assembly pointed out, they are bound together because they have received the same baptism and share in the same eucharist; they recognize each other's members and ministries. They are one in their common commitment to confess the Gospel of Christ by proclamation and service to the world. To this end each church aims at maintaining sustained and sustaining relationships with her sister churches, expressed in conciliar gatherings whenever required for the fulfillment of their common calling.[32]

By characterizing "truly united churches" as a "conciliar fellowship," the World Council's Faith and Order Commission began to utilize a concept of unity with a history that predates the Protestant Reformation. As Brian Tierney has shown in his scholarly work *Foundations of the Conciliar Theory,*[33] the concept developed in the late Middle Ages, when concern about the unity of the church had been exacerbated by the Great Schism of 1378. Tierney's words relate the concept of unity to the exercise of corporate authority, which is the principle of church unity.

> The urgent, widespread desire for unity in the Church was the very life-blood of the Conciliar Movement. . . . At the beginning of the fourteenth century [there existed] . . . a theory which stressed the corporate association of the members of a church as the true principle of ecclesiastical unity, and which envisaged an exercise of corporate authority by the members of a church even in the absence of an effective head.[34]

It is noteworthy that this medieval concept was translated into Protestant terms as the newly "reformed" church sought to resolve the issues of authority and unity. Tierney's interpretation of the fourteenth-century vision of unity is echoed by John McNeill in his discussion of the development of Protestant perspectives in the sixteenth century. For example, Tierney wrote: "The appeal to the underlying authority of the Church, understood as the *congregatio fidelium,* was the very essence of the conciliar position."[35] Here the constitutional principle of the church is the *congregation of the faithful,* thus also the reality of unity. Concerning the Reformation view, McNeill wrote: "The virtue of Protestantism is neither obedience nor 'private judgment,' but communion. *Conciliarism* is the constitutional principle which gives at once order and freedom to the exercise of the spirit of communion and the priesthood of the people."[36]

As a constitutional principle of the church, conciliarism has been given varied expression throughout Protestant history especially. Its twentieth-century reemergence as a principle of unity coincides with two developments: (1) widespread involvement of the Roman Catholic Church in interconfessional dialogues and Faith and Order discussions; and (2) a growing awareness that "the visibility of unity" can never be limited to visible form but requires qualities and features that identify essential unity. The increasing participation of the Roman Catholic Church is, of course, more than coincidence. It is also a result of the use of the conciliar principle, permitting demonstrations of essential unity without compromising identity and form.

Conciliarity as a *mode* of unity *shifts the focus from visible form to experienced substance.* It is, therefore, not a substitute for organic unity in whatever visible form that may be. Taking a cue from the earliest concepts of conciliarity, as discussed above, we can characterize conciliarity as a mode of unity in two ways: (1) as the essential modus operandi of the united church; and (2) as the *quality* of life where organic union prevails.

As an essential manner or style of functioning, conciliarity utilizes the constitutional principle of authority located in the congregation of the faithful. To function in a conciliar way is to act *in council* where subordination, each to the other, is in Christ. The headship of Christ in the church is thus never exhibited solely in a person or an office, but in shared acceptance of responsibility for the needs of the other as well as of the body corporate. To put it another way, the conciliar mode permits and requires living out what Martin Luther taught as "the priesthood of every Christian,

57

. . . a function to be exercised on behalf, not of himself, but of every other Christian."[37] Conciliarity thus assumes the corporate nature of the Christian life in the church. When extended beyond the local church to churches related regionally and/or confessionally, the conciliar mode functions in the same way. It thus expresses the essential unity of "all in each place" and of the "whole Christian fellowship in all places and ages."[38]

Conciliarity, as the *quality of life* of the united church, refers to the acceptance of a new identity in which reconciliation and a new experience of freedom predominate.[39] As a conciliar community the church is able to demonstrate freedom and wholeness in a society where alienation breeds hostility, and where over-zealous individualism is expressed in adversarial relationships. As a united church demonstrates and is recognized by this conciliar quality, it becomes the sign of hope for the unity of humankind.

In varying degrees the conciliar principle is the foundational principle of most Protestant church governments. The role of conciliarism in the ecumenical goal of Christian unity has become the occasion for united churches especially to re-learn its potential and make use of it creatively. The United Church of Christ in its ecclesial journey has special reason to explore more fully the meaning of conciliarity. Its heritage in conciliar Congregationalism[40] and in the representative form of government in the Evangelical and Reformed tradition yields important insights for being a *united* and *uniting* church.

SUMMARY

In relating the United Church of Christ ecclesial journey as a united church to the general experience of united churches I have sought to underline both possibilities and problems. As one form of organic unity, united churches have had and will continue to have important responsibilities as partners in the ecumenical enterprise. Three of these have been identified: interconfessional dialogue; expanding and intensified faith and order studies and consultations; and sharing in the exploration of a conciliar mode of church unity.

In succeeding chapters this background material is employed as I consider three sets of relationships and involvements in which the UCC seeks to meet the responsibilities of its ecumenical vocation.

The Ecumenical Vocation: Full Communion

A landmark event for the United Church of Christ as well as for uniting churches worldwide took place at General Synod XIII, June 30, 1981. In a celebrative session the Synod enacted a resolution sealing a "covenant of mission and faith" with the Evangelical Church of the Union of both the German Democratic Republic (GDR of East Germany) and of the Federal Republic of Germany (FRG of West Germany). The occasion was a signal response to the concept of unity defined in 1961 by the New Delhi Assembly of the World Council of Churches.[1] It marked the official beginning of a "conciliar fellowship" in which truly united churches are in full communion, sharing the fullness of catholicity in the apostolic faith, and acknowledging each other's sacraments, members, and ministry; and entrusting themselves to the guidance of the same spirit.[2] It was a significant step in fulfillment of the United Church of Christ ecumenical vocation.

The action of General Synod XIII culminated more than twenty years of dialogue, visits, exchanges of pastoral and theological leadership, and deliberate consultation about a shared ecumenical vocation. It issued in a relationship between the Evangelische Kirche der Union (the Evangelical Church of the Union) and the United Church of Christ* that displays a remarkable interweaving of the obligations of historical consciousness and ecumenical commitment. Tracing this in its historical context, and identifying and assessing the evidence of ecumenical commitment throughout, can

―――――――――――――――――――――――――――――

*Hereinafter designated EKU and UCC respectively wherever the discussion involves both.

illuminate some of the most significant, yet less well known, aspects of the United Church of Christ ecclesial journey.

There are important questions to be answered. Why a covenant of full communion with a European church? And why a German church, for example, rather than one from Britain or some other nation? For those acquainted with the details of UCC history, the answers may seem obvious. However, it is in the interweaving of the threads of historical consciousness and a shared ecumenical vocation that one can discover understanding and renewed vision.

ON THE WAY TO FULL COMMUNION

The immediate historical context of the full communion covenant is of importance for UCC understanding of its ecclesial journey, especially since it touches on some little-known aspects of UCC history. Beyond that, however, it is of significance to other united churches in their perception of their place in the realization of visible unity.

The convergence of particular developments, events, and special circumstances can yield clarified vision and decisive action. Such was the case when the objective of full communion began to engage the attention of the UCC and the EKU. The story of that convergence is in itself quite complex, but even more so when placed within the context of a longer history of relationships.

The first development, bearing a direct relationship to the full communion covenant, issued from two events separated by more than a decade.

The first event occurred in 1957, shortly after the United Church of Christ headquarters were provisionally established in New York, where co-presidents Fred Hoskins and James E. Wagner met with two officers of the EKU.[3] Dr. Heinrich Held, president of the Evangelical Church in the Rhineland, and Prof. Dr. Joachim Beckman, vice-president of the Executive Council of the EKU, had come to New York to pursue the question of closer ties with the UCC. The formation of the UCC had been of great interest to the EKU for reasons that will become clear later in this account. That church had been represented at the Uniting General Synod in June

60

of 1957 by Dr. Hans Thimme, president. The New York meeting with the co-presidents resulted in an action of the UCC Executive Council which declared: "The Council rejoices in the conviction that such matters as intercommunion and mutual recognition of each other's ministries constitute no problem in the relations between the United Church of Christ and the Evangelical Church of the Union in Germany."[4]

Although the Council referred the matter to General Synod II, there is no record of a follow-up action. This is not surprising since the all-consuming concerns of that session were the proposed Constitution and Bylaws and the Statement of Faith. Nevertheless, the Synod did listen to Dr. Gunther Harder of the EKU, who gave a brief but impassioned description of the conditions faced by the EKU in East Germany. Moreover, UCC sensitivity to the East German situation was reflected in the delegated visit to Germany in 1960 by Professors Roger Hazelton and John Dillenberger. Their report to the Commission on Christian Unity and Ecumenical Study and Service led to a resolution urging deeper ties between the UCC and the EKU. Nevertheless, it is clear that UCC preoccupation with its own pressing organizational matters was largely responsible for failure to respond in any substantive way at that time to what amounted to a "reaching out" of a "sister church" for understanding and support in a most difficult time. Through the remainder of that decade UCC concentration on its own development, and efforts to meet the social turmoil of the 1960s, left no room for official and definitive response to the EKU situation. This was countered, however, by continued informal visits and contacts, which led to the second event in the early '70s. That was a visit to East Germany by a delegation led by President Robert V. Moss in November of 1973.*

The Moss delegation visit came as a direct response to an invitation from the EKU (GDR), where there was a growing concern that the intention of the UCC Executive Council resolution be given concrete expression. In many respects the affirmation of "The Ecumenical Stance of the UCC" by General Synod IX in June 1973 was of great encouragement to the EKU. That extensive

---

*Those accompanying President Moss were Louise Wallace, Theodore A. Ledbetter, and Scott Libbey.

61

and detailed statement, as shown earlier, was a turning point in the UCC handling of its ecumenical vocation.[5]

At the same time, the significance of the Moss visit cannot be appreciated apart from two other sets of circumstances that made possible the interweaving of the strands of historical consciousness and ecumenical commitment. Two strands of UCC history and ecumenical commitment, dating from the World War II era, produce a single thread of surprising strength—a thread still to be tested in the EKU/UCC "covenant of mission and faith." One had its genesis in the work of the former Congregational Christian Service Committee and its continuation in a special project of the United Church Board for World Ministries. The other strand developed out of historic ties between Evangelical and Reformed and German Congregational people and their forebears. Those ties were renewed and strengthened in postwar reconstruction and relief projects, and they indirectly nurtured a pastoral exchange program developed under the leadership of Harold H. Wilke, then executive director of the UCC Council for Church and Ministry. Greater detail about these two strands will underline their contributions to the covenant of full communion enacted in June of 1981.

In 1942, anticipating the immense and crucial task of reconciliation and reconstruction to be laid on the churches at the war's end, the American Board of Commissioners for Foreign Missions (one of the predecessors of the UCBWM) was encouraged by the General Council at Durham to undertake "A Mission of Fellowship to the Churches of Europe."[6] Theodore C. Hume, a Chicago pastor, was designated as the emissary to carry out the mission from "listening posts" outside of occupied Europe—London, Stockholm, and Lisbon. The mission was temporarily halted by the tragic death of Hume a few months later when the plane in which he was traveling to Stockholm was shot down. In 1946 the mission was renewed when Howard F. Schomer was appointed director, and began the ministry of reconciliation. Schomer served as the Congregational Christian field representative in Europe over a period of thirteen years, working with and through ecclesiastical and civil authorities to rebuild relationships essential to the church's mission of reconciliation. Although his mission related to the whole western European scene, his contacts in Germany with the EKU became important links in the subsequent relationships with the UCC.

Nearly a decade later, when he became the Europe Secretary for the UCBWM, these contacts were of invaluable significance.

Complementing Schomer's wide-ranging ministry was the position of "fraternal worker" in Berlin. The narrower focus of this position was a response to the extremely difficult situation of the EKU in that divided city. The position was created initially by the Congregational Christian Service Committee. Preparatory work was done by Carlton Lee. In 1957 he was succeeded by Robert B. Starbuck, who served first with the Gossner mission in West Berlin. Later, under direction of the UCBWM, he assumed a dual position with the ecumenical offices of the EKU West and the EKU East. Peter J. Meister succeeded Starbuck at the end of the 1960s and served until 1976, when the fraternal worker position was eliminated.

Starbuck and Meister served in Germany during some of the most critical years in the life of the Evangelical Church of the Union. The postwar division of Germany into two separate states— one continuing an essentially capitalist economic/political tradition and the other claimed by a socialist government—placed the church in an extremely difficult situation. The role of fraternal workers, combined with the work of Howard Schomer in the mission of fellowship of the UCC, was mediatorial, maintaining contacts across political borders, channeling information in the reconstruction tasks, building bridges of understanding and cooperation. It was a *servant* ministry of one united church to another. When the Evangelical Church of the Union was divided into separate synods in 1972, to correspond to the political partitioning, the contacts established through the years of that ministry proved invaluable to those synods as well as to the UCC. In the reshaping of united church life in postwar Germany and in the formation of a new united church in the United States (1957–1975), a significant strand of united church experience and history was woven.[7]

That strand was interwoven with another through relationships that had their origins in the common ethnic tradition that many Evangelical and Reformed and German Congregational people of the UCC had with the German people. Some of these began in pre-World War II days through informal contacts that had developed between seminary teachers, students, and churches in Germany and the United States, most notably through the efforts of Prof.

Carl E. Schneider of Eden Seminary. His relationships with German church leaders in the tension-filled days of the 1930s forged links of special importance for postwar reconstruction as German churches turned toward their ethnic-related fellow-Christians in American churches.* Some of those links were formed through personal relationships developed between United States military chaplains of Evangelical and Reformed background and German pastors with whom they came into contact. Henry Koch and Harold Wilke, in their ministries to United States service personnel during the war, helped direct the flow of material and financial aid from Evangelical and Reformed churches, chiefly through World Council of Churches channels. Howard K. Hammelmann, a German Congregationalist, was recruited from Hartford Seminary in 1947 to serve a three-year term with the Wuerttemberg Evangelical Church as a youth worker. Pastoral exchanges between EKU and Evangelical and Reformed churches naturally developed in an informal way during this period. These became important links with the about-to-be-formed UCC in the late 1950s.

It was almost inevitable, then, that a more formal pastoral exchange program would develop as the UCC's new organizational structure was set in place. In 1964 Harold H. Wilke, executive director of the Council for Church and Ministry, because of his experience and involvement with the German church, became the shaper of that program, which has nurtured strong ties between UCC and EKU local congregations and prepared the way for full communion. Through Wilke's efforts, supplemented by President Ben M. Herbster's official support and contacts, four EKU leaders visited UCC churches between 1958 and 1965. These included two bishops: Otto Dibelius and his successor, Kurt Scharf; Gunther Harder; and Dr. Ferdinand Schlingensiepen, who was the EKU ecumenical officer. On the occasion of the latter's visit to the United States, when he addressed General Synod IV in 1963,

---

*It is of special note that because of his relationships with the German churches, Schneider was one of the first persons called to Geneva by the World Council of Churches in 1945 to assist in interchurch aid efforts. His was a key role in channeling vast amounts of food and clothing from the churches of America to the war victims in Europe. (From an unpublished paper by Lowell H. Zuck, "Appreciation for the Life of Carl E. Schneider").

agreement was reached that the chief objectives of the pastoral exchange program would be "continuing ministerial education" and the "nurture of ecumenical relationships." This exchange program became the responsibility of the Europe Secretary of the Board for World Ministries in 1974, following the close of Harold Wilke's ministry as director of the Council for Church and Ministry. Peter J. Meister, as fraternal worker for the Board for World Ministries with the EKU, became the contact person in Germany in this transfer of responsibilities.

Through the years since its formal establishment in 1964 more than two hundred pastors, about evenly divided between the UCC and the EKU, have been involved in this exchange program. Obviously the exact benefits to both churches are difficult to measure. It is clear, however, that the establishment of full communion between these two united churches had considerable solid ground in shared understandings and purposes. In many respects the circumstances leading to the EKU/UCC exchange program can be viewed as a providentially-given opportunity to these united church bodies to understand each other's faith foundations and mission consciousness.

Perhaps the most helpful perspective on the significance of the interweaving of these two strands of history, as we have discussed them above, is to see them as testimony to the power of the gospel of reconciliation. The story so briefly told here is astonishing in its implications. The memory of the agony of war, of unmitigated cruelty and suffering, of senseless waste, of human stupidity and human evil as seen in World War II, has dimmed. But the reality of alienation, of psychic scars, of human problems compounded by that war experience, remains deeply embedded in the fabric of the modern world's life. Reconciliation remains a fundamental, yes urgent, need. The story recounted here suggests clearly that in the wisdom of God the UCC/EKU relationship of full communion was destined for even more total immersion in the ministry of reconciliation in the years to come.

There is ample reason to claim that the "reaching out" of the Evangelical Church of the Union, in its time of suffering and need, to the UCC has become in many ways a reconciling experience as well for UCC people on their own ecclesial journey. This will be discussed more fully later in this chapter. However, in recounting

65

the weaving together of two strands of wartime and postwar relationships with the German church, I have underlined the reality that the ethnic differences exhibited in the English and German elements of the UCC are not barriers in the unity we seek and claim. The ministry of reconciliation is always a reconciling experience to those who thus serve. The *koinonia*, which is God's gift, is the creation of the reconciling spirit and act.[8]

The second development bearing on the move toward a covenant of full communion grew out of an event that has had continuing influence on united churches in their ecumenical vocation. This was the Toronto Consultation of United Churches held in June 1975.[9] In that third worldwide consultation, clearly-defined steps toward the realization of unity were laid out and urgently recommended. Possibilities and risks were faced. Because "united churches validate the universality of the Church rather through their adaptability to culture than through worldwide uniformity," there is always the risk of over-identification with a particular sociocultural ethos. "For this reason they need strong links beyond national boundaries."[10]

That perception is of crucial importance, since organic unions almost always take place within particular geographical and political boundaries. The point applies not only to unions in Third World countries where the majority of united churches have been formed, but also in Britain and the United States where cultural diversity tends to be homogenized by the all-pervasive influence of a technocratic society. Links beyond national boundaries provide experience in critical self-awareness, always a necessary antidote to provincialism.

This awareness led the participants in the Toronto Consultation to see the distinctive responsibility of united churches in terms that had been elaborated in the World Council of Churches' statement on "the one church as a conciliar fellowship." That definition, proposed by the Faith and Order Commission, was to be presented to the Nairobi Assembly of the World Council in December of that year. United churches, therefore, "should be prepared to be in full communion with other united churches,"[11] accepting the requirement of conciliar fellowship—full commitment to the fellowship shared in Christ. The Consultation, recommending specific steps to achieve this, urged that:

1. United churches covenant to support one another and to promote together, within the whole ecumenical movement, the fuller manifestation of the unity of the Church;
2. Each united church make the explicit declaration that it recognizes the other united churches as true churches of Jesus Christ . . . ;
3. Each united church declare that it regards the ministry of the other united churches as blessed by the Spirit and effective in the preaching of the Gospel and the administration of the Sacraments.[12]

The Toronto Consultation gave impetus to the deepening relationship between the EKU East and the UCC—a relationship that had had its official beginning in 1973 when President Robert V. Moss and three other delegates met in Berlin with the EKU/GDR.[13] Less than a month after Toronto, an EKU/GDR delegation[14] made an official visit to the United States and heard President Moss at General Synod X pledge the commitment of the UCC to "a shared ministry of reconciliation, peace and justice" with the EKU East. The significance of that pledge is heightened when it is recalled that the East German Synod of the EKU had known a separate existence only since 1972. In the twenty years immediately following World War II, the EKU had struggled to maintain its unity in ministry and mission under two separate governments—in the East a socialist state, and in the West a capitalist state. The tensions in the two societies exacerbated tensions in the church. The separation into two synods in 1972 was a step into the unknown for the EKU East. It required both synods to find new ways to be one church. UCC relations with the EKU West continued in well-established patterns, but a new official relationship had to be worked out with the EKU East. General Synod X action placed a seal of recognition on the EKU East path of reconciliation.

Events moved swiftly in the remaining months of 1975, reflecting the influence of the Toronto Consultation. The EKU East Synod was especially concerned to structure the relationship with the UCC in ways that would make it possible for "both sides to learn from each other how to offer Christian witness and service in their respective societies."[15] On the UCC side, the task of nurturing this relationship fell to Howard Schomer, Europe Secretary for the Board for World Ministries, and Peter Meister, who was serving as the BWM's fraternal worker in Berlin. Ernst-Eugen Meckel, Oberkirchenrat of the EKU, was the key figure in all developing plans with Schomer and Meister. His vision of and commitment to EKU East relationships with the West proved invaluable.*

A meeting in New York was planned for September of 1975. The agenda for the meeting called for decisions that reflected the ecumenical responsibilities and goals of united churches as set out in Toronto. It included the concern that "the goal of ecumenical contacts between the EKU and the UCC should be a joint declaration of church fellowship, signifying mutual recognition of ministries and fellowship of pulpit and altar."[16] All the plans for shared activities and study projects, and for "learning from one another", were designed to lead to that goal. The pastoral exchange program, so helpful in UCC/EKU West experience, would be extended in the EKU East. Of special importance was a plan to locate Peter Meister in East Berlin as fraternal worker—a plan supported by both the East and West synods.[17] A major element in the mutual learning projections was a planned lecture tour by two UCC theologians. Although the special situation and needs of the EKU East generated the central thrust of the steps toward full communion, the agenda of the September 1975 planning meeting reflected as well the shared hopes of the EKU West.

The third development of importance in the movement toward full communion between the EKU and the UCC was precipitated by the visit and lecture tour of Prof. M. Douglas Meeks, of Eden Theological Seminary and Max L. Stackhouse, of Andover Newton Theological School, in May and June of 1976. This visit, arranged by invitation from the EKU East, and facilitated by the Board for World Ministries, led to the establishment of the UCC/EKU Working Group which, on the UCC side, had as one of its principal

---

*All of them worked closely with President Robert V. Moss until his death in late 1976; subsequently with Interim President Joseph Evans and with President Avery Post.

objectives the "investigation of the possibility of establishing inter-communion between the UCC and the EKU."*

During their time in East Germany, Meeks and Stackhouse had opportunity to learn of the depth of the interest and commitment with which the EKU East was seeking to extend and strengthen the relationships with the UCC dating from the 1973 and 1975 official visits. Encouraged by Peter Meister to explore the possibility of joint work, the EKU Synod created a UCC *Arbeitsgruppe* (working group) to investigate and implement possibilities. At the close of their lecture tour, Meeks and Stackhouse met with the *Kirchenrat* (Council of Bishops) and were convinced that an analogous UCC/EKU Working Group should be established by the UCC to forward the common interests and concerns of these two church bodies.[18] Their recommendations were approved by the Board for World Ministries, and subsequently by the UCC Executive Council.†

The establishment of the UCC/EKU Working Group in the closing months of 1976 began a new chapter in the relationship of these two united churches. As the foregoing account shows, that relationship was not simply a continuation of traditional ethnic and ecclesiastical ties, but rather a culmination of events and developments having their origins in the special circumstances of church life in the post-World War II era and in the modern ecumenical movement. *The new responsibilities of these churches were being defined by those special circumstances, and only in a refracted way by common historical roots.* The question and possibility of full communion, although continually in the foreground of the Working Group's attention, was now encompassed by a wider range of concerns that had been identified in agreement with the UCC

---

*Other visits by UCC persons in the late 1970s and early '80s contributed indirectly to the growing relationship with the EKU. Besides various educational tour groups, the UCC had representatives at several of the German Kirchentag religious festivals, including Dr. Ruben H. Huenemann, Prof. Paul Bock, and Prof. Lowell Zuck—all of whom made written reports to the church.

†The initial membership of the UCC/EKU Working Group included: M. Douglas Meeks as chairperson, Frederick Herzog, Scott Libbey, Max Stackhouse, Robert B. Starbuck, and Frederick R. Trost. Howard Schomer and Peter Meister served in an ex officio capacity.

Arbeitsgruppe in the EKU East: theological education; theological imperatives for church and society; formation of the congregation/ organization and leadership of the church; sacraments and orders/ offices; common ministry of the EKU and UCC to the Third World.[19]

The move toward full communion became more focused in the Working Group as a result of a meeting in March 1979 in the United Church Board for World Ministries offices. The chief ecumenical officers of the EKU East and EKU West, Pfarrerin Christa Grengel and Dr. Reinhard Groscurth, respectively, were present for discussions. President Avery Post and David Stowe (UCBWM executive) also participated.[20] In those and subsequent discussions looking toward the declaration of full communion, two united churches were seeking to forge links, not only beyond national boundaries and across great geographical distances, but across the barriers of social and political ideologies as well.

The enhancement of critical self-awareness in the process of forging such links at this 1979 meeting resulted largely from a series of questions *(Anfragen)* submitted by the EKU representatives. Differing perceptions of the place of doctrine, confessional statements, the sacraments, order, and mission in the two communions, underlined for both groups the need for clarity in ecclesiological self-understanding. Complicating aspects of current developments in each church body emerged as factors to be faced together. For the UCC, these included especially their involvement in the Consultation on Church Union and conversations with the Christian Church (Disciples). For the EKU East, many of the pending ecclesiastical issues are related to the confessionalist position of the dominant Lutheran bodies in the German Democratic Republic. In differing ways the UCC and the EKU face a common problem of united churches: how to maintain openness in confessional theology (i.e., official recognition of several confessions) while seeking full communion with a church body having a singular confessional stance. The pressing question—wherein lies the church's teaching authority?—would continue to be an agenda item for both the EKU and the UCC.

Three events in 1980 became definitive final steps toward the realization of full communion. On May 18 the Synod of the Evangelical Church of the Union, East Region (EKU/GDR), voted to enter into *Kirchengemeinschaft* (full church community—full communion) with the United Church of Christ. Frederick R. Trost, a member of the UCC/EKU Working Group, represented the UCC at that meeting. The resolution voted on that occasion in East Berlin came before the Evangelical Church of the Union, West Region (EKU/FRG), June 15 for adoption. Frederick Herzog represented the UCC at the West Synod.* On June 6–12 a joint meeting of the UCC/EKU Working Group and the EKU/UCC *Arbeitsgruppe* had been held in East Berlin. That consultation was designed to further the process and prepare for a presentation to the UCC General Synod XIII in 1981.

The resolution adopted by the two synods affirmed the long-held intention "to nurture and deepen relationships to the united and uniting churches." Acknowledging with gratitude the twenty years of "dialogue, mutual visits, and concerted theological work . . . between the EKU and the United Church of Christ," the resolution claimed that "there has been practiced and there has grown *full communion* as elaborated by the ecumenical commissions." Noting that there are neither theological nor legal obstacles to full communion with the UCC, the resolution claimed that the EKU "is ready to acknowledge the baptism, holy communion, and ministry of the UCC." In its conclusion of the resolution, the synods expressed hope and expectancy that "through continuing theological dialogue regarding our common understanding of the gospel, *full communion* between the EKU and the UCC will deepen, and that concrete steps on the pilgrimage to yet stronger communion will be taken."[21]

With this resolution in hand the joint consultation of the two working groups, meeting June 6–12, 1980, spent nearly a week sharing their perception of the significance of full communion, with special reference to their respective traditions, practices, and circumstances. What significance does it have for those traditions? In what ways will ongoing conversations concerning further union in both countries be influenced? What new opportunities and obligations will be, or could be, drawn from this new relationship?

---

*In this connection it should be noted that the resolution engendered considerable debate in both the EKU East and the EKU West, where faith and order concerns were considered critical.

A Summary Report, prepared by the Consultation for the "Governing Councils (Instrumentalities, Boards and Agencies) of the Evangelical Church of the Union and the United Church of Christ," set forth conclusions about questions to be addressed and tasks to be undertaken in the future. These conclusions were based on the clear affirmation that "the effort toward Full Communion between the EKU and the UCC is oriented in what the World Council of Churches formulated as elementary ecumenical convictions of its member churches. The ecumenical movement is tending toward full communion of mutually accountable churches. Each enactment of Full Communion can be only one step toward this goal."[22]

As a means of gaining clarity about the meaning of full communion between these united churches, the Consultation recommended that four questions be addressed as priority matters in ongoing theological conversations between these churches:

1. How can the covenant notion *(Bundesgedanke)* and the Doctrine of Justification *(Rechtfertigungslehre)* be related more strongly to each other and *what might it entail for the understanding of Church and Society?*

2. What is the meaning of Baptism and Eucharist for the life of the congregation *in society?*

3. How in sound teaching and sound preaching are theology and congregation, *faith and action,* related to each other?

4. *What is the point of confessing and confession in a world in which the majority of human beings are poor and oppressed and where in hunger and violence they are pitted against each other?*[23]

The concerns identified in these questions reflect to a great extent the profound interest in, and appreciation for, the UCC document "Toward the Task of Sound Teaching in the United Church of Christ," prepared by a seminar sponsored by the Office for Church Life and Leadership in 1977.[24] Sound teaching (accountable teaching) assumes crucial importance in a socialist society where the church is not only in a minority position but also must be able to give reason for its work and life in a hostile environment. For the EKU East the "Liberation Affirmation" of the "Sound Teaching" document, touching especially on issues of God and state, church and state, and church and culture, was an encouraging witness from a related united church. The Consultation report was thus addressing the EKU churches in an awareness of their situation, but the UCC congregations as well in theirs, when it urged: "With special emphasis we wish to point once more to the discovery that Full Communion can grow only to the extent that in local settings congregations accountably make it their own. Only if congregations and church leaders become accountable to each other will sound teaching be possible."[25]

In its concluding section the Summary Report listed projects that would give nurturing substance to full communion: a theological conference in 1983 bringing together the mainstreams of the Reformation; a consultation on Peace, Justice, and the Church; introduction into seminary curriculums of courses on the history of the related churches; inclusion of seminaries and the pastors' collegium in the well-established exchange; common work in relation to another country, e.g. Tanzania, China, or an Islamic nation; a common position on "One Baptism, One Eucharist, One Ministry."[26]

LIVING IN FULL COMMUNION

The reciprocal action of UCC General Synod XIII in June 1981 to the *Kirchengemeinschaft* votes of the two EKU Synods reflects the interweaving of the obligations of historical consciousness and ecumenical vocation. In the introductory paragraphs of its response resolution the General Synod, acknowledging gratitude for the "gift" of *Kirchengemeinschaft*, alluded to the special historical ties with the EKU and the new possibilities offered in this "ecumenical moment"[27]: "in renewing our common faith in Jesus Christ as the Lord of history; in sharing our heritage as reformed and reforming churches; in responding together to the Gospel call to enact hope for all humankind." The ecumenical moment, which comes as a gift of the Spirit, includes awareness of the "stark realism and urgency" in "a world agonizing in the pain of East/ West and North/South conflicts; a world teetering on the threshold of nuclear destruction; a world with hundreds of millions of persons suffering violent oppression and living in absolute poverty."

The substance of the General Synod response to the gift of *Kirchengemeinschaft* from the EKU was based on the constitutional declaration of intention to "acknowledge as kindred in Christ all who share in the confession of Jesus Christ, Son of God and Savior as sole head of the Church," and to be "a uniting church." Five points are then delineated in which the General Synod:

1. Celebrates the global partnerships in the one mission which the UCBWM makes possible for the whole United Church of Christ, and recognizes each of these partners as "kindred in Christ";
2. Affirms the UCBWM and the President of the United Church of Christ in deepening our relationships with the Evangelical Church of the Union;
3. Gratefully acknowledges and celebrates the action of *Kirchengemeinschaft* voted by the EKU, and looks forward to shared ministries and the sacraments;
4. Recognizes a growing relationship between our churches as a mandate for renewal in mission and faith:
   • Renewal in mission coming from stirring one another up to respond together to the world's cry for justice and peace;
   • Renewal in faith as, mindful of our roots in the Reformation, we seek to meet the complex needs of faith today and to revitalize the local congregation in the whole range of its witness;
5. Urges the UCBWM, in continuing consultation with the Council for Ecumenism and the President, to pursue the development and implementation of a covenant with the EKU, in which our two churches will
   a. Develop, in cooperation with the Office for Church in Society and the EKU counterparts, strategies for witness in common tasks of justice and peace for the whole world;
   b. Develop, in cooperation with the Office for Church Life and Leadership and EKU counterparts, strategies for exploring and recasting the catholic, evangelical, reformed, and covenantal aspects of our theology for issues of faith today, and for providing resources to local churches for performing the tasks which God requires of us now;
   c. Explore these forms of mission and faith action for their possible significance in the relationships of our two churches with the other churches with whom we are jointly called to discipleship.

It is clear that the action of the General Synod placed the

primary significance of the covenant of full communion in the context of unity and mission. This was consistent, of course, with the central affirmations of the preamble of the *Basis of Union* and of the first paragraph of the Preamble of the Constitution. In this respect the covenant of full communion with the EKU provided an encouraging and strengthening consistency for the UCC on its ecclesial journey. That is the thrust of paragraph 4, where *renewal in mission and faith* is linked in consideration of the needs of the world and the roots of faith traditions.

Implementation of the covenant of full communion was given to the Board for World Ministries, with the Council for Ecumenism and the President of the Church having a consultative relationship and responsibility. That action illustrates an anomaly in UCC organization that often leads to ambiguous situations. The ambiguity in this relationship is underlined by the fact that the President is the chief ecumenical officer of the church, and the Council for Ecumenism is the advisory and planning body for the President's execution of the church's ecumenical programs and relationships.

In part this circumstance is simply the outcome of historical relationships, most of which were developed under the auspices of the Board for World Ministries and its predecessor body. In the postwar "Mission of Fellowship to the Churches of Europe" and the "fraternal worker" post, the Board for World Ministries' focus was on mission. That mission was an expression of an *assumed unity* rather than an ecclesiastically established unity. Its concern was to fulfill the obligations of Christian fellowship. It was "life and work" ecumenicity.[28] Likewise, after 1974 the pastoral exchange program, developed by the Council for Church and Ministry under Harold Wilke in the previous decade, became a responsibility of the Board for World Ministries. In that process, the program became even more explicitly an expression of "life and work" ecumenicity. The EKU concern for full communion, however—understood in terms defined in Toronto—introduced issues of "faith and order" ecumenicity. That action called forth the affirming covenant vote by the UCC General Synod, emphasizing both "life and work" and "faith and order," thereby thrusting a growing but largely hidden ambiguity into the very center of UCC organizational structure. Faith and order concerns are primary in the work of the Council for

Ecumenism and in the President's ecumenical leadership responsibilities.* In the UCC/EKU relationship, then, ways to deal with
such concerns were, by implication, a matter of negotiation between the Board for World Ministries and the Council and President.

This circumstance, underlined rather starkly by the wording of
the action of General Synod XIII, points to anomalous features in
the UCC organizational system. Obviously some negative conclusions can be drawn, but for the purpose of understanding its
meaning for the UCC ecclesial journey it is—at least in this connection—more important to see the potential of particular arrangements and actions. As is well known, all organizations have
anomalous features, and force their adherents into ambiguous actions. Such ambiguities may be the occasion for creativity rather
than difficulty.

In a clear acknowledgment of the original mission role of the
Board for World Ministries, the General Synod resolution (see
paragraph 1) placed the EKU/UCC covenant of full communion in
the context of the "partners in mission" program, which had become an outstanding symbol of its global mission strategy. By
implication this makes the *full communion covenant* synonymous
with *partners in mission agreements*. What is not clear from any
reading of the resolution, or from any other documents, is exactly
how these two concepts are related and what that means for fulfillment of the covenant. On the one hand, it is a continuation of the
question of how mission and unity are related. On the other hand,
however, the apparent identification of the "covenant of full communion" with the "partners in mission" concept raised very sensitive issues for the UCC.

The UCC/EKU Working Group was not unaware of the com-
plications. At its first meeting following the General Synod action,
the Working Group

---

*For example, involvement in the World Council of Churches and the National
Council of Churches, in the World Alliance of Reformed Churches, in interconfessional dialogues, in the Consultation on Church Union and the conversations with
the Christian Church (Disciples), all belong to the President's office.

urged the United Church Board for World Ministries in continuing consultation with the Council for Ecumenism and the President of the Church to pursue the development and implementation of a covenant with the EKU in which our two churches will: (a) create, in cooperation with the OCIS (Office for Church in Society) and the EKU, *strategies for witness in common tasks of justice and peace* for the whole world, and (b) create, in cooperation with the OCLL (Office for Church Life and Leadership) and the EKU *strategies for exploring and recasting the catholic, evangelical, reformed, and covenantal aspects of our theology for issues of faith today,* and (c) *explore these forms of mission and faith action for their possible significance in the relationship of our two churches with the other churches with whom we are jointly called to discipleship.*[29]

At the heart of this resolution is the Working Group's desire to dispel any fear that the UCC/EKU relationship was of such a special nature that other partners in mission were in a less favored situation. Was "full communion" a privileged position or a more fully elaborated responsibility in ecumenical relationships? In most situations the United Church Board for World Ministries, as the initiator of partnerships in mission, would need to carry the burden of interpreting the UCC/EKU covenant in terms of responsibility rather than privilege or position. At the same time, the covenant clearly underlined the faith and order elements of the UCC/EKU full communion, thus introducing a dimension that had not been a primary feature of the partners in mission relationship. All this pointed to unfinished work in fulfillment of the UCC's own perception of the ecumenical vocation. The fact that the concern for mission—its definition and enactment—was part of the EKU's agenda in seeking full communion with the UCC was in itself a promising sign.[30]

In the years following the 1981 "covenant in mission and faith" action by the General Synod, the Working Group continued to be the ad hoc agency with responsibility for implementation of full communion. Its membership was enlarged to include representatives of the Office for Church in Society and the Office for Church Life and Leadership as implied in the implementing instructions that were part of the covenant resolution. To pursue the responsibilities involved in the covenant, the Working Group divided into subsections (Peace/Justice and Theology/Worship): one to give attention to peace and justice concerns, and the other to theological issues—all of which had been identified at the Consultation in June 1980 in East Berlin. In addition, the Working Group continued to have responsibilities that had gradually accrued to it since its establishment in 1976 and the relationship with the EKU had begun to deepen. These included the pastoral exchange program; visits of theologians; and informing the church at large of the developing relationship.[31]

It is sufficient for the purposes of this account to refer to two major gatherings and to some ongoing interchanges of papers as illustrations of the fulfilling of the covenant of mission and faith adopted by the EKU and the UCC.

A Peace Convocation at the Evangelical Academy at Iserlohn in Westphalia, in June 1982, involved UCC and Presbyterian delegations from the United States. The theme—"Peace as a Priority Issue: The Pastoral and Prophetic Tasks of Ministers and Church Boards in Different Social and Cultural Contexts"—was of special interest to the UCC in view of the Peace Priority established by the 1981 General Synod. The opportunity to gather in Europe, where East and West tensions were acute, made this conference a significant part of UCC peace and justice programs. The Working Group and the Office for Church in Society selected UCC delegates from an overwhelming list of applicants. In this and succeeding conferences in which the two churches were fully engaged, differing perceptions of the nature of the church, *the role of faith confession and doctrinal substance, and their relation to fulfillment of the mandates of mission*—particularly peace and justice—gave evidence of the nature of the task of working *in full communion.*

Theological issues were the focus of another conference arranged by the EKU. In June 1983 the EKU East gathered a consultation at Erfurt to discuss "Reformation Theology for Today." In addition to delegates from the United States and Canada, there were also representatives of Third World churches. The peace/ justice theme was the larger context of the conference, with subthemes of justification and covenant introduced, respectively, in papers by Joachim Rogge of the EKU and Max Stackhouse of the UCC. The ensuing discussion exhibited the possibilities as well as the problems to be resolved by these two united churches. The

Reformed concept of the church, grounded in God's covenanting action, prevails in the UCC despite a strong Lutheran influence. The Lutheran concept, grounded in God's justifying action in Christ, prevails especially in the EKU East, while the EKU West includes more of the Reformed tradition, especially in the Rhineland.

EKU interest in UCC theological development had been expressed on many occasions. The EKU East Synod underlined that interest in a document entitled "Beschluss der Synode der Evangelischen Kirche der Union-Bereich DDR," with special reference to expectations concerning *Kirchengemeinschaft*. For that Synod the possibility of "further theological discussions surrounding our common understanding of the Gospel" was an especially important expectation.[32] Seeking to be the church in a civil environment that had been deliberately secularized, the EKU East church was much in need of the support of the wider Christian church as it dealt with fundamental theological issues. UCC theological concerns as expressed, for example, in the "Sound Teaching" document of the Office for Church Life and Leadership, had existential significance for the EKU East. In its own struggle to be faithful as the church, the EKU East Synod found its "full communion" with the UCC to be a "window open to the West"—an opportunity not usually available to churches in the eastern bloc of nations. Hence an "encounter between Europe and America," facilitated by a church with significant roots in the German "union church" model, was seen as a promise of support in the struggle.

Theological concerns in the "full communion" relationship were equally important for the EKU West, although for obviously different reasons. While the urgency for enactment of "full communion" was not as great as it was for the East Synod, the churches in the EKU West Synod had followed UCC theological developments with much interest through the years. The UCC Statement of Faith (in both the original and the Moss revision forms) and the "Sound Teaching" document provided opportunity for theological discussion of special importance to union churches. In 1981 the Theological Commission of the EKU in the Rhineland submitted an extensive commentary with questions concerning these documents. In that process the "faith and order" issues that are so critical in the union church context were opened for discussion. Foremost among them is the nature and place of confessions of faith in the life of the church.

Here again, the "encounter between Europe and America" is real. The role of a definitive confession of faith in Europe, where state and church are so intimately linked, is clearly not the same for U.S. churches. The EKU perception of the confessional principle has obvious implications for the UCC, where confessions are not seen as definitive of the nature of the church. In terms of its ecumenical vocation, the UCC stake in this kind of discussion is crucial. As a means of broadening the discussion, the Working Group sought responses to the Rhineland commission's commentary from the seven closely-related UCC seminaries. As would be expected, those responses tended to be essentially reflective of the diverse UCC understandings of "confessions, creeds, and traditions," illustrating again the persistent UCC ambivalence in ecclesiological matters. Nevertheless, the ongoing dialogue with the EKU has the potential of significant theological gifts for churches in both America and Europe.

A pressing concern of the Working Groups in both the UCC and the EKU was to further full communion, with all its implications, among local congregations and parishes. Both groups recognized that "we will have to develop a couple of models in this area which would indicate how the *local congregation* sees its ecumenical mandate and tries to fulfill it. . . . [In other words] what will it now amount to on grounds of Full Communion to act accountably in ecumenical terms?"[33] Experimental efforts to develop models resulted in relationships between "sister churches" in Germany and the United States. These involved exchanges of pastors and laypersons. Equally important was shared commitment to address major issues in both communions. In this process, UCC conference officers have assumed increasing responsibility.

FULL COMMUNION AND THE UCC ECCLESIAL JOURNEY

In writing a report about the resolution of the General Synod in 1981 to enter into a "covenant of mission and faith" with the EKU,

Frederick R. Trost underlined a perspective of special importance to the UCC ecclesial journey. He wrote:

> Kirchengemeinschaft (full communion) is more than a moment in history. It is more than a series of significant historic events. It thrusts us into the future, and is a gift which is bringing two parts of the Body of Christ together for a purpose. There is hard work ahead as we think through and live out the meaning of Kirchengemeinschaft. What of the common witness of the church, in East and West, to a just peace among the nations? What of our calling in a world fractured by social injustice as witnesses to the righteousness of God: What would it look like were we to engage in significant theological reflection, exchange and action together?[34]

Trost's words bring to mind the metaphor used earlier in this chapter to interpret the significance of the thread that binds the EKU and the UCC together in full communion, a thread made of the interweaving of the strands of historical consciousness and ecumenical commitment. Historical consciousness—that is, a sense of history—is the awareness that the "moment" has a context of past, present, and future; but, even more, it is the awareness of the obligations implied in the acknowledgment of the context. For the church, the obligations of historical consciousness have theological and moral dimensions. Both dimensions are illustrated in the primary agenda items of the major consultations involving the two churches: the 1980 East Berlin consultation where respective faith/theological identities were set in the context of the church's responsibility in the world; the 1982 Iserlohn Peace Conference; and the 1983 Erfurt Consultation that considered Reformation theology themes in relation to a just peace.

The historic "moment," however, is underlined by still other aspects of the obligations of historical consciousness for the UCC and the EKU. At the beginning of this chapter the question was posed: Why a covenant of mission and faith—of full communion—with a German church? Why not some others? Our tracing of the events leading to the covenant decision discloses the answer in several ways, including reference to ethnic ties and a shared sixteenth-century Reformation rootage. But of greater importance was *the reaching out* of the German church in its time of dire need and its turning to the UCC, whose spirit of ecumenical commitment originally exhibited in its antecedent bodies (CC and E&R) was focused on the task of reconciliation in a war-torn world.

We would be unfaithful to our calling were we to fail to see that this convergence of desperate need and commitment to reconciliation *was not our choice but the gift of God.* In a sermon given at the 1981 General Synod, President Joachim Rogge of the EKU East, emphasized the point:

> Certainly we come together with different understandings of the church and with different political convictions. Yet, nevertheless, we are all one. This unity is not true because we are so excellent or because we are so full of everlasting faith; but because Jesus Christ has prayed for us, that we may be one (John 17:21). . . . To the gift of being united belongs the task of each to seek out other parts of the body in other parts of the world and to relate to them in new ways. . . . You have sought (us) just as we sought you. This new mutuality is a fruit of the spirit, *primarily not the result of our efforts.*[35]

Historical consciousness is energized by commitment to the ecumenical vocation. As the UCC was being formed in the late 1950s by the power of that perceived vocation, its historical consciousness was alerted and its sense of obligation (responsibility) brought into focus on the task of reconciliation between East and West. The points of reconciliation are wide-ranging. They relate not only to sociopolitical and economic matters—each of which is of incalculable dimensions today—but to the theological, and especially ecclesiological, issues that continue to be crucial in this ecumenical age. Reconciliation of differing perceptions of the gospel, of the nature of doctrine, of the nature of the church *and its mission,* is also part of the full communion commitment of these two united churches—the Evangelical Church of the Union and the United Church of Christ.

In this way, full communion can be thankfully received as a special gift for the UCC on its ecclesial journey. For, as it is worked out and its obligations explored, we will be sensitized to other outstretched hands, especially those that in their own stringent and often disastrous circumstances will require new perceptions of the task of reconciliation. *Kirchengemeinschaft* is essentially "the reconciled and reconciling community." It is, therefore, a way of life to be learned for the sake of God's *oikumene,* in which nations, races, and oppressed people yearn for the hand of reconciliation and hope.

Perhaps the dimensions of that gift are suggested most helpfully by calling attention to some especially significant lines in the action of the General Synod of 1981. By the covenant of full communion the General Synod

> Recognizes a growing relationship between our churches as a mandate for renewal in mission and faith:
> • Renewal in *mission* coming from stirring one another up to respond together to the world's cry for justice and peace;
> • Renewal in *faith* as, mindful of our roots in the Reformation, we seek to meet the complex needs of faith today and to revitalize the local congregation in the whole range of its witness.[36]

Renewal in mission and faith constitutes the heart of the full communion expectations of both the EKU and the UCC. As illustrated by both the Erfurt and Iserlohn consultations, mission and faith are seen as integral elements of every expression of the church's faithfulness. The ever-changing world frames new contexts for mission as it does also, simultaneously, for faith. The new contexts were visible in the persons from Third World countries at Erfurt; but also in the peace and justice issues at Iserlohn. For the EKU, both East and West, the new contexts of mission had a special meaning because of circumstances laid on them by the prevailing Reformation tradition and by postwar developments.* But for the UCC the context in which mission and faith are framed today has a somewhat different promise, of equally critical importance.

This is illustrated by the fact that in the thirty years of its ecclesial journey, the UCC has given itself with considerable devotion to "mission," defined in terms that describe the transformation rather than the evangelization of the world. In that same period, as was discussed in chapter 2, the UCC has not come to grips with the faith heritage—theological tradition—which, in principle, undergirds that concept of mission. The consequences have been se-

---

*The contributions of Robert Starbuck, Howard Schomer and Peter Meister in assisting the EKU East especially to see the new possibilities is a story in itself.

rious—if not, as some feel, nearly disastrous. The consequent ecclesiological deficit has drained the energies of the church in many ways still unrecognized. Program efforts at faith nurture and spiritual renewal will always be mortgaged by that deficit until attention is given to the requirements of "being the Church of Jesus Christ" in this age.

The requirements of being the church in this age will be discussed more fully in the last two chapters of this book. It is important, however, to underline at this point the special opportunity of the UCC, by means of full communion with the EKU, to come to a new level of accountability in ecclesial matters. If the EKU/UCC full communion relationship is seen in terms of the moral obligations of historical consciousness (exhibited so dramatically by the "fellowship and reconciliation missions" as well as by historic ethnic ties), and ecumenical commitment, there is bright promise. The UCC can begin to discover the immense potential of the constitutional affirmation of its faith tradition and its responsibility to "make that faith its own."

However, full communion expressed only through denominational channels will not accomplish the needed renewal. That will come, as the Working Group reports have emphasized, only when local congregations become involved and accountable to the whole church. Local church involvement and accountability in the UCC, though, will continue to be unrealizable until, under the moral obligations of historical consciousness and the claims of the God-given ecumenical vocation, there is a readiness to acknowledge that the ever-damaging ecclesiological deficit has its anchor in the ambiguities of the UCC Constitution. Full communion, whether with the EKU or any other church, exposes the contradictions of UCC ecclesial existence. "Where there is full communion the churches are free to address one another with *critical questions*. They are compelled to *confront one another in love*." That is the reality of this "moment in history." Full communion, then, is a distinctive mark and dimension of the UCC ecumenical vocation, pointing to a special aspect of its history that holds both responsibility and promise.

The Ecumenical Vocation:
Ecumenical Partnership

The decade of the 1980s brought important new perceptions of the ecumenical vocation to the United Church of Christ on its ecclesial journey. Of decisive significance were those issuing from intensive involvement in two sets of church union discussions: with the Christian Church (Disciples of Christ) and the Consultation on Church Union. As concurrent involvements, they became intimately interwoven. However, for assessment of their importance to UCC ecclesial experience they must be considered separately in this and the following chapter.

When General Synod XV voted in July of 1985 to declare a new "Ecumenical Partnership Between the United Church of Christ and the Christian Church (Disciples of Christ)" it was setting forth in specific detail some steps to be taken as concrete expression of the unity given in Christ.[1] This action, with the concurring vote of the General Assembly of the Christian Church, culminated six years of covenanted conversations between these two church bodies at a time in the ecumenical movement when the focus in the mode of unity had begun to shift from "visible form to experienced substance," in other words, to the mode of conciliarity.[2] That shift in focus reflected the ever-widening consensus that "The one Church is to be envisioned as a *conciliar fellowship* . . . [in which] each local church possesses . . . the fulness of catholicity, witnesses to the same apostolic faith . . . [and all] are bound together because they have received the same baptism and share in the same eucharist."[3]

The full meaning of the "Declaration of Ecumenical Partnership" with the Christian Church (Disciples of Christ) will become known only as it is experienced in its implementation. Much of its significance lies in the history of a relationship that had its beginnings in the 1940s. That longer history, however, is illuminated and set into perspective by the substance of the partnership agreement and the process in which it was formed. For that reason it is important, before recounting that history, to identify and interpret the requirements of the partnership. These, in turn, will then serve to underline the aspects of that history which present the special problems and possibilities of the partnership process in ecumenical responsibility. This is, of course, an acknowledgment that the history of the UCC/Disciples relationship has features of quite unusual significance in the ecumenical scene.

A NEW ECUMENICAL PARTNERSHIP*

The proposal for an ecumenical partnership between the United Church of Christ and the Christian Church (Disciples of Christ) grew out of a covenant adopted by these two communions in 1979 "to work together towards embodying God's gift of oneness in Jesus Christ."[4] A six-year period of work and study (1979–1985) was undertaken with direction from a steering committee composed of twenty persons, ten from each denomination. In its 1985 report this committee recommended a declaration of "ecumenical partnership" between the two churches. The committee, working under the covenant mandate, had arranged a wide-ranging involvement of persons, churches, and administrative bodies in its work and study. The focus was on:

1. The theology and practice of Baptism and the Lord's Supper . . . ;
2. The nature, task and equipping of ministry, both lay and ordained;
3. The identifying of and responding to the continually emerging new forms and tasks of God's mission, with special attention given to the constant need of the church to reform itself.[5]

---

*The text of the Declaration of Partnership is given in Appendix A.

By use of a "Covenant Study Packet," widely distributed in both bodies, the committee elicited responses from local churches, wherever possible involving churches from each communion studying together. Linking these with its own study the committee reached two foundational midpoint conclusions in 1982:

1. The God of Jesus Christ who gives the unity of the Church requires the pursuit of union by all its parts for the sake of *the reconciliation of humankind and the fulfillment of God's mission;*
2. As part of the context of our wider search for the visible unity of Christ's church, it is necessary to pursue further embodiment of union between our two churches (United Church of Christ and Disciples) in order to be faithful to God's call to unity in Christ.[6]

Based on these conclusions, a working paper was prepared on "Shared Life: A New Approach to Church Union," and circulated throughout the churches, with a request for responses. Specific examples of "shared life" in five key areas of church life were: mission, mutual recognition of members, theology, ordained ministry, and eucharistic fellowship. Responses to the "Shared Life" working paper were both negative and positive. When placed in the context of the committee's own study and discussion they confirmed the growing perception that the times called for new and creative ways of "embodying God's gift of oneness in Jesus Christ." From that matrix of listening and study, the concept of an "ecumenical partnership" came to birth.

The distinctive features of the "ecumenical partnership" proposal were brought into sharper focus by the committee's report concerning its major insights. Through the study of scripture and tradition, combined with the contemporary witness of the church, the committee "heard again the imperative of the Gospel for oneness among Christ's followers and reconciliation within the church," and affirmed "the gift of unity-in-diversity which is already ours in Christ Jesus."[7] This careful linking of oneness and reconciliation reflected the awareness of the seemingly intractable problem of making unity visible for the world's faith in Christ while the Body of Christ seemed continually torn apart, not simply by disagreement but by diversity of gifts and traditions. The authenticity of unity was seen as dependent on God's reconciling act in

Christ. For a *uniting* church, that understanding is the sine qua non of the effectiveness of its witness.

In like manner, the committee's listening to scripture *and tradition* yielded understanding "that commitment to the unity of the church is central to each of our churches' histories—for the Disciples of Christ, unity is the 'polar star'; for the UCC, its first principle is to be 'united and uniting.' "[8] Those histories and identity marks were seen in the context of current ecumenical involvements and commitments, especially in relation to the Consultation on Church Union, requiring a clear determination to "seek greater unity between our two churches" only within the "wider ecumenical context." Grasping those histories, in which Christian unity is the singular benchmark, yields a clearer understanding of the potentialities of an ecumenical partnership. As we shall see later in this chapter, the history of the relationship between the United Church of Christ and the Disciples of Christ is uniquely enriching for the ecclesial journey.

In its time of listening and reflection the committee "heard again the cries of the world's oppressed, and [had] seen again the evil of segregation and other forms of brokenness within society which denies the fulness of God's creation to and for each human being."[9] Elimination of all barriers of race, sex, age, class, and disabling conditions "will be a sign of healing in the renewal of true human community." Claiming that "a union of churches which does not address the systemic nature" of these divisions is "not acceptable to us or, we believe, to God," authentic unity was seen in new terms. "To affirm authentic unity within the church is *not to set our sights on organizational oneness,* but, as stated in the New Testament, it is to seek to eliminate all barriers between persons and to live in anticipation of God's promised kingdom of peace and justice."[10] The indissoluble link between unity and mission was fundamental to the vision of an ecumenical partnership.

The committee listed as its final major insight an awareness "of the changing character of the search for unity and union itself." Seeing that the goal of unity is not simply organizational and institutional merger, it became clear to the committee that there is "need for a more dynamic understanding of both the goal and the steps required in achieving that goal." Therefore, "the focus would be upon mutual sharing of gifts rather than a compromise of theological positions or practices." This requires "an approach to unity . . . which is dynamic, growing and responsive to the gospel and to the condition of the church in its present context and this historic moment."[11] In that insight the move was clearly from "visible form to experienced substance," an affirmation of the mode of unity envisioned at New Delhi in 1961 and elaborated at Uppsala in 1968.

In all the foregoing learnings, which became foundational for the ecumenical partnership proposal, the influence of wider ecumenical development can be seen. This is especially true in relation to the Consultation on Church Union and the work of the Faith and Order Commission of the World Council. For this reason, the experience of the committee, of obvious importance for both churches, was particularly significant for the UCC. It provided a thorough in-depth reworking of the implications of the ecumenical vocation at a critical juncture in the UCC ecclesial journey. Most important of all, it gave new intentionality to the commitment to be a uniting church. The specifications of the ecumenical partnership, as in the case of the "full communion" covenant with the Evangelical Church of the Union (see chapter 4), called for concrete steps that take into account the tradition of ecumenical responsibility envisioned in the UCC ecclesial journey. In that respect the ecumenical partnership with the Christian Church (Disciples of Christ) represents a means of renewal of the vision through greater clarity about its requirements. A brief summary of the major provisions of the "Declaration of Ecumenical Partnership" bears this out.

Ten "Theological Affirmations for Our Life as Ecumenical Partners" provide the basis for the joint declaration. The centerpiece consists of three affirmations that are then spelled out in the areas of particular concern in the proposed partnership:

> Affirming that "all are one in Christ Jesus," and that "Christ is our peace," we hear with urgency God's call to our two churches to *claim together the signs of a fuller communion,* namely, the recognition of one baptism and one eucharist, the mutual recognition of members, the recognition and reconciliation of ministries, the common commitment to confess the Gospel of Christ by proclamation and service to the world, and *openness to common decision-making.*

We affirm that God, who in the crucified and risen Christ acted to bring the world to wholeness, calls for *our obedience and sacrifice* from every center of pain and injustice, hunger and homelessness, violence and peril of war, and all wasted and endangered environments.

We affirm these essential elements in the common journey to be God's people: *life in a worshipping community, the treasuring of Scripture and the apostolic faith,* and *self-giving discipleship in and for the world.* These, together with other graces from God, nourish members of the one church and support God's saving mission to the whole creation.[12]

These affirmations underline the areas of the life and work of the two churches in which the ecumenical partnership is to be carried out: mission, theological work, and worship.[13]

1. In commitment to a common *mission* on local, regional and national levels, the emphasis is on "coordinated planning and, wherever possible, joint staffing in areas of mission such as: education, evangelism, peace with justice, economic justice and human equality."[14] It is clear that *the partnership in mission area represents a major test point* for both church bodies. On all levels, joint enterprises in mission require *extra* effort, not simply in the expenditure of time and money but chiefly in overcoming long-standing habits of mind, and patterns of action. Any "breakthrough" in new models of mission partnership will be evidence of commitment to the ecumenical vocation. Examples, of course, already exist, especially in missions beyond national borders. Much more is needed, however, on local and regional levels where the "competitive mentality" of American social structures inhibits the surrender of self-assuring habits.

2. In commitment to shared *theological work,* the emphasis is on "receiving and claiming the theological convergence of the World Council of Churches" in the *Baptism, Eucharist and Ministry* documents, and the "theological consensus of the Consultation on Church Union" expressed through *In Quest of a Church of Christ Uniting.* The intention of this emphasis on "the theology of Christian unity" is to give opportunity to these two churches to enter into "*full communion . . .* which includes mutual recognition

90

of baptism, full eucharistic fellowship, the mutual recognition of members and ordained ministers, the common commitment to confess the Gospel of Christ by proclamation and service to the world, and *common decision-making.*"[15] Here again, the objective is in keeping with the mode of Christian unity that has dominated the ecumenical scene ever since New Delhi in 1961. Its special importance lies in its potential as a witness also on the American scene, where denominational self-defensiveness seems ever more solidly entrenched. As a bilateral move within the context of a shared commitment to the Consultation on Church Union, the partnership is a demonstration of the Consultation's achievements in its own journey.

3. The commitment to shared *worship* is recognition of "the centrality of worship in the life and witness of the church." As a means of underlining that point and of giving a common point of reference to both churches, the "ecumenical partnership" is to be celebrated in local churches and in national and regional gatherings with a service of Word and Sacrament prepared especially for such occasions. In this area of partnership life, as with mission, a testing of commitment will be felt at all levels. In worship the linkage between symbol and tradition is more often protected by experiential and affective perceptions than by cognitive and rational understanding. In the two churches represented in this partnership, as shall be seen in the next section of this chapter, the experiential and affective grasp of worship represents a diversity that underlines some of the major divisions in Protestant church life. This very fact gives great importance not only to shared worship, but also to a common effort in education in worship as envisioned in the partnership plan.

My discussion of the "Declaration of Ecumenical Partnership," and the process by which the Declaration was developed, provides a perspective for understanding the special role of the relationship between the United Church of Christ and the Christian Church (Disciples of Christ) in the broader ecumenical scene. By the same token it can serve the UCC in its ecclesial journey by bringing into focus some of the special responsibilities that have accrued to its ecumenical vocation in the years of conversations with the Christian Church. Those years have an important and fascinating history.

91

PARALLEL JOURNEYS AND FELLOW-TRAVELERS

The UCC/Disciples* story is about two *quite different but parallel ecclesial journeys.* After nearly thirty years of tentative engagement they entered a period of convergence. The model of convergence is unique, as I have noted, in that it became possible by setting aside (for the foreseeable future) the goal of organizational union. It is a model required by the special histories of these two churches as shown in the experiences of their separate yet parallel ecclesial journeys.[16] The convergence of these journeys, modeled in ecumenical partnership, makes the people of the United Church of Christ and the Christian Church (Disciples of Christ) "fellow-travelers" in a venture filled with imaginative potential and testing questions for the entire ecumenical enterprise.

The requirements of this ecumenical partnership are much more than a matter of simply "comparing notes," as fellow-travelers are inclined to do when their journeys converge. In order to fulfill mutual responsibilities in common mission, in theological work, and in shared worship, an intensity of experience and understanding will be required that has the potential for transforming both church bodies. "Comparing notes" may be the entry level of ecumenical relationships. "Discovery of each other's history," however, is the critical second level—an experience that can be both exhilarating and disconcerting. The third level is "mutual responsibility in mission," where commitment is tested. The fourth is the "transforming experience of oneness."

In the discovery of each other's history the UCC/Disciples partnership will expose the formative elements of some of the essential features of the American denominational system that continue to impede the actualization of Christian unity. But of even greater importance is the contribution of shared histories to the self-understanding of both churches. Although this is not unlike the process that is typical in church unions, there is, in this partnership, a significantly different context in which the shared histories are explored and reappraised. In the church union context,

---

*In this section, for the sake of convenience, "UCC" and "Disciples" refer, respectively, to the United Church of Christ and the Christian Church (Disciples of Christ).

shared histories often become stereotyped, thus foreclosing the discoveries that are important to unity of spirit and will. This became a major problem in the union that produced the United Church of Christ, where historical self-understanding continues to be dominated by false images. The result has been a failure to acknowledge and become accountable to the history in which the claim to be united and uniting can be validated. In relation to the American scene, at least, the obligations of historical consciousness tend to be avoided in the UCC. In the UCC/Disciples ecumenical partnership, mutual historical self-understanding will require a sustained effort to arrive at a shared ownership of each other's histories as an integral part of the common enterprise in mission, theological work, and worship.

A sustained effort of this kind will yield constructive understanding if undertaken as an essential aspect of the ecumenical vocation. In that context the disconcerting impact of fundamental differences can yield to the reconciling power of the gift of unity in Christ. When such differences are not faced openly, and are not addressed as responsibilities in the ecumenical task, they become festering wounds in the community of faith.

Some indication of areas in which mutual historical understanding is critical can point us not only to demanding tasks but also to promising possibilities. The sharp underlining of differences is here intended to show the nature of the task to be faced. One can focus attention on four areas where differences rooted in their histories have both *attracted and repelled* the UCC and the Disciples in their parallel ecclesial journeys: sociocultural context, theological experience, ecclesiological development, and ecumenical vision.

A. In sociocultural terms there are marked contrasts as well as shared perspectives in the separate histories of the UCC and the Disciples. Both may be described as "American religious movements,"[17] sharing many characteristics that are common to this nation's religious ethos: self-determination, individual initiative, commitment to free enterprise in organization and promotion, and confidence in the dominance of the Protestant movement. However, the nurturing influence of each of these has been conditioned by other factors that tend to highlight the contrasts.

There is, first, a marked difference of *place* when both groups are described as American religious movements. The Disciples represent a nineteenth-century American religious phenomenon, exhibiting the influence of three sociocultural factors: the opening midwestern frontier, the exciting promise to common people in Jeffersonian democracy, and the Second Great Awakening. In contrast, more than one half of the congregations in the UCC (in the Congregational tradition) trace their origins to the earliest settlements in New England nearly two hundred years earlier, representing a very different set of sociocultural realities: the first establishment in the New World of the religiosocial impulses of the revolutionary movements that had broken the unity of medieval Christendom; the breaking of the domination of ecclesiastical/political hierarchies; and the emergence of the voluntaristic principle in human society.

Second, there is a difference in *self-perception* between these two church bodies as they see themselves as representative of the American religious phenomenon. The Disciples, moved by the factors identified above, represented a movement in radical discontinuity from the Old World. This was more than the lure of the tabula rasa (the clean slate) dream; it was a maturing of individual and group self-determination that had been tested in the American revolution and the birth of the nation, thus nurturing the self-reliance required on the frontier. It was also a rejection of the dependency models implicit in hierarchical and authoritarian social structures; in that rejection was the birth of an egalitarian spirit unknown in the Old World. In all this the Disciples identified themselves with the common people of America's heartland in a continuing concern for the individual person's freedom.

In contrast, the *self-perception* of the Congregationalist portion of the UCC through the seventeenth and eighteenth centuries, and to a considerable extent in the nineteenth, reflected a continuing tension between continuity and discontinuity. Old World social/intellectual habits and perceptions were not easily adaptable to the New World's raw wilderness, but they persisted. Thus continuity, reflected in reliance on the old, resulted in giving congregationalism an "establishment" image that dominated New England for decades. The dream of establishing a "city set upon a hill" was oriented to the Old World. The new existed to save the old. But discontinuities were underlined by the circumstances of the New World—

a wilderness to be pushed back, ever new demands for self-reliant decisions and actions. In consequence, although individual liberty and self-determination were affirmed, the social structures of New England did not tend toward the egalitarian vision of the frontier regions.

A third point of difference in sociocultural terms between the UCC and the Disciples is *demographic*. With its longer history in this country, the Congregational portion of the UCC has inevitably become more urban, while the Disciples have a much larger rural constituency. Of greater significance, however, is the UCC absorption of continental European immigration. In the Congregational portion, that involved significant numbers of Germans migrating from their settlements in Russia in the last half of the nineteenth century. In the Evangelical and Reformed portion there were German Reformed immigrants in the early eighteenth century, long before the Revolutionary War; German Reformed and German Evangelical people through much of the nineteenth century; and smaller groups of Swiss and Hungarian people.[18] In these the UCC encompasses an amalgam of sociocultural traditions little known to the Disciples' movement, which was almost untouched by nineteenth-century immigration and remained dominantly Anglo-Saxon. There is, in other words, in the Disciples' sociocultural ethos a singularity of composition shaped by the frontier, while in the UCC a complex interplay of ethnic, racial, and generational factors makes for a highly pluralistic composition.

A fourth point of difference is related: the *intellectual* roots of the sociocultural matrix of the Disciples are relatively singular in contrast to the plural and more complex roots of the UCC. Such a generalization tends to oversimplify, but in philosophical terms the point can be underlined. The dominant Anglo-Saxon composition of Disciples membership from earliest days is reflected in a *nominalist* bent that *accentuates the precedence of the individual over the whole*.[19] That intellectual predilection was unusually receptive to some of the prevailing thought of the late eighteenth and early nineteenth centuries on the American frontier, represented chiefly by the English philosopher John Locke, and the subjective individualism of the Romantic era. It was the age of widespread Enlightenment influence, of the growing impact of rationalism and pragmatism.[20]

In contrast, the plural roots of UCC intellectual life represent not only the diverse expressions of Anglo-Saxon and Teutonic culture but the major shifts in human thought that had their inception in the Renaissance and the Reformation. German realism and idealism, *accentuating the precedence of the whole over the individual*—making the individual derivative—is in tension with the Anglo-Saxon nominalism at almost every point of UCC life. This has been one of the continuing barriers to a reconciled ecclesiology in the UCC, as will be noted more fully in succeeding paragraphs. The plurality/complexity of the UCC intellectual ethos can be illustrated in many other ways, of course, but it is sufficient here simply to indicate its contrast with the Disciples' intellectual ethos.

B. Theological differences and similarities between these ecumenical partners are suggested, of course, in the preceding paragraphs, especially in the discussion of intellectual roots. However, some of the distinctive features of Disciples theological thought and teaching that underline the differences should be noted. Many of them are derived from the basic teachings of Thomas and Alexander Campbell, Walter Scott, and Barton W. Stone, the major shapers of Disciples thought.[21] At the same time, the influence of the founders, although pervasive at many levels even today, is countered particularly by some major developments in the period following World War II.[22] These, too, must be noted, for the Disciples of this later period represent a clear movement toward and identification with the historic mainstream of Protestant thought.

It is equally important to identify aspects of the UCC theological temper in terms of both their classic form and their later development. This is, as intimated earlier, a highly complex matter due in part to a much longer history and in part to the plurality of theological traditions. An exhaustive discussion of the UCC theological ethos would be required if attention were given to the interplay of the diverse elements in UCC theology, and that is clearly impossible in this connection.

Three subjects of central importance in all theological discussion can be used illustratively to identify similarities and differences of critical significance between these ecumenical partners: the nature of faith; the authority of the Bible; the place and function of tradition.

1. The prevailing understanding of the nature of faith among Congregationalists of early Puritan days, and even of the early nineteenth century, stands in sharp contrast to classic Disciples thinking. For the Puritans, faith, on the one hand, was a gift from God, the work of the Spirit; on the other hand, it involved an intense subjectivism by the insistence that the reality of faith required evidence for which the believer was at least a responsible party. Experientially, the "blessed assurance" of faith was rarely entered except through the agonizing hallways of self-examination and submission to community correction; for, after all, it is God who chooses and justifies, and true faith must not violate divine sovereignty. By the seventeenth century, and until the early nineteenth, the pathway of the Christian was, for many, a time of all-consuming anxiety for assurance. Faith was a fundamentally experiential matter, in which rational powers tended to be at the mercy of the hopes and anxieties of the heart.

The classic Disciples perception of faith was, in contrast, marked by simplicity and rationality. While the Puritan tradition in the UCC heritage took seriously the Reformation teaching of justification by grace through faith—a teaching that presupposed innate human sinfulness—the Disciples, shaped in the milieu of Enlightenment philosophy and Lockean psychology, affirmed basic human goodness and consequently took faith to be a matter of *belief* in the scriptural evidence that, in Christ, God has saved humanity. In that stance, human rationality—examining and believing the evidence—made the experience of faith simple. Walter Scott, close colleague of Alexander Campbell, used this understanding of faith to design a "primitive gospel" suited to the frontier mind and spirit. This involved three human steps in order to be a Christian: belief in Christ on evidence of the scriptures; confession of belief; and baptism. God's response to this was also threefold: remission of sins, the gift of the Holy Spirit, and eternal life.[23] This simple "gospel" was a welcome word on the midwestern frontier, where all life was a matter of straightforward transactions.

Modern-day Disciples, of course, have moved far beyond this simplistic formula of a "faith transaction," just as in Congregationalism the intense subjectivistic strain of faith gave way to a more rational, intellectual approach. The emphases of Lockeanism have never disappeared completely, however. Americans opt for

97

"reasonable Christianity," whether expressed in either conservative or liberal modes. It is fair to say that by the early decades of the twentieth century both traditions had absorbed the same major theological emphases and, therefore, were much closer together with respect to their understanding of the nature of faith. What Ralph G. Wilburn wrote concerning the Disciples in 1963 could be used also as a quite faithful portrayal of twentieth-century UCC people of Congregational background:

> The combination in Disciple thought, of a critical approach to the study of the Bible, and a Christ-centered religious orientation have made possible a liberation of Disciples of Christ from the doctrinaire view of faith and led them to adopt a personalistic view. In the Disciples' syntheses of faith and reason . . . faith is more inclusive than reason . . . . [It] characterizes the primal life-relationship between God and man . . . the response of personality to the call and claim of God in Christ . . . in absolute trust and commitment; only in such total commitment to the claim of God does one receive the power of God's Spirit . . . [and] is the mind of man redeemed from sinful self-centeredness of personality. Yet reason also has a part to play, . . . a kind of John the Baptist role, in so far as it prepares the way for the coming of faith; . . . it has a part to play in the total response of faith . . . [which] is intellectual as well as volitional and emotional; . . . [and it] has an apologetical function to perform. . . . It must show the relevance of the gospel . . . to man's actual situation.[24]

The same characterization would apply, of course, to the Christian denomination, which has many of the same roots as the Disciples through Barton W. Stone and became part of the Congregational fellowship in 1931. But what about the Evangelical and Reformed tradition in the UCC? Does Wilburn's interpretation fit? In terms of confessional teaching (official doctrine) the differences appear in greater specificity and in the link to the catholic evangelical tradition of the sixteenth-century Reformation. In that tradition, faith is always *assensus* and *fiducia,* the believing and trusting in the living Word of God in Christ. But the *fiducia*—the trusting as a fruit of the Spirit—precedes the assent and commitment of the heart and mind. The role of reason is essentially complementary, and dependent on the "complete trust" of the repentant and surrendered heart.[25] Such trust is not the product of rational analysis but of awareness of being confronted personally by God in the good news of Christ. It is a trust generated by the Holy Spirit. Faith, then, in the Reformation tradition, is a gift to be received, and the response is a thankful life of obedience.

In the Reformation tradition it is God's initiative that counts in the generation of faith. That was distinctively Calvin's emphasis and, when combined with Luther's emphasis on God's initiative as justifying grace, it became not only the dynamic impulse of the Protestant movement but especially of the Evangelical and Reformed tradition. It brought a freedom to the human spirit that undercut sacerdotal ecclesiasticism and generated a piety in which thankful obedience to God became the binding element of the life of the community of faith. This perception of the nature of faith was the fundamental shaping influence on the spirit and mode of Evangelical and Reformed church life.

All of the above illustrates the impossibility of a singular characterization of the UCC understanding of the nature of faith. The diversity fits the modern mood, which sees it as essential to individual freedom. That same diversity brings the Disciples and UCC somewhat closer together despite the quite striking dissimilarities exhibited in the originating perceptions of the nature of faith. It also, however, underlines the importance and dimensions of the common tasks of worship, theological interpretation, and mission in the ecumenical partnership.

2. Two of the three subjects I have identified as important for discussion of theological similarities and differences between the ecumenical partners must be considered together: the authority of the Bible and of tradition. In this, again, present-day perspectives are quite different from those prevailing in originating times among both partners.

For American Christians in the first two and one-half centuries, especially those of Anglo-Saxon origin, the Bible was *the* book. It was *the authority for faith* for both Congregationalists and Disciples. But that authority was understood in different ways. The Puritan forebears of Congregationalism, bred in the sixteenth-century Reformers' reliance on the Bible and sharing their basic interpretation, used biblical authority to break ecclesiastical domination of the life of faith. Relying on Divine Sovereignty and calling, they found their way lighted by the scriptures, making them a "pilgrim people" even as the people of Israel had been called to rely on the Divine Sovereignty. In that emphasis they depended heavily on the Old Testament. Two hundred years later, as the midwestern frontier opened, the Bible became for Thomas and Alexander Campbell also the book of authority for dissent. In their case, resistance was directed not only to ecclesiastical authority but to the authority of traditions—doctrinal/theological—most of which they had experienced under the scholastic Calvinism of Scottish Presbyterian teaching.

Using the Bible as an instrument of dissent from the bonds of ecclesiastical and theological tradition was not the only expression of its authority. For the Puritans the scriptures bore authoritative witness to the Word of Life in Jesus Christ. The biblical witness to the action and will of the sovereign God came alive in the community of faith as the Word was proclaimed by those called to minister that Word to the gathered community, interpreting and teaching in the context of a tradition formed in the Continental Reformation. Study and interpretation of the scriptures by the individual believer, with an aim to sanctification and righteousness, was always subordinate to the teaching of the community of faith, exemplified in the office of the minister.[26] Puritan use of the Bible did not reject tradition but served as the means of critical assessment of the same.

Under the influence of the Enlightenment nearly two hundred years later, the Campbells and their co-reformers—especially Walter Scott and Robert Richardson—saw the authority of the Bible and tradition in quite different ways. Two principles ruled: "The Bible is the Book of God" and "Private judgment is the right and duty of man."[27] No human authority stands between the believer and God. The "facts" of God's purpose and activity can be discerned by any person and interpreted for the individual's own situation. All interpretation is in the nature of *human opinion* and is not binding on anyone else. This essentially nullified "tradition." In fact, however, *a Disciples tradition* did emerge and become authoritative for the followers of the Campbells—a tradition concerning the ordinances of baptism and the Lord's Supper, and the form of church order derived from the New Testament. The Disciples movement was initially "restorationist," claiming the New Testament model of faith and life as the true order for the followers of Christ. George A. Beazley Jr. summed up the founders' position:

Within such a context we may readily discern the power of their appeal: "We take the Bible, the whole Bible, and nothing but the Bible as the foundation of all Christian union and communion." Here was an authority universally acknowledged . . . , accessible to all, and free of the subtleties of academic theology. Their appeal to Scripture, however dogmatic and legalistic it may sound to a later generation was liberating in intent and in effect, as it served to release men from arbitrary human authorities and from the divisiveness of conflicting theologies.[28]

By the nineteenth century Congregationalism, losing much of the Puritan accent, had moved closer to the Disciples' founding principles, especially with regard to the "right and duty of private judgment," largely under the same Enlightenment influences. The growing impact of modern biblical scholarship was felt in all Protestant denominations, opening the way for new perspectives in affirming biblical authority. Private judgment was enshrined in slogans that claimed individual freedom as a *natural right* and not as the gift of God in the new creation in Christ. The consequence for twentieth-century Protestantism generally, as well as for the UCC specifically, was a pluralistic approach to the place of the Bible and tradition in the life of faith.

Another facet of the UCC understanding of the roles of the Bible and tradition is shown in its Evangelical and Reformed segment. Formed primarily in the matrix of continental European Protestant thought, Evangelical and Reformed self-understanding exhibited the mark of being "reformed according to the Word of God," and known as "one of the family of churches which confesses the Holy Scriptures to be the supreme standard of its faith and life."[29] Added to that affirmation is a qualification that had become the mark of the creative piety of the late nineteenth century among the churches of the Reformed and Evangelical families of faith. Elmer J. F. Arndt, writing with the counsel of a theological committee of the Evangelical and Reformed denomination, underlined the distinctive *Reformed* conviction:

It [the church] believes not only that God has spoken . . . of old, but also that he speaks today through the Bible. . . . Through the testimony of the Holy Spirit, . . . he speaks his living Word to us through the Scriptures. Hence, the Bible is authoritative. . . . The church lives under the Bible. . . . It knows the Bible as its "rule of faith and life." . . . Yet the Evangelical and Reformed Church has sought also to keep clearly before it the fact that there is a difference between "faith in the grace of God" and the creeds and confessions. . . . It knows . . . that faith in God is primarily trust . . . rather than . . . intellectual assent to doctrines about God. Its doctrines are those expressed in the ancient creeds, . . . together with the Augsburg Confession, Luther's Catechism, and the Heidelberg Catechism. These creeds are revered as conformable to the biblical teaching and as historic confessions of faith. . . . [They] are not substitutes for the Bible; their authority is dependent on the Bible.[30]

Thus, although formally a "confessional body," the Evangelical and Reformed Church gave primary place to the authority of the Bible. Its confessional stance was reflected chiefly in the programs of Christian nurture and liturgical life, but less so in its preaching. As in other "union" churches with diverse traditions, the plural confessional stance tended to be minimized. Nevertheless, this stance gave a much greater emphasis to the church's catholicity in which continuity is honored above discontinuity and dissent. It accentuated the corporate nature of the faith rather than its individual expression. "Evangelical catholicity" continues, therefore, to be a force in UCC life for which there is no exact historical parallel in Disciples experience, nor, for that matter, in Congregational Christian experience. The persistent questions around the authority of the Bible and tradition in UCC life are underlined in the ecumenical partnership with the Disciples.

C. Ecclesiological perspectives and principles of these ecumenical partners exhibit similar differences and parallels. In what is, perhaps, an oversimplified way of differentiating among the several ecclesiological perspectives, it is possible to say that the factor of *dissent* is decisive. Dissent required, for both Congregationalists and Disciples, a new way of defining the church as a visible community of faith. That task colored and shaped their histories in ways never experienced by the Evangelical and Reformed segment of the UCC; consequently for the UCC it is an unfinished task. Can the lived experience of ecumenical partnership bring new and creative insight into the ecclesiological problem?

The Puritan forebears of Congregationalism were as bent on

purifying and reviving the church as the founders of the Disciples movement were committed to reforming it. But the settings were different, literally worlds apart. The influence of the different settings is strikingly shown by comparing the basic documents of the Disciples founders with those of Puritan Congregationalism, for example: Thomas Campbell's *Declaration and Address,*[31] Alexander Campbell's *The Christian System,*[32] and Barton W. Stone's *Last Will and Testament of the Springfield Presbytery,*[33] which reflect the immense influence of John Locke's *The Reasonableness of Christianity*[34] as Christians faced the new experiences of the midwestern frontier; and, comparatively, Williston Walker's classic *The Creeds and Platforms of Congregationalism,*[35] particularly chapters one through ten, in which a series of creeds, confessions, articles, and platforms of Congregationalism seek to preserve continuity with the church catholic and reformed while exercising dissenting convictions. The common feature of both settings was a new sociocultural context in which centuries-old societal patterns were disappearing. The sharp differences lay in the way the early Congregationalists had to struggle with the authenticity of tradition while offering dissent, and the need of Disciples (two hundred years later) to adapt to the requirements of a nonstructured societal milieu in which old patterns of organization and government were incongruent.

Puritan Congregational ecclesiology had its foundations in the Reformed teachings of John Calvin and the Rhineland reformers of Germany—particularly Martin Bucer and Heinrich Bullinger. But the social matrix in which it developed was the English Puritan revolution when new models of social organization opened the way for fresh perceptions of church order and government. That new ecclesiology received its classic expression in the *Cambridge Platform* of 1646–48 in New England. It also marked the end of the distinctive Puritan era in the process of defining the church. Subsequent church-defining efforts in the last half of the seventeenth century and through the eighteenth were *accommodations* to the emerging voluntaristic society of that era, shaped by the Enlightenment. As a result, Congregational ecclesiology by the twentieth century found no impediment to a union with the Christian Church (1931), which had its origins in the same social matrix as did the Disciples. As an ecclesiology accommodated to Enlightenment thought it exhibited the marks of Anglo-Saxon nominalism: the particular, the individual, is real; the universal only an intellectual construct. In this, of course, the gap between the *Disciples* and *Congregationalists,* caused by settings two centuries apart, was at least partially closed.

The Congregational facet of UCC ecclesiology, however, is far more complex than the foregoing discussion seems to suggest. Denominational formation, thrust upon the Congregationalists by the realities of American church life throughout the nineteenth century, renewed the need for self-definition as church. That need became more urgent with the rise of the modern ecumenical movement. It was this need that moved twentieth-century Congregationalism to seek a "new form" of the church in the process of union with the Evangelical and Reformed Church. The impulses were diverse, but the concern for defining themselves ecclesiologically had deep roots in the Puritan tradition.[36] Those roots had been nurtured in the same ecclesiology prevailing in continental Reformed church life from which the Evangelical and Reformed Church drew its own perceptions of the church.

The common rootage, however, should not conceal the impact of the *dissent* factor discussed earlier in this section. Just as dissent gave a distinctive shape to Puritan ecclesiology, so the *absence of dissent* in the German Reformed experience was definitive for the immigrants from Germany in the eighteenth and nineteenth centuries who later formed the Evangelical and Reformed Church. In that tradition the church was prior to the individual, who was incorporated into the church by baptism. Local congregations were organized by laypersons as units of the church. The church, called into being by the Word and the Spirit, is, in Calvin's terms, "mother of the faithful." Evangelical and Reformed ecclesiology, therefore, had a functional view of the visible form of the church, wherein all aspects of its organization and government are determined by its mission. That mission, for the most part, did not include the modeling of a new and transformed society, as was the case for both Puritan Congregationalism and the early Disciples' movement.

The ecclesiological presuppositions of the founders of the Disciples movement were framed in quite another sociocultural context. Although the "restorationist" impulse is evident in appeals to the New Testament record of primitive Christianity, Disciples ecclesiology exhibits a variegated pattern of influences that tend to qualify and nullify that impulse.[37] However, the New Testament foundation led to a "high" view of the church as "the incarnation of Christ," thus giving to the church the authority of Christ himself. Although conceived as an "organic fellowship of all believers" in which the wisdom and grace of God are revealed, in the actual organization of the church the sociopolitical conditions of the frontier tended to prevail. Ralph G. Wilburn argues that

> early Disciple ecclesiology . . . failed to see with sufficient clarity that at no time in history has the inner, permanent element of the church's being existed apart from transient, structural elements. . . . Time has demonstrated that the restoration method not only did *not* effect the goal of unity but has actually served . . . to perpetuate and even to further the disunity of God's people.[38]

Sectarianism, the very evil that the Campbells resisted, captured their movement when the restorationist ideal was given expression in a social situation dominated by Lockean principles of the religious life and social organization. In that process a subtle but persistent anticlericalism gained a foothold in the movement, interpreting Luther's teaching of the "priesthood of all believers" in Lockean egalitarian terms. In like manner, the covenant of grace at the heart of the church as an organic fellowship, was enshrouded in the garments of the Lockean social contract.

As a result, the Disciples ecclesial journey reached a point of crisis.[39] It was a movement seeking to be the church—reformed and restored—in an age of the burgeoning of the denominational form of the church, a force that contradicted the Disciples vision. The ambiguities thus produced were exemplified in the restructuring experience when the name, The Christian Church (Disciples of Christ) was taken. That experience was accompanied by agonizing division and disruption. Disciples ecclesiology has been marked by stages of development in which the tensions between the original vision with its limitations and the changing ecclesial perceptions in American Protestantism generally have left confusion not unlike that prevailing in the UCC.

D. The ecumenical commitments of both the UCC and the Disciples would suggest more similarities than differences between these ecumenical partners. However, the differences are significant, and they account, in part at least, not only for the diffidence toward definitive unions, but also for the difficulties to be faced. Both partners exhibit in their own histories the reality that ecumenical vision and the commitment to unity are often far apart.

The Disciples experience illustrates this. The founders, particularly the Campbells, took the unity of the church as a fundamental premise. Thomas Campbell's famous dictum remains deeply embedded in the Disciples ecclesial consciousness:

> The Church of Christ upon earth is essentially, intentionally, and constitutionally one; consisting of all those in every place that confess their faith in Christ and obedience to him in all things according to the Scriptures, and that manifest the same by their tempers and conduct and of none else, as none else can be truly and properly called Christian.[40]

When implemented by the New Testament restorationist vision this dictum lost its touch with reality. As the Campbells developed their ideas, the reality of the divisive effect of scripturally based "principles" and "practices" was clear. As Ronald E. Osborn has said, the founders were not the "ecumenical pioneers" Disciples mythology has claimed.[41]

At the same time, the fundamental affirmation of the unity of Christ's church is the ground of an ecumenical commitment that has deeply involved Disciples leaders in the worldwide ecumenical movement. They and the National Council of Congregational Churches were the only American church bodies to respond initially to the invitation of the American Episcopal church, through Bishop Charles Brent, which led to the Faith and Order Movement. Given that commitment, the inevitable question arises: Why have the Disciples experienced divisions more than unity?

The answer is complex, but in a perceptive essay, "A Theology of Denominations and Principles,"[42] published in 1963, Ronald E. Osborn attributes the problem to the ambiguity permeating all Disciples history: the pressure to become a denomination in order to be a visible form of the church while having origins in the conviction that the denomination is destructive of the unity of the church. That dilemma persists, and is a constant companion in the Disciples ecclesial journey. At the same time it undergirds the

Disciples persistence and leadership in all ecumenical efforts to deal with the issue.

The UCC ecumenical stance is not unlike that of the Disciples, even as there are parallels of circumstance and experience. The UCC stance, discussed at length in the first three chapters, needs no elaboration here. It is important, however, to point out that both ecumenical partners face the same dilemma: the reality that the denominational form of the visible church is, because of its historical relativity, a continually inhibiting factor in both unity and mission. It is noteworthy that from the beginnings of denominational self-consciousness, especially from 1852 on, the concern for Christian unity was continually reiterated by the Congregational national-level gatherings. The concern for faithfulness to the given unity of Christ's church was the counterpoint to denominational formation, as it was for the Disciples.

HISTORICAL POSTSCRIPT AND SUMMARY

The foregoing discussion of historically rooted differences that have both attracted and repelled the UCC and the Disciples in their parallel ecclesial journeys, underlines some of the substantive factors of the relationship that had its beginnings at the birth of the UCC in 1957. These gain significance when viewed in relation to circumstantial factors that impeded the hope of an early union involving the Disciples.

The Disciples interest in a union effort had been expressed as early as 1947, when the International Convention of the Disciples of Christ* authorized their Association for the Promotion of Christian Unity* to explore the possibility of sharing in the proposed union of the Congregational Christian Churches and the Evangelical and Reformed Church. That authorization was reiterated in 1956, and resulted in a joint invitation to the Disciples from the Congregational Christian General Council and the Administrative

---

*Later designated The Christian Church (Disciples) and the Council on Christian Unity, respectively.

Committee of the Evangelical and Reformed General Council to send a fraternal delegation to the Uniting General Synod in June of 1957. In the period of 1957–61 the Disciples, by invitation from the UCC Executive Council, were observer-consultants with the UCC Commissions on the Constitution and Bylaws and the Statement of Faith.

This early-on intimate relationship seemed to indicate a real possibility of almost immediate union developments. Four joint meetings between the Disciples Council on Christian Unity and the UCC Commission on Christian Unity and Ecumenical Study and Service were held between 1962 and 1966. Two complicating circumstances introduced uncertainties into these joint efforts: (1) The need of the UCC Commission on Christian Unity and Ecumenical Study and Service to gain clarity about its role and authority in union negotiations and all ecumenical relationships[43]; (2) the formation in 1962 of the Consultation on Church Union, which involved the UCC from the beginning and the Disciples subsequently. The first circumstance was the natural accompaniment of the work of a new organization, and it was especially inhibiting when working with the Disciples' counterpart body, which had a long history of experience in ecumenical affairs.

The second circumstance, the creation of the Consultation on Church Union (COCU), immediately introduced the question of the advisability of bilateral negotiations. To what extent would the UCC/Disciples union conversations contribute to or detract from the COCU goal? As the records show, increasing involvement in the Consultation's work raised pressing questions about bilateral efforts.[44] By 1966 both the UCC Commission and the Disciples' Council on Unity could find no justification for continuing bilaterally. The suspension of UCC/Disciples talks can be seen in positive terms when understood in relation to the direction and progress of the COCU discussions. That will become clearer in the following chapter, in which the particular contributions of the COCU discussions and studies to the UCC/Disciples ecumenical partnership are traced.

It is fair to say that in the mid-1960s neither the UCC nor the Disciples were ready for union, or even for serious union negotiations. UCC ecclesial self-understanding at that point was coming under the pressure of critical examination in light of newly emerging concepts of the mission of the church as these developed in ecumenical circles. If anything, that began to expose the ecclesiological deficit that had been built into the UCC structure. The Disciples faced a crisis of their own, as discussed earlier in this chapter. The ensuing task of restructuring, when completed in 1968, left that communion with a new and somewhat chastened ecclesial self-understanding.

Resumption of the bilateral conversations in 1977, therefore, came with the prospects of important learnings about the ecumenical vocation to which both church bodies were committed. Those learnings came from difficult and trying circumstances in both groups in the 1960s and early '70s but especially from full involvement in the Consultation on Church Union. From those learnings the ecumenical partnership concept emerged as a new direction in the experience of unity.

If taken with shared commitment, the ecumenical partnership between the United Church of Christ and the Christian Church (Disciples of Christ) has the potential for radical changes in both communions—changes that can mean much for all those churches which have given priority to the ecumenical vocation. They portend the promising move from a concern for visible unity in organization structure to a concern to experience its substance in mission. For the United Church of Christ ecclesial journey it means new horizons and new hopes which, in turn, depend on a readiness to be reequipped for the new circumstances of the ecclesial journey. When set alongside the obligations of full communion with the Evangelical Church of the Union in Germany, it is clear that this ecumenical partnership will require new levels of commitment and involvement that go far beyond cooperation, goodwill, and casual fellowship. The "essential elements in the common journey to be God's people" are the testing points of full communion for every local congregation: "life in a *worshipping community, the treasuring of Scripture and the apostolic faith*, and self-giving *discipleship in and for the world.*"[45] In each of these responsibilities, clarity and consensus about faith, scripture, and tradition can be expected as the fundamental equipment for authentic witness. Ecumenical partnership is, in this way, another distinctive mark of the UCC ecclesial vocation, formed in a particular aspect of its ecclesial journey, and pointing to a new era of promise and responsibility.

6

The Ecumenical Vocation: Consensus and Covenanting

The closing years of the third decade of the United Church of Christ ecclesial journey were filled with events and developments that called for significant ecumenical decisions. In a space of six years, 1981–87, the General Synod took actions which, on the one hand, marked the consummation of years of ecumenical involvement and, on the other hand, set the UCC ecclesial journey on a new course. Each involvement has left definitive marks on its ecumenical vocabulary and vocation. To *full communion* with the Evangelical Church of the Union and a new *ecumenical partnership* with the Christian Church (Disciples) were added *covenanting and consensus*—two marks of the UCC ecumenical vocation that came to the foreground in 1985-87 through participation in the Consultation on Church Union.* Consideration of this participation rounds out our discussion of the three ecumenical involvements dealing directly with the issues of church union that have become test marks of UCC ecumenical commitment.

It is of no small significance that in all three involvements the United Church of Christ has not been the initiator. In view of the aim to be a united and uniting church one might have assumed that union initiatives would become a mark of UCC existence. The facts are otherwise. Why? That is an especially appropriate question to raise in examining and assessing involvement in the COCU process of church union. The invitation to respond to the COCU *consensus* and *covenanting proposal* will test UCC ecumenical commitment

*Hereinafter designated COCU, or Consultation. It is important to note that as of this writing the United Church of Christ action on the COCU proposals was "in process," with General Synod voting scheduled for 1987. Regardless of the nature of the vote, the terms *consensus* and *covenanting* are fixed in ecumenical awareness.

in matters that remain, at this time, untouched in the *full communion* and *ecumenical partnership* arrangements.[1] As will be seen, the COCU proposal asked not only for recognition of "consensus" but for action that would express and forward that consensus. In this respect the proposal asks much more of the UCC than did the "convergence" document on *Baptism, Eucharist and Ministry*, which was received in 1983 from the World Council of Churches.* The response to the COCU proposal requires an in-depth effort on the part of the UCC to recognize and accept the dimensions of accountability as a united and uniting church. If this is done it has the promise of realizing the benefits of accepting the obligations of its historical consciousness.

TWENTY-FIVE YEARS IN COCU

Some perspectives on the UCC/COCU relationship can be gained by recalling that in the years of its birth and formation the ecumenical movement experienced a critical turn of events affecting the entire Christian world, Roman Catholic and Orthodox as well as Protestant. Enthusiasm and optimism marked the cause of Christian unity in the period between 1957, when the United Church of Christ was born, and 1962 when the Consultation on Church Union came into being. The Third Assembly of the World Council of Churches in 1961 at New Delhi gave expression to new hope for a fragmented world, symbolized in the cause for Christian unity. That hope had been voiced initially at Evanston in 1954 and had become the central thrust of the ecumenical movement.[2] When the Eastern Orthodox Church became a member of the World Council in 1960 it appeared that unity had made a major stride toward the goal. Vatican II, announced by Pope John XXIII in January 1959, was the beginning of several years of a radical new openness and ecumenical consciousness on the part of the Roman Catholic hierarchy. Ecumenical vision and fervor were being matched by actions and events that formed the matrix of both UCC and COCU developments. Church vitality, especially in America, had known nearly a decade of expansion. Theological renewal, related to the

---

*See the discussion in the closing section of chapter 3.

resurgence of biblical studies and the influence of neoorthodoxy, gave strength to vision and commitment.

Ironically, the optimism yielded by this impressive convergence of promising developments in the worldwide Christian communities was short-lived. The 1960s, especially by mid-decade, brought a chilling awareness that the world's dis-ease found little or no assurance in all the ecclesiastical achievements and promises of that time. Increasingly hostile forces in the society aimed critical barbs at all institutions, including the churches. By 1965 the General Synod of the United Church of Christ faced up to that reality in a major effort to shape its organization into an effective instrument of mission. The focus of attention was: In what ways can church structures be designed for mission in a time of anti-institutional commitment? That became a major concern of all the mainline denominations as organizational inadequacies emerged in the confrontations that were characteristic of the times. Unfortunately, in many cases it was a time of denominational self-defensive preoccupation that seemed to throw "cold water" on the prospects for Christian unity.

In this very atmosphere of challenge to traditional ecclesial structures the Consultation on Church Union came to birth. To some it seemed to be born out-of-time, an anachronism, a last futile effort to justify institutional religion. To others it was an underlining of the very hope that the ecumenical vision had nurtured for so many years—the hope that the visible unity of the church could become an unmistakable sign of God's reconciling presence in the world. COCU was proposed as a vision of what *church union* could accomplish and as an instrument for making that vision a reality. In this respect the vision that produced COCU corresponds closely to the vision that gave birth to the United Church of Christ. At the same time there were significantly different perceptions of what was needed to give substance to the vision. Those differences require attention if the UCC/COCU relationship is to be understood. The consequent difficulties and tensions need candid evaluation if the potentials of the *covenanting* process and the *consensus* instrument, proposed by COCU, are to be realized.

There was an inevitability about UCC involvement in COCU. When Eugene Carson Blake, the proposer of the COCU concept in 1960, was asked some years later why the UCC was invited to become one of the founding participants, he responded: "Because I felt they would likely say yes."[3] The UCC example of church union had commanded the attention of all ecumenically minded persons and churches. Thus its response was positive and immediate, giving it a voice in all the critical initiating steps.[4] At that point in December 1960, of course, the United Church of Christ organization was not yet accomplished. Its Constitution and Bylaws had been adopted that summer, but were not declared operative until June 1961. Thus, in the most critical years of its organizational formation, the United Church of Christ became a participant in a wider concept of church union.

What seemed to be a natural step, however, was actually more complicated. This becomes clear when attention is given to the central thrust of the proposal that led to the establishing of the Consultation. It was a proposal to explore the establishment of a "united church, *truly catholic, truly evangelical, truly reformed,*"[5] thus clearly giving priority to "faith and order" issues as foundational matters in union. That direction was given greater specificity when the Episcopal Church made its participation in the Consultation conditional upon agreement concerning the "Holy Scriptures, the Creeds, the Sacraments, and the Historic Episcopate."[6]

The UCC experience in church union, as has been seen, stands in sharp contrast to such emphases on faith and order.* Formed under the dynamic impulses of "socio-moral ecumenicity," which had dominated the ecumenical scene in the 1920s and '30s when its union process began, the UCC had concentrated on devising a viable form of church structure that would give expression to a unity in faith assumed and confessed. Matters of faith and order could be expected to reach a consensus level through faithful witness in mission and ministry. Doctrinal differences were subordinated to the goal of organic unity, but some form of consensus became an obligation for the future. Differences were *continuing questions* for a united church but not *preconditions* for union.

Participation in COCU, therefore, seemed, on the one hand, to present the opportunity needed for the UCC to begin its own deferred work on matters of faith and order. On the other hand, engaging in a church union effort in which faith and order questions

---

*See the discussion of this in chapter 2.

are preconditions, introduced tensions in the UCC/COCU relationship that have persisted. In principle, the potential benefit for the UCC was obvious. In actual fact, that benefit was not realized to the degree anticipated by some. The reasons are complex; in part, circumstantial, relating to the influence of radical social change and concomitant changes in ecumenical vision; but also foundational, relating to some of the ambiguities in UCC ecclesial self-perception.

At the same time, UCC involvement in and commitment to the Consultation should not be minimized. From the beginning the UCC contributed significant leadership. David G. Colwell, chairperson of the UCC Commission on Christian Unity and Ecumenical Study and Service, was deeply involved in the Consultation, serving as chair of COCU's Executive Committee, 1966–68. Profs. Elmer J. F. Arndt, John Dillenberger, and Roger Hazelton, along with Gerhard Grauer, Truman B. Douglass, President Ben Herbster, and Helen Baker, had part in the discussions leading to the first major document of COCU—*Principles of Church Union,* published in 1966. In succeeding years many other persons were members of the UCC delegations and continued to give service to the COCU vision.

It is, nevertheless, important to acknowledge that the Consultation has never been a high priority concern of the UCC as a whole. In large part this reflects the many circumstantial factors cited in chapter 1 that have inhibited fulfillment of the ecumenical vocation. In the same years COCU was working out "the principles of church union," with a focus on faith and order, the UCC's grounding in a life and work orientation was being confirmed in its ever-deepening responses to the emerging social crises of the '60s. As a consequence, the Consultation did not claim the UCC ecumenical vision and commitment at the grass roots level. The energies and attention of the church on all levels were absorbed by the special needs of that time. In view of this, the negative response of the UCC to the *Plan of Union* proposed by the Consultation in 1970 might well have ended the UCC/COCU relationship. The fact that this did not happen can be traced to changes in both the UCC and COCU that have produced some points of convergence of perspectives about unity and union.

In the case of the UCC, the changes are linked to the growing

114

awareness of the need to address faith and order matters with greater intentionality in the effort to fulfill its ecumenical vocation. As discussed in the concluding section of chapter 2, claiming a particular "ecclesiological location" requires clarity about the faith declared. Seeking such clarity meant some convergence with the basic design of the COCU discussions that from the beginning, had concentrated on the faith ground of church union.

Of equal importance were the changes in the Consultation itself. The failure of the 1970 *Plan of Union* to gain support among member churches led the Consultation in 1973 to review the approach it had taken to accomplish a multiparty church union. The result was a transformation of the Consultation, giving it a dynamic character that commands attention throughout the ecumenical movement. The transformation confirmed the vision and understanding that had been growing among many of those who had been intimately involved. Thus, in 1972 Stephen C. Rose could characterize the Consultation as

> an *authoritative conciliar process* on the Protestant ecumenical scene, dealing with "Faith and Order" issues and forwarding a process of *participatory ecumenism* that integrates the institutional churches involved with the new ecumenism of "all in each place." By refining principles of union, renewal, and mission, and by inaugurating a plan of union that will involve the church in each place in common conversation, COCU . . . exhibits authority evidenced by the free response of divided churches to its prayer and vision.[7]

In many respects it can be said that the Consultation had "come of age," representing a kind of breakthrough in what seemed to be a stalemate in all efforts to move from denominational autonomy toward union. Instead of a continuing focus on "designing church union from the top down," a deliberate decision was made to enter into a process of "living [a] way toward union, especially in growing together in local and regional expressions of the church."[8] That decision meant an entirely new style of church union effort in the final quarter of twentieth-century ecumenism.

> Living our way to union offers two heartening revelations . . . .: First, to speak of living our way to union should *encourage congregations and middle judicatories to experience union,* to seek reconciliation

at their levels. If this happens, church union will not be something that seems alien to their Christian experience, but a response that arises out of their faithfulness to the Gospel in their locale. Secondly, their method *allows the churches themselves to contribute to the shape of a united church*. . . . The Consultation is now committed to sharing the ownership of the vision, to help the whole people of God travel the road to union.[9]

Without question this change in direction and style had the potential for adding entirely new dimensions of experiences to the church union process. Perhaps few could have anticipated the developments of the remainder of the decade. A new era had begun for the Consultation and it took on new life.[10] Living the way to union became a time of surprising discovery.

A first step in this new direction involved a revision of those portions of *The Plan of Union* (submitted to the churches in 1970) having to do with faith, worship, and ministry. The intention in undertaking that revision was to provide "a theological basis for working toward *mutual recognition of members and ministries,* and further development of a plan of union."[11] Clearly, such mutual recognition was a sine qua non for developing ways to live toward union. This meant meeting head-on some of the most difficult and divisive issues in church union.

In many respects, however, the most significant feature of the 1976 report of the Theological Commission of the Consultation to which the revision task had been assigned, was an appended section entitled: "An Alert on the New Church-Dividing Potential of Some Persistent Issues." The "alert" underlined the divisive nature of four nontheological issues: racism, sexism, institutionalism, and exclusivistic congregationalism. The inclusion of reference to these nontheological church-dividing issues in the report dealing with faith, worship, and ministry, marked the conjoining of "faith and order" and "life and work" concerns in the *context of concrete church union efforts.* That conjunction was a watershed in the COCU enterprise.

Of course, facing up to these alienating and divisive issues was simply a reflection of the tensions in all of American church life. The social turmoil of the 1960s left indelible marks on every major denomination. As a result, the '70s became a time not only for agonizing self-examination and searching for ways to deal responsibly with these issues, but also a time of raising anew the fundamental questions about *the church as God's reconciling mission* in the world. Within each denomination the initial responses to these divisive issues tended to be organizational/political, dominated generally, as Albert Outler has suggested, by "the philosophical virtues of prudence and justice rather more than . . . from the theological virtue of charity."[12] Toward the end of the decade, when organizational/political responses were perceived as lacking the fundamental spirit and substance of the church as God's reconciling community, a vigorous theological response began to address the issues of racism and sexism especially. Generated in large part by black and women theologians, this response has become a most significant component of late twentieth-century theology.

Although the church-dividing issues of racism and sexism received continuing, but not always consistent, attention in the Consultation's member denominations, the issues of institutionalism and exclusivistic congregationalism* were rarely addressed with the same intensity. Deeply embedded in the denominational form of the church as the bastion of privatistic religious life, denominations are not generally penetrable by reform efforts from within.[13] Denominationalism is, as Bishop J. Lesslie Newbigin has charged, simply the "institutional form of privatized religion." It is the "visible form of an inward and spiritual surrender to the ideology of our culture."[14] It is equally the case that exclusivistic congregationalism is a surrender to the culture of privatized religion. It was in the Consultation, however, that all these issues have been addressed most directly. At least three circumstances gave the Consultation freedom to do this in ways that most denominations do not have available.

First, the COCU experience of a decade of church union planning had been focused on a wider spectrum of ecclesiological perspectives than is generally available to any single denomination. The intentional concern to understand the church in its catholic, evangelical, and reformed dimensions *from the beginning* gave the Consultation freedom from the self-serving definitions that plague

---

* "Congregationalism" as used here denotes the emphasis on the primacy of the congregation in the church consciousness of the people. As has been said: "Congregationalism is the mode of church life in all American denominations."

117

denominational perspectives on the nature of the church. In that freedom the Consultation moved from the arena of negotiation of differences between uniting bodies, into the *arena of mutual discovery*.* It permitted a direct approach, especially to the problems of institutionalism and exclusivistic congregationalism, under the critical purview of the faith.

Second, the presence of three black denominations in the Consultation had the effect of introducing a style of change that is *movement-oriented* rather than *institution-oriented*. That is to say, the ethos of the black churches in the 1950s and '60s was characterized by *liberation* concerns rather than institutional concerns per se. The movement-orientation of these churches thus became a powerful factor in the generating of a liberation thrust in the Consultation's perception of its mission. Canon Burgess Carr of the All Africa Conference of Churches, in addressing the Consultation's 13th Plenary in 1976, identified the change in the COCU focus:

> Therefore, in a real sense, the significance of COCU is not merely a search for the organic union of nine of the major denominations of this country. It is really a challenge to allow Christ to *liberate* you from your ecclesiastical fetters and set you free to share in the union he shares with the Father. . . . Is overcoming our theological snobbishness toward one another the most urgent priority of any of our churches? Or is it overcoming the disparities in human living, and conditions caused by poverty, racism, exploitation in old and new forms, and sexism in the world.[15]

Third, the concomitant factor of the growing influence of the *feminist movement* added another dynamic in the early '70s, reinforcing the liberation perspective in the Consultation's concern for a united church truly catholic, evangelical, and reformed. Feminist goals especially gave a new orientation to consideration of theological issues couched in traditional terms. When supplemented by the vigorous and creative leadership of ever-larger numbers of women delegates to the Consultation, this orientation had immense influence. It was particularly helpful in opening the understanding of the

---

*The UCC experience is an example. Mutual discovery in the pursuit of a new model of church organization was continually inhibited by the denominational mind-set that sees negotiation as the solution to divisive matters.

participating churches to the subtleties and persistence of church-dividing issues rooted in the patterns of human society.

THE UCC AND THE TRANSFORMED CONSULTATION

It is clear that many of the changes in the Consultation gave it an orientation quite congruent with the major concerns of the UCC through the decade of the '70s. The liberationist perspective of the Consultation was harmonious with the socio-moral roots of the UCC union experience. Nevertheless, as indicated earlier, tensions persisted and UCC involvement in the COCU proposals for advancing church union continued to exhibit ambivalence and restraint. Earlier in this chapter I attributed this to some ambiguities in UCC ecclesial self-perception.

Perhaps the most helpful illustration of these ambiguities can be found in the UCC official response to chapter VII, "The Ministry," in *In Quest of a Church of Christ Uniting*.[16] This chapter represented the last of a series of "consensus" chapters to which the participating member churches of COCU were asked to respond. The "Introduction" to the UCC response to the chapter on ministry described the reception and study process.

> We are pleased to note and report that the chapter has been studied extensively in the United Church of Christ, in a variety of settings in all sections of the Church. While an open invitation was given to the whole church, special effort was made to have the chapter studied by the Executive Council, the Boards and Staff of National bodies and Conferences, all Church and Ministry Committees in Associations, Special Interest Groups, and Seminaries. . . . The study process has involved both clergy and laity, and has included persons in key leadership roles across the denomination.[17]

The UCC response included two summations that can be helpful in understanding UCC ambivalence toward the COCU proposals. First,

> the sub-sections on "The Ministry of Jesus Christ and the Ministry of God's People" and "The Ministry of Lay Persons" received *the*

strongest affirmation by far and the fewest reservations or sugges-
tions for change. There was a high degree of comfort and agreement
with those sections.

Second,

> the sub-section on "The Ministry of Bishops" received the *most*
> *frequent and intense reservations and suggestions for changes and*
> *the fewest affirmations.* Comments on "The Ordained Ministry" and
> "The Ordering of Ministry" generally were influenced by or reflec-
> tive of comments concerning "The Ministry of Bishops." While
> some of the comments are reactive to the word "Bishop," most are
> of a substantive nature.[18]

The tenor of these responses reflects what almost every member
would recognize as being characteristic of many persons in the
UCC. Some of these positions are shared to a degree in several of
the member churches of the Consultation as well. That is to say,
they are not ones held solely by the UCC, but belong to the wider
milieu of a significant segment of American Protestantism. It is for
this reason that consensus on the ministry has been the most
difficult to achieve in the Consultation. The report of COCU's
Theology Commission makes the clear point that:

> On the one hand, statements about ministry can be—and frequently
> are—understood in terms of *questions about organization, function,*
> *effectiveness, and power.* On the other hand, the same statements are
> sometimes understood in terms of *questions about the active imag-*
> *ing or symbolizing, in and for the church, of the truth or reality by,*
> *and out of which, it lives.* Both of these . . . are necessary.[19]

Is a consensus on ministry, then, a real possibility? As will be
shown later in this chapter, the Consultation, utilizing the responses of the churches, made some important revisions and proposed a "process" by which commonalities in shared experience
could be expected to build bridges across the differences in the
theory and practice of ministry. In that process each church's
particularities with reference to ministry will be tested.

For the UCC such a process can be salutary; some of the same
differences, as defined above by the COCU Theology Commission,

exist *within the UCC* and continue to inhibit the free expression of the church in its mission. For this reason, the ambiguities in UCC self-perception, which contribute to a continuing ambivalence toward COCU, must be faced. Two persistent conditions in the UCC nurture these ambiguities: first, a long-time neglect of *the catholic tradition* in which the unity and continuity of the church in Jesus Christ is *conveyed authoritatively in the creeds, sacraments, and the ministry;* and, second, a failure to take into account and acknowledge the effects of the *anti-ecclesial bias* inherited from *the Enlightenment* and *magnified in the individualistic/privatistic religiosity of Western Christianity.* These conditions obviously intertwine, but can be most helpfully considered if taken separately.

Neglect of the *catholic tradition,* of course, can be traced in part to prejudices that are the stock of Protestant lore, especially in America. The persistence of such prejudices, however, is "out of character" in a church of the Reformed tradition, and certainly inconsistent with the focal faith affirmations of the *Basis of Union* and the Constitution and Bylaws. In the act of declaring the *Basis of Union* as the foundational document of the union in 1957, the UCC affirmed not only "our membership in the *holy catholic church* but also that:

> The faith which unites us and to which we bear witness is that faith in God which the Scriptures of the Old and New Testaments set forth, *which the ancient Church expressed in the ecumenical creeds,* to which our spiritual fathers gave utterance in *the evangelical confessions of the Reformation,* and which *we are duty bound to express in words of our time as God Himself gives us light.* In all our expressions of faith *we seek to preserve unity of heart and spirit with those who have gone before us as well as those who now labor with us.**

The same emphases on the *catholic tradition* (ecumenical creeds) are at the heart of paragraph two in the Preamble to the UCC *Constitution.* To express it in another way, one can say that the UCC *commitment to unity clearly affirms the continuity of the Church in the catholic tradition.*

---

*From the Preamble to the *Basis of Union.* Italics added.

121

Those emphases on the catholic tradition belong to all the major Reformed confessions and doctrinal statements—the Belgic, the Scots, the Westminster, and the Second Helvetic Confessions, as well as the Heidelberg Catechism and the *Confessio Catholica* of the Hungarian Church. All of them affirm, without qualification, the definitive declarations of the Apostles' and Nicene Creeds in which the church is, respectively, "the holy catholic church" and "the one holy catholic and apostolic church."[20]

The persistent anti-catholic prejudice that flies in the face of this central Reformed commitment *has its origins* in a distorted view of catholicity, symbolized by medievalist papal authoritarianism and obscurantism, and resistant to all forms of ecclesiastical power and all concepts of orthodoxy and ecclesial continuity.[21] What is usually not recognized, however, is the *reinforcement of such prejudice* by some of the central accents of the Renaissance (e.g., secular individualism), subsequently magnified in Enlightenment concepts of religious individualism, egalitarianism, and anti-hierarchicalism—all of which add up to an anti-ecclesial bias essentially resistant to the *catholic tradition*. This is the second condition in the UCC that nurtures ambiguities in ecclesial understanding.

An illustration can be drawn from one of the responses included in the UCC report on the COCU consensus document on "The Ministry." The report makes the point that behind the reservations about the ordering of the church and the ministry are "implicit affirmations of certain values of the Free Church tradition." The report then quotes an extended comment that had been received from a study committee:

> It is not just a reservation that this committee has, but an out-and-out dislike for the concept of Episcopacy in church government as described in chapter VII. Episcopal and congregational concepts and forms are mutually exclusive. The committee feels it is impossible to have both or some form which combines both. We are not willing to sacrifice the congregational form in favor of the episcopal structure outlined in chapter VII. We do not like the bishops administering discipline; being responsible for church tradition; presiding at services of baptism, confirmation, ordination; administering discipline over ordained ministers; having administrative and pastoral responsibility for candidates for ordained ministry. We do not like all presbyters being ordained by the church through the bishop. . . . These are a few

specifics; however, as indicated above, *we are opposed to the whole concept of episcopal ministry as described in this chapter.*[22]

Although this quoted section is directed at an episcopal ministry, its presupposition is twofold: (1) that episcopal ministry is hierarchical and authoritarian by definition, and (2) that "certain values of the Free Church tradition" stand in irrevocable opposition to the concept of *episcopé*. But what are the values of the free church tradition that would rule out any form of episcopacy? This was not made clear in the UCC response, nor, for that matter, in any other negative response to the episcopacy as outlined in chapter VII of the COCU consensus.[23] *It seems fair to say that the constructive contribution of the free church tradition to a consensus on ministry was not offered in the UCC response because that tradition has not been sufficiently examined and understood in its historical context.*

In this matter certainly, the moral obligations of historical consciousness must be faced. Those obligations, as I have said in a variety of ways, require the "owning" of one's history, both its *negative* and *positive* aspects, in the context of the faith grounded in God's act in Jesus Christ. In that context *both the catholic and the free church traditions* must be claimed. But to claim them, and to understand their complementarity, demands an honest facing of the distortions both have suffered in popular imaging. The essential contributions of both traditions can never be understood as long as the distortions are absolutized. Just as the catholic tradition has been distorted in the popular mind by ignorance of history, especially the history of the late medieval period, so also the free church tradition has been distorted by ignorance of its history.

The factors involved in that distortion are complex, but for the purpose of illustrating the problem it will suffice to focus on one predominant characteristic of the free church tradition—the *subordination of the church to the individual believer.* The subsequent loss of a corporate sense of the church can be traced to two influences, one more characteristically religious, the other more secular: pietism and the Enlightenment.

Continental as well as English *pietism* accentuated the *faith experience of the individual, seeing the corporate setting as only enabling the individual's concerns.* The church became solely a means to individual salvation. In its more extreme form this reduction of the corporate nature of the faith was expressed in conventicle forms of worship, thus reducing catholic awareness to a minimum. In both the Puritan migration to New England in the seventeenth century and the German Reformed migration to the Middle Atlantic colonies in the eighteenth century, the emphasis on individual salvation supplanted the "catholic" sense of being the church. The subsequent influence of the Great Awakenings radically changed the Puritan movement into the Congregationalism of the nineteenth century, which was increasingly individualistic; and it wreaked havoc in the German Reformed Church where the corporate sense was already strained by lack of pastoral leadership. The countervailing forces—the central affirmation of the lordship of Jesus Christ among Congregationalists, and the later "catholicity" of the Mercersburg Theology in the German Reformed Church—in the long run did not stem the tides of ecclesial reductionism.

The loss of the corporate sense of the church, while feeding human religiosity, proved to be a disastrous distortion of the special contribution of the free church tradition to the cause of the gospel. That contribution, expressed in the profound sense of God's sovereignty, of grace expressed in the lordship of Jesus Christ, of God's freedom to call into being and nurture a community of people for the divine service of reconciliation without dictation by any human authority, of the vocation of a mutual "priesthood," had the potential of enabling the catholic tradition to regain the freedom it has often lost by both ecclesiastical and civil presumption of supremacy.

The words Paul M. Harrison has used to describe the difficulty of maintaining the free church tradition among American Baptists fit very well the situation of most of the so-called free churches:

> Pressed by the secular spirit of individualism current in the eighteenth and nineteenth centuries, and proud of their religious contribution to the movement, later Baptists slipped *off their theological base and cooperated in the support of an ideology grounded in the spirit of individual voluntarism.*[24]

Modern Protestants claiming the free church tradition do not take into account the changes that have occurred in that tradition. In fastening on its eighteenth- and nineteenth-century expression, and failing to acknowledge the secularization and falsification of its most popular tenet—the freedom and dignity of the individual *before God*—free church adherents today tend to fail the moral obligations of their history. The result is a form of idolatry that expresses "the glorification of the human individual and the apotheosizing of the intimate fellowship to which he belongs."[25]

It has been argued, of course, that the special contribution of the free church tradition to the Consultation's consensus on ministry lies primarily in the emphasis on the ministry of the laity. But the foundational teaching concerning the ministry of the laity is biblical. Without that foundation, expressed in "The Ministry of God's People," the section of the consensus document treating "The Sharing and Ordering of Ministry" would have little theological significance.[26] It is in this latter section that free church concepts are most evident, with accents on a ministry that is "personal, collegial, and communal."

In the foregoing discussion I have simply sought to indicate that the free church tradition does not stand as a negative counterpoint to the catholic tradition. Neither in principle nor in its originating development does it deny the basic catholic tradition. Based on a clear conviction of God's sovereignty and grace in Christ, the free church tradition was born in resistance to the *distortions* of authority and power *exercised in the structures of both ecclesiastical and civil government*. Neither the catholic tradition nor the free church tradition can tolerate the tyrannies of human pretension and contrivance, whether they be of ecclesiasticism or of individualistic privatism.

As I have said, the COCU consensus process can be salutary for the UCC. It provides an opportunity for honest testing of long-held assumptions and misunderstandings about the catholic tradition—and, in particular, about ministry—that underlie popular attitudes but have not been examined in their historical context. And it provides an equally significant opportunity to test our claims about the free church tradition—a tradition that has become so culture-embracing as to have little to say to the secularized privatism of modern persons. An attitude of blasé indifference to the Consultation and the opportunity offered therein is not as harmless as some may think. Much is at stake, not only for the UCC but for the whole Christian cause of reconciling unity. The culture-embracing habits of a thoughtlessly-claimed free church tradition tend to feed the divisive forces of sexism, racism, institutionalism, and congregational exclusivism. Until the radical claims of the gospel have overcome our acculturated acceptance of such alienating forces, the UCC will have gained little on its ecclesial journey as a result of its involvement with COCU.

CONSENSUS AND COVENANTING: ESSENTIAL ELEMENTS OF AN ECCLESIAL JOURNEY

The terms *consensus* and *covenanting* denote concepts that emerged in the Consultation's commitment in 1973, following rejection of the *Plan of Union,* to find a means for participating churches to "live their way toward a united church," truly catholic, truly evangelical, truly reformed. They are terms that reflect the reality of the consultation as a focused effort in one nation to implement concepts of unity that had evolved in the worldwide ecumenical movement. The Consultation thus "mirrors" the ecumenical movement as it relates to the particularities of denominational church life on the North American scene.

In this context the *consensus* concept holds special promise for those who have feared the consultation's aims as a way of imposing uniformity that tolerates no disagreement in a united church. But as developed in the Consultation, consensus theology

is shaped by constructive rather than dogmatic or apologetic concerns. One may enter discussion chiefly conscious of his role as a trustee of a particular tradition, but soon enough it becomes evident that one is called into the work of giving new visibility, new embodiment to the Church that lives in the midst of the churches. What urges forward this common work is no pre-conceived ecumenical harmony, contingent on negotiated agreements; *the impulse is found rather in that sense of wholeness in the Church which embraces both the protestant and the catholic principle.* . . . Instead then of searching for some least common denominator, consensus theology keeps in view the unity of faith which can reform and renew the churches.[27]

126

By the 1980s, experience with the consensus process had generated a firm confidence in the Consultation that it could serve as the "key element" in the next stage of "living the way to union." What had come to be known as *The COCU Consensus* was a document representing a "maturing consensus" that had been tested among the churches and had established its "ecumenical credentials" in recognition of, and correspondence with, the development of the *Baptism, Eucharist and Ministry* agreement of the Faith and Order Commission of the World Council of Churches. [28] Concluding that the *consensus* document was "relatively finished" (although always subject to review and change), the Consultation forwarded it to the churches for their reception in late 1984. Participating churches were asked "to find in this document 'an expression' of the great Apostolic tradition they hold in common, an anticipation of what they intend together to become, and an expression of those things 'sufficient' to make next steps . . . possible." [29]

In asking the participating churches to "claim" the *COCU Consensus*, the consultation was not asking each church to give up its own faith tradition by officially adopting the *Consensus*. Rather,

(1) The document, *The COCU Consensus*, . . . is intended to encourage the development of a common language for the expression of a common faith.

(2) The question before each church is, "Do you recognize in this text an expression of the faith of the Church?" The question is not, "How does this consensus agree or disagree with our particular communion's theology?"

(3) Consensus as used here does not imply complete unanimity or uniformity of doctrinal understanding. "Consensus" does, however, point toward the fuller confession of our common faith that can be made only on the basis of *life together within one ecclesial fellowship.*

(4) It is important to remember that this consensus is "emerging"; it is an ecumenical witness of a group of churches that are on a pilgrimage of faith and reconciliation. [30]

The COCU Consensus thus anticipates that "life together in one ecclesial fellowship" has the potential of overcoming inherited doctrinal differences in a "fuller confession of our common faith." From that life together, held firmly in a higher loyalty than that attached to particularized traditions, an experience and visible expression of unity in Christ can be expected. In that way the *consensus* is the key element in the shaping of the "Church of Christ Uniting." And in that way the Consultation's efforts give a particular expression to the "one conciliar fellowship" model of unity that had emerged definitively in the World Council of Churches in 1973. The definition bears repeating here:

> The one Church is to be envisioned as a conciliar fellowship of local churches which are themselves truly united. In this conciliar fellowship, each local church possesses, in common with the others, the fulness of catholicity, witnesses to the same apostolic faith, and, therefore, recognizes the others as belonging to the same Church of Christ and guided by the same Spirit.[31]

Recognition of the *Consensus* by the participating churches was seen by the Consultation to be the key element in a *covenanting* process proposed by the 16th Plenary, in November 1984, as the means by which the member churches "might live their way toward a uniting church." "The Covenanting Proposal" and the "Liturgies for Covenanting" were submitted to the member churches in 1985–86 for study and response. Reception and implementation of the proposals will follow revision based on responses.

UCC people have quickly recognized that both the *Consensus* process and the *Covenanting* proposed are, in principle, consonant with the vision and potentiality that moved the founders of their fellowship to set out on their ecclesial journey. In many respects the UCC vision and experience represent a "trial run" of a model of ecclesial unity that is now, in COCU, more broadly conceived and elaborated. Despite the parallels, of course, there are significant differences. The UCC journey began with a "consensus assumed" but not worked through, whereas the Consultation spent nearly two decades arriving at a consensus that calls for recognition of the central tenets of the apostolic faith.

Likewise, the UCC journey was made possible by a "covenant"—the *Basis of Union,* subsequently elaborated in the Constitution and Bylaws. That covenant, however, is markedly different from the Consultation's *covenanting* proposal. The UCC "covenant" is fundamentally juridical, and only implicitly theological, whereas the Consultation's *covenanting* proposal is "three dimen-

128

sional: theological, juridical, and liturgical."[32] This represents, as I have noted earlier in this chapter, the fundamental difference between the UCC and COCU approaches to the goal of visible unity: for COCU, "consensus" was always a precondition of the ordering of a visible structure of unity, whereas for the UCC, "consensus" could be assumed and then spelled out under the juridical provisions of the covenant.

The Consultation's *covenanting* proposal remains to be tested, of course. It has meanings of far-reaching significance as implied in the constitutive elements of covenanting, all of which exhibit the interrelation of the theological, juridical, and liturgical dimensions. The proposal clearly states that:

> In covenanting the churches will pledge themselves formally to become visibly one, *entering upon a solemn and sacred journey together,* doing whatever things may be necessary, under God, to become one church. During the covenanting period the individual communions will continue to function internally according to their own policies and practices. Prior to the covenanting agreement, *each communion may feel the necessity of making some polity changes,* particularly with reference to preparation for reconciliation of ministries. As they grow together in covenanting, it is likely and desirable that the communions will begin to make additional polity changes. . . . *Such changes will be voluntary responses . . . to the workings of the Holy Spirit in covenanting.*[33]

Here again the parallels with UCC experience are clear: a journey together to make the church visibly one; the necessity of polity changes (although not considered as a prior step to the UCC union, a commitment to polity change was implied); and dependence on the leading of the Holy Spirit in all changes. The constitutive elements of covenanting, as proposed by the Consultation,[34] also identify parallels in UCC experience:

COCU	UCC
1. Claiming the *Consensus*	1. Assuming *Consensus*
2. Mutual recognition of one another as churches.	2. Recognition was implicit in the E&R/CC proposal for union.
3. Mutual recognition of members in one baptism.	3. Recognition was implied, even though there were divergent emphases in baptism.
4. Recognition and reconciliation of ordained ministries.	4. No stipulations were made; thus recognition was given despite diverse principles and practices.
5. Engaging together in mission and evangelism.	5. Immediate steps to merge agencies and programs.
6. Formation of Councils of Oversight.	6. No parallel in UCC experience since the covenant was juridical and provided permanent structures.
7. Establishing regular eucharistic fellowship.	7. No parallel since local churches acted autonomously.

Obviously the parallels are less meaningful when it is remembered that in the Consultation's *covenanting* process the member churches are provided with a means for "realizing and making unity visible," with organic union as the ultimate though distant goal. In the UCC case the *covenant* elaborated in the Constitution is a means of living in a structural unity already developed but still to be realized in its fullness. In the COCU covenanting process the member churches retain their structures, with only such changes as may be necessary to "live the way to unity." In that provision there is a deliberate attempt to make structural design and organizational development subservient and subsequent to the experience of unity identified in the seven constitutive elements. The UCC effort to develop an organization to *give expression to unity through a focus on mission* placed the emphasis on the juridical dimension of the visible unity of the church.

The parallels and differences identified in the foregoing discussion can be instructive for the UCC as it continues on its ecclesial journey. Assuming that participation in the Consultation will continue, and that some form of recognition will be given to the *Consensus* as a partner in the *covenanting* process, the UCC may be given opportunity to work at the *theological and liturgical* dimensions of the unity envisioned. As has been noted, these are areas of unfinished business as the church continues its ecclesial journey. To work at these dimensions in dialogue with the other member churches of the Consultation has the potential of a broader and more wholistic perspective on theological and liturgical matters. It is a way of utilizing the conciliar mode of unity* to overcome the innate parochialism of any denominationally oriented theological effort.

COCU, THE DISCIPLES, AND THE UCC

It is important, in the concluding paragraphs of this chapter, to evaluate the interweaving of the development of the Consultation and of the ecumenical partnership of the Christian Church (Disciples of Christ) and the United Church of Christ. Covering essentially the same period of years, motivated by the same commitment of Christian unity, and nurtured in the same ecumenical milieu, both developments inevitably exhibit particular, and sometimes diverse, facets of the one ecumenical movement. COCU, as a multilateral move toward unity, gives opportunity to address the wider dimensions and diverse aspects of being a "church uniting." The UCC/Disciples ecumenical partnership, as a bilateral move, allows for specificity in addressing issues. The two thus serve the ecumenical vocations in a complementary way. In like manner, both developments have exposed ambiguities† in the UCC effort to fulfill its ecumenical vocation. As discussed earlier in this chapter, those ambiguities subtly influence UCC participation in both movements, making for ambivalence, some resistance, and considerable indifference on almost all levels of the church's life. Thus, while commitment to the ecumenical vocation is always reaffirmed, actual involvement is uneven and sometimes almost casual.[35]

The decisions required at this time by the *COCU Consensus*

---

*See the concluding section of chapter 3 for a discussion of the conciliar process.

†Exposure of ambiguities is the common experience of communities and organizations when they seek to make themselves understood to others in working toward common goals.

and the *Covenanting* proposal, and the responsibilities assumed in the ecumenical partnership with the Christian Church (Disciples) therefore are clearly times of testing for the United Church of Christ. I have sought to show the potential benefits to the UCC on its ecclesial journey. The histories of these two developments (COCU and the Ecumenical Partnership) are also UCC history. We are bound together in our journey with others with whom the vision is shared. The hope of continued in-depth involvement with the Consultation and the Christian Church (Disciples) is that the inevitable lethargy of a lengthy journey will be countered and overcome by a shared experience of the unity of the Spirit. "There is one body and one Spirit, . . . one hope that belongs to your call, one Lord, one faith, one baptism, one God . . . of us all [Eph. 4:4–6]."

Learnings from the Ecclesial Journey: Challenges and Responsibilities

In the foregoing chapters I have sought to illustrate some of the key ideas and motivating factors of the United Church of Christ ecclesial journey in relation to both general and particular developments in the modern ecumenical era. The account of that journey has included concomitant discussion of the implications of the experience of ecclesial formation. It is important at this point to summarize and evaluate the meaning of that experience, with specific reference to two major points made in the introductory chapters.

1. The vision and commitment to be a united and uniting church included a clear aim to develop a new form of the visible church that would be a faithful response to the claims of the gospel. Ecclesial formation was, therefore, the essence of the United Church of Christ ecumenical vocation.

2. The goal of developing a new form of the visible church was deprived, from the beginning, of a clearly articulated ecclesiology. Subordination of doctrinal matters to the goal of union resulted in the neglect of a much-needed ecclesiological dialogue. Although the essential principles of faith and order were assumed at the time of the union, they were not critically examined for their implications for polity and organization. The consequent confusion about polity principles—the form of the church's government—became a constant companion on the ecclesial journey.

With these points in mind we can undertake an assessment of the meaning of the UCC ecclesial experience of the past three decades. The three sections of this chapter deal successively with (a) affirmations of the UCC model of ecclesial formation as seen in the ecclesial journey; (b) an assessment of the implications of the ecclesial understandings gained in the three ecumenical engagements described in chapters 4 through 6; and (c) an analysis and evaluation of some little-recognized issues and unfinished tasks as the UCC continues its ecclesial journey.

AFFIRMATIONS OF THE UCC ECCLESIAL MODEL

A listing of the affirmations of the UCC ecclesial model gained by organizational experience and ecumenical engagement, is appropriate simply on the ground that the commitment to be a "united and uniting church" was a faith response to the prayer of our Lord that "they may all be one [John 17:21]." To acknowledge affirmations of the effort is an expression of a continuing faith in the leading of the Spirit, and of gratitude for our ecumenical calling.

The United Church of Christ was seeking to become a new form of organized church life on the American scene at the very time when most major denominational bodies were undergoing extensive reorganization.[1] Whether by new organization or reorganization, the objective was to overcome the severely inhibiting aspects of the traditional denominational form of church life. At the time of its inception the UCC model seemed to some observers to be only a simulated conflation of two traditional polities in which adjustments were reached by compromising long-cherished principles. The perception that the model was actually new came slowly, both to those within the UCC and to many without.[2] As Reuben A. Sheares II has noted, the traditional ways of classifying church polities do not apply when one seeks to characterize the UCC ecclesial model; in fact, they can lead to confusion and distortion.[3] Consequently, the distinctively new character of the UCC ecclesial model was not immediately perceived.

A systematic characterization of this model will be developed in the concluding chapter of this book. However, we can gain some helpful perspectives by noting the affirmations yielded by three decades of experience in the ecclesial journey. These speak to

several critically important features of the new model now wi̇ᶜ
not universally, confirmed in ecumenical relationships. Since eᶜ
feature has been discussed at some length in connection with
particular ecumenical experiences and developments, it is necessary to add only a few points of elaboration here.

First, ecumenical experience has confirmed the UCC principle
of *living its way toward unity** even while affirming unity as the
God-given reality of life in the Spirit. Church union, whatever form
it may take, is seen as a means to the end that it express the visible
unity of all in Christ. Living toward unity, then, is a way of characterizing the style of life of a united church. That, as has been seen,
requires an intentionality that goes far beyond adjustments in organizational habits so as to "get on" with the mission of the church.
It has involved fundamental rethinking of the requirements of the
mission of the church in matters of faith and order, a process that
could not be done in advance of union but is an ongoing task. It is
indeed an ecclesial journey in which the UCC has had to give a
fresh account of its faith in every new circumstance.

The awesomeness of that responsibility can be overwhelming,
as United Church of Christ people can testify. The temptation to
draw back and seek a return to less demanding ways of fulfilling the
requirements of unity is always present. As implied in earlier chapters, we have drawn back from the major task by settling somewhat
comfortably in a standard denominational mode. Learning to be
accountable to Christ and Christ's Body requires a radical transformation for which many may not be ready. Nevertheless, that is
what is necessary in living toward unity. Although there have been
many faltering steps on the journey, the rightness of the way has
been continually validated both in experience and in the wider
Christian community.

United churches have contributed invaluable experience to the
entire ecumenical movement by demonstrating the possibilities in
living toward unity.[4] They exhibit the reality that theological con-

---

*The phrase "living the way toward unity" is my amendment of "living the way
toward *union*," which came into ecumenical discussion primarily through the Consultation on Church Union, as noted in chapter 6. However, it was employed even
earlier in the pre-union and early union days of the UCC as a way of rationalizing the
implementing features of the *Basis of Union*.

absolute precondition of union but the continuing, exhilarating, task of the community of faith living er of the gift of unity. The special freedom to move na of the negotiation of differences between uniting he arena of mutual discovery" is not always immeed in a newly united church. Awareness of the significance of that freedom grows slowly, as has been the case for the United Church of Christ. Living toward unity implied a promise that, in principle, under the power of the Spirit's gift of unity, UCC people would be able to shake off the bonds of being liberal or conservative, evangelical or "mainline Protestant," Congregational Christian or Evangelical and Reformed, as they sought to be faithful in the tasks given to them by the "Head of the Church." This has also meant that in living its way to unity the UCC has had to shape and reshape its organization and its government to be faithful to the leading of the Spirit in every new situation. It has meant living with a "polity-in-process," learning continuously how to govern the life of the church in faithfulness to Christ its head.*

The ecclesial journey is, then, an experience in "life together in the bonds of the Spirit." "It is," as Bishop J. Lesslie Newbigin has said, "just being *in Christ* and *recognizing one another in Christ*."[5] At the same time, the fundamental condition of *being in Christ* "has to be made explicit in more elaborate statements as to its basis in the revelation to which the Scriptures witness, its explication in the ecumenical creeds, its effectual signs in the sacraments and its visible incorporation in the historic church unified around the apostolic ministry."[6] Newbigin's point serves as a reminder that, although affirmed in its experience of living toward unity, much remains to be done in the UCC in terms of ecumenical responsibility.

The second feature of the new ecclesial model projected by the United Church of Christ, and now widely confirmed in ecumenical developments, is its dependence on the *covenant concept of ecclesial formation*. In the preceding chapter we illustrated the UCC use of the covenant principle by comparing it with its use in the Consultation on Church Union. The subject merits a more extended

---

*"Polity-in-process" was the characterization used by the seminar *Toward the Task of Sound Teaching in the United Church of Christ*.

discussion, however, if one is to appreciate the importance of the influence of ecumenical insights on the UCC experience with covenanting.

It is of no small significance that although the covenant concept is interwoven with the histories of both predecessor bodies of the UCC, the word covenant is not used in either the *Basis of Union* or the early editions of the Constitution and Bylaws. Nevertheless, the language employed in both documents expresses the essential elements of the covenanting act: <u>mutual commitment and agreement as to what steps are necessary</u> to be one church.[7] They are, therefore, covenantal documents in which the details of agreement focus almost entirely on the political principles (polity) that provide the linkages among the various units of church life—local churches, regional, and national bodies. In this way, then, the UCC covenantal style emerged as a *juridicial* expression of the covenant relationship, with little or no elaboration of the implicit *theological* dimensions affirmed in paragraph 2 of the Preamble of the Constitution: "The United Church of Christ acknowledges as its sole head, Jesus Christ, Son of God and Savior."

In all polity developments the critical issue is the location of authority in reference to its contingent aspects.[8] For the church, in which Christ is acknowledged as the head, *the permanent aspects of authority* lie in the institutions of Word, Sacraments, and Ministry. *The contingent aspects of authority* are expressed in those polity principles that delineate lines and levels of responsibility. Because contingent authority never escapes the corruption of human sin, its location must be bounded with care.* To some, locating contingent authority in the congregation narrows the boundaries of sinful possibilities while, to others, placing it in a synod or an ecclesiastical office seems simply to elevate these possibilities to more public view. In one way or another, common consent of the governed, motivated by self-interest, wages a relentless battle against the freedom that is the gift of responsibility

---

*In historical perspective the location of contingent authority in the congregation (as in Congregationalism) was less a defense of the freedom of believers than an affirmation of the freedom of God, untrammeled by human ecclesiastical systems. This concern for the freedom of God was grounded in the doctrine of justification by grace through faith.

given by God. Freedom to fulfill the responsibilities of fellowship under the lordship of Christ is a freedom never to be won or claimed; it is the gift of a gracious God in whose love humans need not justify themselves *nor claim their rights*. To the extent that contingent authority is often arrogated to the service of human presumption, the church is divided into competing segments, each of which claims its special place and builds boundaries around it.

It was in recognition of this that the writers of the *Basis of Union* sought to introduce a new understanding of the organization of the church's life. Their vision reflects a singular awareness of the ecclesiological principles that are always at the heart of the Reformed faith: *autonomy understood not as independence but as responsibility for self-rule in the awareness that in Jesus Christ all are one body in communion with him and with one another*. In this way order and organization are linked so as to place contingent authority in a subordinate relationship to the authority of Christ. When the United Church of Christ developed its Constitution and Bylaws on the *Basis of Union* principles, it did in fact give expression to a principle of order *new* in American denominational church life. That *new element was a covenanted relationship among autonomous units of church life—a relationship delineated but not regulated by a constitution and bylaws*.

The implications of that covenantal basis of organized church life have emerged slowly, and sometimes tentatively, among UCC people. For thirty years we have lived in a covenanted relationship that was never intentionally explored in its *theological* dimensions. Self-consciousness about the principle of autonomy was reflected in uncertainty about the limits of mutual responsibility. The fear of infringing on the freedom of others often resulted in indecisiveness and frustration. The focus on the institutional decision-making process—the juridical aspect of the covenant—was skewed by the social contract language of paragraph 15 in Article IV of the UCC Constitution in such a way as to *shift all attention from mutual responsibility to the protection of rights*. In principle, and *in fact, that tended to subordinate the freedom of God in the community of faith to the bounded territories of individual and group self-interest*.

In historical perspective, it is fair to say that, despite our failure ~ ll·· covenanted people, the United Church of Christ has

138

experienced the binding together that is the Spirit's work. No one can disregard the weaknesses and failures resulting from inattention to the foundational meanings of the covenanted relationship discussed above. Those weaknesses and failures, as intimated earlier, have not only produced a malaise of spirit among us, along with dissatisfaction and frustration, but also have raised serious questions about *our credibility as church.* At the heart of this questioning is the matter of a more intentional and knowledgeable implementation of the theological and liturgical aspects of living in covenant under the faith that Christ is the head of the church. When autonomy in social contract terms is seen as a denial of the headship of Christ, the importance of the covenantal mode is magnified.

A third feature of the new model of church life for the UCC, confirmed in its own experience and in ecumenical relationships, is the emphasis on the *church as a conciliar fellowship.* John T. McNeill's point bears repeating: "Conciliarism is the constitutional principle which gives at once order and freedom to the exercise of the spirit of communion and the priesthood of the people."[9] Although never explicitly expressed in the UCC Constitution, the conciliar principle undergirds the covenantal assumptions throughout. Conciliarity is the style of organizational functioning that makes the covenantal principle viable.

It is clear, however, to anyone who has followed the forming of the UCC spirit and style from the beginning, that commitment to the conciliar mode throughout the 1960s and '70s stemmed as much from the spirit of the times *(Zeitgeist)* as from theological understanding and conviction. Insistent demands for the rights of the individual, and thus the freedom to have voice and power in all decision-making, became the mark of Western culture—particularly of American individualism. A concomitant resistance to all forms of hierarchical authority and order was a feature of organized church life in all major religious traditions. This came to a peak in the UCC in the period between 1967 and 1971.[10] Individual freedom and rights expressed in sociocultural ideals were rarely examined critically in relation to the Christian doctrines of freedom and order. A widespread popular assumption that individual rights and freedom are grounded in the doctrine of the priesthood of all believers was never seriously challenged.

Conciliar fellowship as a distinctive mode of UCC church life was affirmed by experience, despite its mixed motivations. Its values are cherished, but its potential for both the present and the future will be limited without a more intentional effort to learn and use its theological (doctrinal) foundations. Perhaps what is most urgent at this time is for UCC people to understand that conciliar fellowship implies much more than a local church experience. In this matter, historical amnesia has denied appreciation of an exceptionally important heritage. Few persons remember that in the formative days of the congregational model of church life, conciliarism was espoused over independency. As Douglas Horton, quoting from *An Apologeticall Narration,* has noted: "The five ranking Congregationalists of the Westminster Assembly [1643] repudiated the idea of sheer independency in local churches: to them it was 'the most to be abhorred maxime . . . that a particular society of men professing the name of Christ . . . should arrogate unto themselves an exemption from giving account' to 'their neighbour churches.' "[11] The conciliar principle, as McNeill has noted, "gives at once order and freedom to the exercise of the spirit of communion and the priesthood of the people" in boundless dimensions. It is an ecumenical principle, breaking down the artificial barriers erected by human religiosity and extending the communion of the Spirit to all who confess Christ. Moreover, it translates the "priesthood of believers" from privilege to responsibility, thus countering privatistic religiosity. Conciliar fellowship characterizes life in God's *oikumene.* This has yet to be more fully discovered by the UCC if it is to be faithful to the vision that created it.

ECUMENICAL CHALLENGES TO THE UCC TODAY

Ecumenical involvement and the UCC experience in ecclesial formation do indeed provide important affirmations. Of greater importance, however, are the critical challenges and questions arising persistently from that experience. It is true, of course, that in each of the several ecumenical engagements requiring the General Synod to respond the UCC has reaffirmed its commitment to be a "united and uniting church that intends to share responsibility for a faithful manifestation of the unity of Christ's church."[12] And along

140

the way there have been many occasions to declare and demonstrate that determination. It can be fairly stated that, measured in terms of *official* ecumenical involvement, the UCC has been *continuously if not always intensively active*. Questions and challenges do not arise at this level.

There is another side to the picture—a side that makes many UCC people feel defensive. That side has to do with the church's continuing confusion in ecclesiological self-understanding. The hampering effects of what we have called our ecclesiological deficit have been felt throughout the ecclesial journey. Events of the 1980s in all ecumenical engagements have elevated the consequent unresolved questions to critical levels. Each of the several major ecumenical involvements underlines such questions. In other words, external relationships bring internal contradictions and weaknesses to a critical focus.

In a very real sense our UCC ecumenical relationships are calling us to give an account of the issues and problems that we have identified along the way. We cannot claim to be a united and uniting church unless we are willing to be tested in the context of the wider Christian community. At this stage in UCC history our ecumenical commitment* requires two crucial responses from the *entire church*—not only from the General Synod but from Conferences, Associations, and local churches, as well as from the several Instrumentalities. They are: (1) a more intentional and disciplined effort to work through the ecclesiological issues that we as a community of faith owe in fulfillment of ecumenical responsibility; and (2) a more defined openness to the witness of the church universal—the church in its catholic, evangelical, and reformed dimensions—and what it has to say to us both critically and affirmatively.

1. The call to be *intentional and disciplined in working through persistent ecclesiological questions* has been sounded with increasing frequency in the mid-'70s. Some were addressed as early as the mid-'60s when the former Theological Commission gave attention

---

*The assumption here, as has been argued throughout the book, is that UCC ecclesial self-understanding depends on full awareness of the formative influence of ecumenical involvement. The UCC is a product of the ecumenical movement.

to the meaning of autonomy. Although a report was published, it received little attention, as was the case with most such efforts in those years of social turmoil.[13]

The first and most extensive effort to be intentional about theological issues—including the ecclesiological questions—was undertaken in the mid-'70s by a seminar, to which I have referred earlier, organized under the auspices of the Office for Church Life and Leadership. The report was entitled *Toward the Task of Sound Teaching in the United Church of Christ*.[14] Although the seminar group eventually involved thirty persons, a smaller group was responsible for the report.*

Some prefatory paragraphs from the seminar report suggest a direction that would have been salutary for the entire church:

> Convinced as we are that our church, along with American churches generally, is excessively accommodated to cultural values and perceptions, our thinking revolved around the conviction that the ministry of the church must become *more intentional and disciplined* in teaching the faith of the church, involving its theological tradition and its responding to the present place of the church in the culture.
>
> Our brief report which we here submit seeks to be faithful to the character of the United Church of Christ. On the one hand, it seeks to articulate those *substantive* concerns pressed upon us by our theological tradition to which we are all accountable. On the other hand, it seeks to initiate a *process* of engagement and exploration which might involve the whole church.[15]

As was noted in the reference to this report in chapter 1, there was little churchwide discussion of the issues raised, and no follow-up with reference to proposals. Additional seminars and consultations arranged by the Office for Church Life and Leadership for theological exploration had limited results. Although other studies and exploratory efforts were made with reference to particularly urgent issues—many arising from societal problems—by other instrumentalities and special groups, there was no coordination of effort, and no focus. Fundamental questions of a systemic nature

---

*Walter Brueggemann served as convener. Others were Paul Hammer, Frederick Herzog, Ralph Quellhorst, Henry Rust, Clyde Steckel, Reuben Sheares, James Smucker, Max Stackhouse, and Peggy Way.

for UCC self-understanding were left unaddressed. It was that situation which led to the effort of thirty-nine UCC seminary teachers in 1983 to secure an Executive Council initiative in a churchwide effort to address such questions.[16] In this again, no intentional and definitive action was taken.

Reference was made in chapter 1 to the "theological ferment" of the last half of the present decade. That ferment is both a positive and a negative indication of the real theological situation in the UCC. Positively, it signals theological concern and vitality that must be applauded and encouraged. Negatively, it signals the absence of focus and responsible intentionality. It is easy to mistake volume for substance. Individually and separately, the many theological forays of this time in the UCC exhibit substantial contributions. However, without focus, even the best of these cannot counter what Gabriel Fackre has called the "theological promiscuity in the UCC [that] hurts our justice witness."[17] Moreover, lacking focus and a common theological language, they fail to communicate what the UCC is all about, especially to the ecumenical community. Nor do they dispel the puzzlement of colleagues in other denominations who "view the UCC as aspiring to be post-Christian, without visible accountability to the covenants and creeds of the ecumenical church."[18] As a result, the UCC ecclesiological deficit grows larger.

In the discussion of developing ecumenical relationships in chapters 4 through 6, reference was made to some of the unresolved issues stemming from UCC ecclesiological confusion. It is important at this point to underline the problems, simply because *further development of those relationships* could be seriously, if not fatally, flawed. In each case the absence of fundamental UCC ecclesiological clarity is a basic problem.

The first example arises from the *full communion* covenant between the UCC and the EKU (of both East and West Germany), enacted in 1981. Assignment of responsibilities for implementation of that relationship was clear and specific.[19] It is not surprising, considering the intricacies of UCC organizational life, that there has been relatively limited realization of the full communion vision.[20] Potentially important plans are being discussed and actions taken on several levels. But full communion, as envisioned in the resolutions adopted, may be in jeopardy and may be unrealizable

143

except in a few symbolic ways, *unless the UCC is more intentional in seeing itself shaped, and being shaped, as the church.* Living toward unity, utilizing covenant concepts, and developing a conciliar style of church life, important as they are as marks of the UCC ecclesial model, do not remove the very real possibility that the UCC is "constitutionally incapable of Full Communion," as Frederick Herzog has intimated.[21] Two issues are yet to be faced in the UCC if full communion is to be a reality: the issue of a faith that identifies the UCC as the church in terms universally acknowledged, and the issue of an organizational structure that expresses the essential unity of the church.

In every ecumenical relationship, paragraph 15 of the UCC Constitution effectually blocks recognition of the UCC as church. That paragraph, as noted in an earlier chapter, was a compromise intended to assure that local churches would have the *responsibility* to determine their own life *without interference from any ecclesiastical body.* However, when cast as it is, in social contract rather than covenantal language, it contradicts all the preceding paragraphs of Article IV and of the Preamble of the Constitution. UCC people have lived with that contradiction so long that its negative impact is not perceived. But *it is perceived by other church bodies as a denial of the unity of the Body of Christ.* When set over against the well-known and now universally acclaimed definition of the unity of the church, formulated in 1961 at the New Delhi Assembly of the World Council of Churches,* it is clear that paragraph 15 nullifies the unity of the UCC as church and calls into question the UCC identification with "the whole Christian fellowship in all places."

---

* The important paragraph reads: "We believe that the unity which is both God's will and his gift to his church is being made visible *as all in each place who are baptized into Jesus Christ and confess him as Lord and Savior are brought by the Holy Spirit into one fully committed fellowship,* holding the one apostolic faith, preaching the one Gospel, breaking the one bread, joining in common prayer, and having a corporate life reaching out in witness and service to all *and who at the same time are united with the whole Christian fellowship in all places and all ages* in such wise that ministry and members are accepted by all, and that all can act and speak together as occasion requires for the tasks to which God calls his people."

Although no reference was made to this issue at General Synod XIII in 1981, the UCC/EKU Working Group was fully aware of the questions raised about the authenticity of the UCC as church. EKU readiness for full communion with the UCC required assurance about fundamental theological affirmations. In both EKU Synods, West and East, faith and order concerns led to questioning about the UCC understanding of the sacraments, ministry, and faith confessions. Both Frederick Herzog and Frederick Trost, who represented the UCC at the Synods of the EKU West and EKU East, respectively, reported on the depth of those concerns and the intensity of the debates.[22] The UCC constitutional capability for full communion was examined and debated from the perspectives of a "united church" with longtime experience in a faith "truly catholic, truly evangelical, and truly reformed."

The concomitant complicating factor in relation to the realization of full communion between the UCC and the EKU is the UCC organizational structure. Two aspects of this are important. The first was noted in chapter 4. Attention was given to anomalous aspects of the UCC structure where full communion implementation requires complicated coordination among several agencies and offices. Inclusion of representatives from the United Church Board for World Ministries, the President's Office, the Council on Ecumenism, the Office for Church in Society, and the Office for Church Life and Leadership in the UCC/EKU Working Group would seem to ensure adequate involvement of appropriate agencies for achieving the objectives of the full communion resolution as adopted in 1981. The positive and reassuring aspect of this arrangement lies in the interest and competence of the involved staff personnel of these several offices and bodies. *The negative aspect* lies in the absence of a "common theological language" that clearly articulates UCC ecclesiological self-understanding and is at the same time congruent with its oft-affirmed ecumenical commitment.

In principle the coordinated involvement of these program agencies of the church has the potential of integrating mission and faith in ways that are of great importance in this time.[23] For realization of full communion with the EKU, that integration is critical. Is the UCC organizational structure capable of a full implementation of the "covenant in mission and faith" enacted in 1981 with the EKU?* An ever-growing appreciation and use of a conciliar style of coordination and decision-making in the UCC is reassuring in this connection. This is exhibited, for example, in the role of the UCC/EKU Working Group, which functions as a coordinating body in the full communion enterprise.

However, each of the instrumentalities and offices involved in the implementation of full communion has other pressing and wide-ranging programmatic responsibilities, thus limiting the attention and resources that can be directed to this shared responsibility. Given these organizational realities, the integration of mission and faith in the full communion relationship with the EKU will require continual focus on the mandate for mission articulated in 1981, which calls for "renewal in *mission* and renewal in *faith*."[24]

The other aspect of the UCC organizational structure impinging on the full communion relationship has to do with local church autonomy. Since the "covenant in mission and faith" binds only the General Synod and the instrumentalities responsible to it, it is obvious that local churches are involved only on a voluntary basis. This means that the mandates quoted above will command no attention or response in local churches except as interest is generated through churchwide promotion.† To put it crassly, the concept of full communion and its mandates must be "marketed" among local churches. Quite apart from the magnitude and complexity of such an effort, the baffling reality is that UCC organizational structure *lacks a binding principle of accountable unity*. Full communion, dependent on a local-church-by-local-church-decision process, appears as an absurdity when considered in practical and logistical terms.

The relationship with the EKU as discussed here simply illustrates, of course, the need for the UCC to be more intentional and disciplined in working through the ecclesiological confusion that hampers ecumenical responsibility. Similar examples can be drawn

---

*See the discussion of this in chapter 4.

†In subsequent developments the UCC/EKU Working Group, in conjunction with its counterpart in the EKU, has devised a procedure for a common addressing of the theme "The Righteousness/Justice of God," with focus on Peace, Economic Justice, Racism, Sexism, and Ecology.

from the ecumenical partnership with the Christian Church (Disciples of Christ) and the projected "covenanting toward union" as planned by the Consultation on Church Union.

Still another example relates to UCC involvement in interconfessional dialogue, specifically the discussions initiated and continued by the Lutheran World Federation and the World Alliance of Reformed Churches. This series of dialogues, beginning in 1962, was concluded with a third round in 1984 with the publication of *An Invitation to Action: The Lutheran-Reformed Dialogue*, Series III, 1981–83.[25] In this important dialogue series the UCC is being tested in ways that expose, perhaps even more sharply, some of the same unresolved issues in its ecclesial journey and ecumenical vocation.

Although a participant in the dialogue by reason of full membership in the World Alliance of Reformed Churches, the UCC is acknowledged to represent "a special development in church history."[26] Aspects of that "special development" were indicated in the following description of the UCC that was included in a listing of the dialogue partners:

> After more than twenty-five years it [the UCC] still finds itself in the process of being a "united church" even in its own life as a denomination. . . . It participates in the Reformed community as well as in other groups with which it has historic ties. Since 1980 it is related to Lutheran traditions also through full communion with the Evangelical Church of the Union in the German Democratic Republic and the Federal German Republic. . . . Acceptance of particular historic creeds (for example, in ordination) is not an explicit point of church by-laws. . . . It differs from the traditional Reformed pattern in that it roots the Confession in Jesus Christ, Son of God and Savior, in the local church as the locus of authority of faith, and its polity is not presbyterian. The United Church of Christ does share many other characteristics of Reformed churches, however, including representative governance, a deep ecumenical commitment, a strong sense of mission, and a great concern for reform and ongoing renewal in the church as well as a live social witness.[27]

Denominations, defined by singular confessional statements, traditionally have difficulty with united churches that embrace more than one confessional and/or creedal statement. Thus the

147

other Reformed bodies involved in the dialogue with the Lutherans—the Reformed Church in America, the Presbyterian Church (USA)—are forced to come to terms with a "Reformed body" of a different history. As indicated in the above quotation, the UCC is recognized as belonging to the Reformed family of churches by reason of (a) history, in which long-standing historic ties cannot be disregarded; and (b) parallels in governance, ecumenical commitment, mission, and social witness. The fact that, in some respects, the other Reformed bodies appear to have less difficulty in arriving at some consensus in dialogue with the Lutheran churches suggests that the issue of multiple confessional standards versus a singular standard poses problems for both the Reformed and Lutheran dialogue partners.

It would be, however, a serious underestimation of UCC ecumenical responsibility to suggest that the Lutheran and the other Reformed bodies bear the chief burden in dealing with the UCC in these dialogues. The reality is that UCC involvement in the dialogue series is continually hampered by its own blurred self-image as church. As intimated earlier,* the contradictions in the Constitution and Bylaws—especially between paragraphs 11 and 15 in Article IV—are *primarily our responsibility*. What appears to many as UCC inconsistency in the Lutheran/Reformed dialogue has led to confused reports in wider church publications.[28] Such reports, unless countered by definitive responses that reflect a clearly articulated ecclesiological self-understanding, fully consistent with the faith affirmations of the Constitution (paragraph 2 in the Preamble, and Article IV, paragraph 11), contribute to a subtle but steady erosion of UCC credibility.† In this and in other ecumenical involvements the UCC responsibility for intentional and disciplined ecclesiological self-understanding is underlined with increasing urgency.

2. The call to *a more defined openness to the witness of the church universal* is a correlate of the call to be intentional and

---

*See the discussion in chapter 2.

†Contributing to the problem of credibility is the lack of a medium of communication that keeps the UCC constituency informed about such issues. Few UCC people are aware of the Lutheran-Reformed dialogues in which so much is at stake.

disciplined in working through ecclesiological issues. This call is especially critical as the UCC is engaged in the major ecumenical responsibilities discussed in this book. It is essentially a call to take with new seriousness the commitments made in 1973 when General Synod IX adopted a statement of the "Ecumenical Stance of the United Church of Christ."*

This statement affirms its foundation in the description of the nature of unity adopted by the New Delhi Assembly of the World Council of Churches in 1961. In so doing it acknowledged that the commitment "to mission and unity is to *symbolize through its worship, its communal and structural life, and its work in the world* the Christian union which points toward the larger union of creation."[29] For the UCC fulfillment of that commitment "our church symbols, common life, ecclesiastical structures, and mission" must reflect the "effective union and wholeness of Christ's Church. . . . We call the whole Church and the communion to which we belong to the task of giving full witness to the *continuing process of uniting in ways known and to be made known to us.*"[30]

The concluding words of the quotation above underline the call to openness to the witness of the church universal. It was an important acknowledgment that the UCC ecumenical vision is still incomplete and in need of further expansion and continual correction. For example:

> Ecumenicity is not an option for us; rather it is a mandate that prohibits a restrictive view that would separate mission from unity, or unity from mission. Whenever we view ecumenicity as mainly cooperative planning and action rather than as the name for those active steps toward the goal of church union for the union of all humankind, we trap ourselves in the false dichotomy of mission vs. unity or unity vs. mission.[31]

Of particular importance was a concluding proposal that an effort be initiated to "examine our communion's Constitution and By-Laws, and the constitutions, by-laws, operating procedures, and rules of instrumentalities, conferences and associations to *discover possible stumblingblocks to ecumenical cooperation and church union. . . .*"[32] This recognition that the UCC polity system,

---

*Portions of this critically important document are reproduced in Appendix C.

as articulated in its official documents, might be a serious inhibiting factor in fulfillment of the ecumenical mandate was, apparently, not widely shared. No examination of structure and constitution was ever undertaken.

Nevertheless, from the perspective of ecumenical developments in the following years the need for such an examination has been confirmed, as has been seen, by the UCC experience in projected covenants of full communion, ecumenical partnership, and mission and faith. To be defensive about such an examination of the polity system is certainly not in keeping with the spirit of open venturesomeness that led to the adoption of the *Basis of Union*. Moreover, if the UCC is truly committed to the ecumenical mandate, critical examination of its own structure and claims is simply an expression of the conciliar process at the heart of that movement.

What is at stake, of course, is not simply a matter of organizational adjustment and repairs, but a fundamental review and rethinking of the ecclesiological foundations of the UCC polity system. The opportunities for entering into such a rethinking effort are at this time providentially available in the major ecumenical covenants discussed. All of them, from a variety of perspectives, offer the witness of the church universal in its catholic, evangelical, and reformed character. In that ecumenical conciliar process the UCC may indeed be called to undergo a radical transformation in which the deleterious effects of its ecclesiological confusion can be removed from its commitment to the mission of unity.

To speak of a needed radical transformation is not to speak idly. In all honesty, it must be admitted that, although it sought at the beginning to be a new form of church life, the UCC has become in most ways simply another "denomination." In a society so acculturated by privatized religion, the denomination appears to have been the church's most viable institutional form.[33] At the same time, denominational survival is highly questionable, both economically and culturally, especially since it is fundamentally self-serving in an age fast disappearing. Conditioned by two centuries of such modeling of institutionally organized religious life, it is difficult for the church today to envision the requirements of a new age. The persistent parochial orientation of denominational life is rarely countered by the claims of the new age of the global village. The new orientation of the church's life needed in the world for this age requires institutional forms that embody the reality of the faith community which is, to use Walter Brueggemann's perceptive point, neither a community of "fate (into which we are locked without choice) or of convenience (in which we have no serious or abiding stake) . . . [but] a *called* community."[34]

The ecclesiology of the "called community" takes its substance and form from the person and work of Jesus Christ, in contrast to that of the "denomination" where both substance and form are derived from the acculturated ideology of private religion.* The radical transformation needed to move from being a denomination to a called community cannot take place in any one community of faith (denomination) apart from the continual corrective vision and support mutually experienced in responsible and accountable ecumenical relationships. It is in such relationships, as discussed earlier in detail, that the possibility of transformation becomes real. In them, openness to the witness of the church catholic, evangelical, and reformed makes for the empowerment to wholeness which is of critical importance to mission and unity. This openness brings a needed change in perspective, as Roger Hazelton has commented, in which one may move from serving consciously as a "trustee of a particular tradition" to the understanding of being "called into the work of giving new visibility, new embodiment to the Church that lives in the midst of churches." The impulse of that is found in the "sense of wholeness in the church which embraces *both the protestant and catholic principle*."[35]

A POSTSCRIPT ON UCC ECCLESIAL ISSUES

By way of concluding this chapter about learnings from the ecclesial journey it is important to comment further on the contradictions and incongruities of the UCC Constitution and By-

---

*It is ironic that the denomination became so acculturated, in light of the missionary impulse that shaped its earliest structures. This, of course, gives point to Paul Tillich's observation that institutions quite inevitably lose their initial vision and purpose and become self-serving.

laws. There is a natural tendency to avoid the issues referred to above. It is not a comfortable exercise to acknowledge that the covenant implied in the constitutional instrument the UCC has used thus far on the journey is fatally flawed. Nevertheless, the moral obligation laid on us by our historical consciousness is to recognize the constraints of both circumstance and limited understanding* that contributed to the constitutional problems. The circumstances cannot be changed, but they remain instructive and can be helpful as we seek to correct the limited understanding of our basic covenant.

In earlier references to the issue I pointed to the distortion of understanding of the Constitution when social contract language intrudes upon covenantal concepts, as it does in Article IV, specifically in paragraph 15. Underlying that intrusion, of course, was the failure to have a "fundamental ecclesiological dialogue" at the time the union took place.[36] Had that dialogue taken place, some critically important ecclesiological principles would have emerged to guide the development of the Constitution—the covenantal instrument by which we order our lives as a community of faith. A full and much-needed discussion of these is not possible here, but *it will become a focal point in the UCC agenda* for the coming decade. Two corollary principles are basic.

First, the church is the community of faith called into being by God in Christ, working through the Spirit. All of the scriptural grounds for this are widely recognized, and they are caught up as well in the well-known and much-loved documents: the UCC Statement of Faith, the *Heidelberg Catechism* (Question and Answer 54), the *Cambridge Platform* (chapter II), the *Evangelical Catechism* (Question and Answer 88–92), and the *Augsburg Confession*. The point of all this testimony is that *the church as the community of faith—the* congregatio fidelium—*is God's creation, not a human organization*. It is the fundamental *article of faith* by which the church is distinguished from all human religious creation.

Second, the church as the community of faith created by God *precedes* the church as a voluntary association of persons who,

---

*"Limited understanding" is used in a nonpejorative sense. It is simply to acknowledge the human condition to which all are subject when historical perspective is lacking.

knowing their calling from God, organize themselves to give visible expression to the working of God in and through them. The community of faith gives normative shape to the voluntary association, whether local church or denomination.

In both principles the Divine action is primary and basic; as expressed in the creation of the community of faith, it is determinative of the purpose and task of the church in its visible and organized form. *This principle,* although implied in the affirmation of the headship of Christ in the church (Preamble: "The UCC acknowledges as its sole Head, Jesus Christ, Son of God and Savior"), is neither *explicitly affirmed nor implemented constitutionally by the UCC.* In fact, Article IV, paragraph 15, effectively negates it by giving all authority to the local church—the voluntary association—and excluding the authority of any voice from the community of faith that in all ages had been "gathered by the Son of God through Word and Spirit."[37] By that limiting of authority to the local voluntary organization, the UCC eliminates what Frederick S. Carney has called "transcendent constitutionalism." Carney explains why such constitutionalism is important:

> When a seriousness of associational vocation (or high calling) is joined with a recognition of the grave possibilities of sin and finitude to disrupt the pursuit of this vocation, a constitutionalism that can keep political authority (and therefore associational vitality) from becoming unduly corrupt or weak is a decided necessity.[38]

The neglect of a consistent and thoroughgoing application of these principles leads to continual distortion of the church's self-understanding. In a society in which the basic form of organization is voluntary, the church as an organized body not only is the beneficiary of the particular humanistic values of the voluntary association model of society but also is subject to its weaknesses and potential distortions.[39] Moreover, failure to acknowledge the tension between the church as the community of faith and the church as a voluntary organization tends to breed false notions of freedom, of the right or privilege of dissent, of ultimate authority. Freedom claimed as a natural right becomes arrogant and dictatorial, lacking the acknowledgment of human self-centeredness and self-justification; whereas freedom as the gift of a gracious and righteous God acknowledges an objective justification that needs to make no claims. Freedom claimed as the ground of all associational authority (the sovereign will of the people) is always at risk of the elitism of attitude and the exclusivism of practice that plague all voluntary associations. Freedom claimed as the ground for disssent easily becomes the primary justification of privatized religion. The church as a voluntary organization has "grave difficulties with the problem of authority in the church, and much more so when the will to belong (the associational need of the individual) replaces the theological principles of the gathered churches."[40] This condition in the UCC tends to go unrecognized and unacknowledged. The most threatening aspect of the present time in UCC history is the real possibility that the particularities of the UCC covenantal system might be defended in their unexamined and uncorrected form.

As the UCC has sought to live out its commitment to be united and uniting, the special privilege given it on its ecclesial journey is the opportunity to hear the witness of the universal community of faith—the church catholic. At the close of the third decade of that journey it is clear that much remains to be done in rethinking and restating the covenant by which the commitment can be fulfilled.

The UCC Ecclesial Model: Order and Polity; Unity and Mission

The possibilities and problems experienced in the formation of the United Church of Christ ecclesial model clearly suggest significant unfinished business. The most urgent of these matters, as suggested in the previous chapter, is a full and intensive examination of the ecclesiological principles, presupposed but never fully implemented, in the covenantal instrument devised for the shaping of our life as God's mission in the world—the Constitution and Bylaws.

That instrument, although flawed in crucial places, has been validated by experience and by its congruence with several important ecclesiological perspectives characteristic of the ecumenical movement. It must be neither disregarded nor abandoned. At the same time, to regard it as "chiseled in stone" would make it unfit for the people of God who know themselves as pilgrims and who have responded to a vision of unity that embraces all humankind. As an instrument for a people of faith, moving under the power of a vision of "that which is yet to be," the Constitution will always be an in-process document. At the same time, its basic convenantal principle, anticipated by the *Basis of Union,* is its defining characteristic, making it a fit and viable instrument for a united and uniting church. To abandon that principle would be to abandon the union. To elaborate that principle's meaning in ever new circumstances is the concomitant mandate.

Making intensive consideration of this covenantal instrument a focal point on the UCC agenda in the coming decade implies a church-wide effort, characterized by the intentionality, discipline, and openness discussed earlier. The goal, however, is not a self-serving awareness of a unique identity, but faithfulness to the ecumenical vocation to be united and uniting for the sake of God's mission. Such faithfulness requires an informed and involved people, and calls for a linking of the *prophetic and teaching tasks* at all levels of the church's life, but especially in local congregations.

This is not the place to design or propose a program for the undertaking of this major effort throughout the church. It is more important, in keeping with the purpose of this account of the UCC ecclesial journey, to identify and illustrate a methodological principle that can be helpfully employed in examining the Constitution as a convenantal document. In doing so, some important steps can be taken to clarify the ecclesiological assumptions that underlie the UCC vision.

In the following sections of this chapter I will (a) identify and illustrate the methodological principle to be used in examining the Constitution; (b) employ that method in relation to a few key aspects of the Constitution; and, (c) show the implications of such a process for UCC continued fulfillment of its ecumenical vocation.

A METHOD FOR EXAMINING THE CONSTITUTION

Interpretation of the church's Constitution, of course, has commanded attention throughout the three decades of the journey, for it is the one document that delineates organizational relationships and responsibilities. What is proposed here is a systematic examination with a focus on implicit assumptions as well as explicit statements, keeping in mind always the announced intention to be a united and uniting church.

In the two preceding chapters there was reference to the UCC covenantal principle, which has been utilized primarily in its juridical dimension, with no attention being given to the theological and liturgical dimensions. The Constitution is almost wholly a juridical treatment of the covenant. It was quite inevitable, therefore, that almost all previous consideration and subsequent amendment of the Constitution would treat the covenant in juridical terms, that is, established (legal) procedure. Through the years numerous intensive efforts have been made to refine constitutional procedures. In only two instances was consideration given to covenantal theological presuppositions. The first occurred in the 1967–69 biennium when the Committee on Structure declared in its prefatory statement that "form and structure . . . must always be subservient to *mission*."[1] That was an implicit reference to the Divine convenant that shapes the church as God's mission. However, the organizational changes made on the basis of that report, as reflected in amendments to both the Constitution and the Bylaws in 1969–71, did not explicitly utilize the mission concept in its theological dimensions. In contrast, amendments to Article V, "The Ministry," adopted in 1983, introduce the term convenantal in a more precise clarification of the relationship among ministers, local churches, and the UCC.[2] However, these amendments also use juridical language.

Other intensive consideration of the Constitution has taken place periodically in the Council of Conference Ministers, the Council of Instrumentality Executives, and the Executive Council. The role and operation of the General Synod was a recurring concern, especially for the Executive Council, which was responsible for planning, agenda, budget, and related matters. In 1973 and again in 1982 the Executive Council sought counsel from various levels of the church's organization in attempts to clarify the role and improve the operation of the General Synod. Again, juridical concerns prevailed, even though the nature of the UCC as church (in theological terms) was always at stake.

To examine the Constitution as a covenantal instrument involves the linking of theological and juridical perspectives. In my judgment this can be most helpfully achieved by employing a principle of differentiation between *order* and *polity*. These terms are often used as synonymous, but technically, in ecumenical circles, they refer to two different aspects of the church's existence.

Order delineates the essential elements of the church as the community of faith, formed at the call of Christ. Those elements, without which the church has no marks of identification, are: gospel, sacraments, and ministry.* These dominical "institutions" of order represent and convey the authority of Christ, who is

---

*Ministry, here identified as an element of *order*, refers to function rather than to office.

confessed as head of the church. Order thus expresses the *permanent aspects of authority* by which the church is continually formed and sustained. By these institutions of order—gospel, sacraments, and ministry—the church, to use the words of Nils Ehrenstrom, "is endowed with a determinate structure which ensures its continuity and identity as a community in history. . . . They provide an ordered pattern for the common life, through which God imparts his gracious love . . . and makes a personal existence in freedom and responsibility manifest."[3]

Polity, however, refers to the principles of organization and government utilized by the church as a visible body of persons formed for mission. Church polity relates the church as a particular, voluntary, gathering of persons, in one or more places, to the church's order as the universal (catholic) community of faith. It enables persons, who know they are called by Jesus Christ to be members of his body, to give visible form to the church through worship, witness, and service. Polity principles naturally reflect the patterns of social organization of the society in which the visible church exists. At the same time, it is an article of the Protestant faith that the church derives its authority from the "will of the gathered group who know themselves *called by God.*" This is *contingent authority,* flexible and always developing in new contexts but always dependent on the *order* of the universal community of faith. In practice, polity principles tend to reflect the juridical aspects of the covenantal relationship established by God in Christ simply because they must be applied in organizations where issues of power and justice require resolution. For this very reason polity principles are often developed and applied without regard for the principles of *order.* It is this tendency that inhibits the UCC as it seeks to establish its credibility as church.

In suggesting this principle of differentiation between order and polity, I am seeking a way to overcome a Protestant mind-set generally exhibited under the banner of the "free church tradition." Reference was made in chapter 6 to popular misunderstandings of that tradition. A major contribution of the ecumenical studies and discussions of the past fifty years has been a new perception among most Protestant church bodies that "church order is not a 'catholic' idiosyncrasy, nor a matter of organizational pragmatism, but an organic aspect of the Christian faith."[4] The fact remains, however, that there is still a widespread misconstrual of the meaning of the "free church" concept that tends not only to neglect, but to reject, the concept of *order* in the life of the church. That misconstrual, as intimated earlier in this book, has roots in the Enlightenment of the eighteenth century. But its manifestation, in twentieth-century America particularly, exhibits extreme forms of individualism and the privatization of religious belief and practice. In this manifestation, the individual's desire and judgment are supreme, rejecting all other authority. The individual's relationship with God is determined, not by Divine will or action, but by personal choice. Thus the "free church" concept is corrupted into "anything goes."[5] "Freedom" becomes a code word for individual license in social relationships and in religious faith.

Using the rubrics of order and polity to understand the UCC convenant as expressed in the Constitution is intended to raise the issues of authority, responsibility, and accountability to the forefront of all our discussions. A false antithesis between "freedom" and "order," which prevails where order is seen as a human contrivance of control, inhibits discussion of such issues. That antithesis is paralleled by a persistent false interpretation of autonomy as independence from obligation to others. The counterpoint to both is rooted in the basic affirmation of Christ as head of the church. From the Christ whose Word and Spirit gather *individuals* into *one body*—the *koinonia*—comes the order that makes for freedom: freedom from the need to justify oneself before God, freedom from the need to establish one's "domain" over against others, freedom to rise above the clamoring and confusing claims of self-interest. "It is through *koinonia* that we attain freedom . . . , the God-given freedom to believe leads to *koinonia*, and *koinonia* is the condition for the possibility of being free."[6] It is in the God-given *koinonia* in and with Christ that authority, responsibility, and accountability become expressions of true freedom. To posit freedom *versus* order, or even to seek to link freedom *and* order conjunctively in the life of the church, is to misunderstand the Divine act of grace in Jesus Christ. Freedom flows *from* order. *Order* expresses the ultimate authority that assures freedom in the life of the church; *polity* expresses the extension of that authority in procedures of responsibility and accountability that become the occasions for the expression of freedom.

ORDER AND POLITY IN THE UCC COVENANT

My concern in this section is to show the usefulness of the principle of differentiation between order and polity in an examination of the UCC Constitution—the covenant that binds us in one body. A few key provisions in that document—those dealing with the units of structure as listed in Article II—will suffice as illustrations, and will underline the distinctiveness of the covenant by which the church is formed and shaped for mission. I have selected only four key provisions, although several others obviously could be used to get at critical issues.

Each of these provisions must be examined and understood in relation to the Preamble.* The three paragraphs of that introductory section make the critical points for understanding the Constitution as a covenantal instrument. The first paragraph makes it clear that the Constitution is the means of expressing "more fully . . . oneness in Christ." Unity given in Christ, as shown throughout this book, is the reason for the existence of this faith community as a united and uniting church. The implication of this declaration in the Preamble is that the UCC Constitution is not a definition of distinction or of differentiation—as is often the case in such documents—but of purpose. That is the UCC ecumenical vocation.

The second paragraph of the Preamble is devoted to the principles of *order,* which identify the UCC as a body belonging to the church universal. Its foundational confession is that Christ is the "sole Head" of the church. In this paragraph, then, the covenant is assumed, identified primarily in the confession of Christ's headship. The UCC sees itself, therefore, as a faith community called into being by Christ; it is not a human creation. This principle of Reformed ecclesiology—the church brought into being by God's call in Christ—is fundamental in UCC order. That call, continued in Christ as head of the body of faith, lays claims and obligations on all who make the confession, calling them to be "kindred in Christ [with] all who share that confession," laying on them the authority of the Word of God in the scriptures and in the power of the Spirit,

---

*The 1984 edition is used throughout.

relating them to the faith of the historic church, giving them the duty of worship and nurture, and calling them to the sacraments. These constitute the faith response to God's covenanting action. By confession and willing acceptance of the obligations set forth, the church exhibits the universal marks of the community of faith in Christ.*

These principles of *order* are, then, foundational doctrine for the church's teaching task. From each affirmation of obligation and responsibility, the church derives those teachings by which each generation learns the faith and is equipped to make the faith its own for new times and circumstances. It is of no small significance that all these responsibilities involved in the covenantal relationship may be subsumed in the church's worship.[7] For in its corporate worship—where the church is most visible as Christ's Body—the authority of the Word, the work of the Spirit, the use of the creeds and the celebration of the sacraments enable each generation to make the faith its own "in honesty of thought and expression, and in purity of heart before God." Thus corporate worship is the critical focal point of the church's existence as church; it is the occasion when the *church's order* becomes a witness to *God's order* for the world—the world for which Christ died. The crucial importance of this point escapes the attention of many in a time when "worship" is seen as a therapeutic experience and the expression of human religious interest. The essential relationship between the church's worship and its order is critical to our understanding of the covenant in which we live.

The third paragraph of the Preamble draws out the principles of *polity* that are implicit in the *order* derived from the basic covenant. The question faced by the framers of the UCC Constitution was: What principle of organization and government will give faithful acknowledgment to the headship of Christ? Behind that pressing question was full awareness of the limitations of traditional polities as well as the earnest desire by the advocates of the union that the UCC develop a new principle of church organization for the new

---

*Traditionally, the marks of the universal community of faith in Christ are the "institutions" of gospel, sacraments, and ministry. The absence of reference to the ministry in the Preamble is striking. Its implications will be considered under discussion of Article V.

age. A conviction rooted in the histories of the uniting communions, and confirmed by the growing witness of the ecumenical movement, led to taking with ultimate seriousness the risk of the covenant model in which responsibility is lodged in the freedom God gives to everyone justified by grace.

The polity principle adopted, then, was designed to give a consonant expression to the principle of order discussed above. If Christ is head of the body of faith, all members of the body—individually and in groups—are engaged in a covenant of mutual responsibility and accountability. In covenantal relationships, autonomous units of church life (self-governing in the responsibility given by freedom in Christ) live by constitutional provisions that delineate but do not regulate their functions. *The polity principle is that of mutual accountability of persons and groups who acknowledge Christ as head.* The absence of regulations to control and ration that responsibility was and continues to be a risk. At the same time, the risk is an expression of a fundamental conviction of the Reformed ecclesiological heritage. Expressed by John Calvin, and later in the *Heidelberg Catechism* and in early Puritan writings, that conviction is both assurance and challenge to all UCC people:

> *We are not our own;* therefore let us not presuppose it as our end to seek what is expedient for us . . . ; let us as far as possible forget ourselves and all things that are ours. On the contrary, *we are God's;* to him, therefore, let us live and die. *We are God's;* therefore let his wisdom and will preside in all our actions. *We are God's;* towards him, therefore, as our only legitimate end, let every part of our lives be directed.[8]

This polity principle places a premium on the exercise of responsible freedom, a freedom always to be understood as a gift. In UCC organizational life that gift of freedom is not regulated, but is set within the witness of guidelines that are modifiable in the context of mission. In this way UCC polity is a pragmatic expression of church *order* that exhibits the headship of Christ in the responsible freedom given by God in the relationship of grace; and, further, it posits the use of the "law" as the means of living the transformed life in the midst of a corrupted and corrupting social order.[9]

It is clear, then, that UCC polity takes with full seriousness the Protestant constitutional principle of *conciliar* responsibility and authority. I refer again to some words of John T. McNeill, quoted partially in chapter 7:

> Obedience is the virtue of a monarchical society. . . . The virtue of Protestantism is neither obedience nor "private judgment," but *communion*. Conciliarism is the constitutional principle which gives at once order and freedom to the exercise of the spirit of communion and the priesthood of the people. No principle of polity is an end in itself. The social experience of communion is the true objective of enlightened Christianity.[10]

UCC polity holds that the responsible exercise of freedom is not a natural right but a deputized responsibility. That responsibility derives solely from God's call in Christ, by which "we are not our own, but God's," claimed to be to others as Christ is to us. This relationship is communion—*koinonia*—in which freedom flows from responsibility.

In summarizing this discussion of the Preamble it is of the greatest importance that we see the intentional linkage of *order* and *polity*—at points, admittedly, more implicit than explicit. The framers of this document were being faithful to the ecumenical vision, which called for openness with regard to the eventual organizational form of the visible church to be called the United Church of Christ. This must be kept in mind as the principles of order and polity are applied in the succeeding paragraphs to key constitutional provisions. It is also important to be alert to the *descriptive* language employed—as in the third paragraph of the Preamble—with reference to all relationships, thus underlining the significance of the *koinonia* that lives by the action of Christ.*

The constitutional provision for the place of *local churches* in the UCC structure, as described in Article IV, is naturally of greatest interest to individual church members. Some of the most critical issues, and the most frequent misunderstandings of the UCC structure, relate to the definitions given in this Article. The *language is*

Prescriptive, rather than descriptive, language is used in those constitutional provisions that *regulate* the General Synod and the instrumentalities related to it.

descriptive but it is also definitive in the sense that the subject is "local churches of the United Church of Christ"; in other words, the description of the relationship of the local church to the United Church of Christ *defines the latter.* That, of course, is the implication of paragraph 7.

The importance of this becomes clearer in paragraphs 8 through 11 in which local churches are defined. Some negative assertions will sharpen the significance of these definitive paragraphs. The local church is *not* defined, nor even described, as a voluntary organization, although in sociological terms it is that. Nor is it defined as a religious organization; nor even as an association of like-minded persons. The specificity of the description makes the paragraphs definitional. Several emphases must be noted.

The purpose of the organization of a local church derives from its constituency. Organized for worship, fellowship (communion), and witness, the local church is made up of persons of a particular set of beliefs that constitute a Christian confession, setting them apart from other religious systems and ideologies. To persons committed to religious pluralism, such a definition seems unnecessarily exclusionary. But it is exclusionary only if the validity and uniqueness of the Christian revelation is denied. It is not intended to identify counterfeit faith, of which much abounds in every generation. Rather, it is to identify the shared faith and understandings that make the organization called "a local church" able to know itself as *the* church. Roger L. Shinn addressed this problem helpfully when he wrote: "Yet we know that we are a church, a community of faith. We are not a national federation of bridge clubs, of used car dealers, of war veterans. . . . The identity of a church must have something to do with a shared faith."[11]

Without definitive language specifying the faith that unites* the larger communion, a local church has no meaningful identity. That same definitive language is crucial to the subsequent paragraphs. For example, paragraph 8 defines the ways in which persons become members of a local church. Profession of faith in Christ, whether by baptism, confirmation, re-profession, or transfer of letter, is the condition of membership. In this definition, as in that of

---

*The *Basis of Union,* from which the Constitution draws its statement in the Preamble, paragraph 2, is specific about faith as the *uniting* principle, thus identifying the local church in no uncertain terms as a Christian community of faith.

a local church, the polity principle used in UCC organization is based on the church's *order,* giving an explicit involvement in the covenant affirmed in the Preamble.

Membership in a local church, however, involves much more. Paragraph 10 links the local church—already structurally defined as a unit of the UCC—to the larger body of persons of other local churches known as the United Church of Christ. And that linkage, of course, extends to the church universal (catholic) as acknowledged in the Preamble. Here again, UCC *polity* takes its cue as an organization of the community of faith from its affirmed principles of order. There is no such thing as an "independent" United Church of Christ. To exist as a United Church of Christ is to acknowledge a covenantal link with the larger communion. In this way UCC polity counters the persistent parochialism that afflicts local churches of all denominations.

In earlier chapters I have quoted paragraph 11 to accentuate a point little understood and only infrequently used in UCC self-understanding: "Congregational Christian Churches and the Evangelical and Reformed Church unite in the United Church of Christ without break in their respective historic continuities and traditions." Its significance for discussion of order and polity lies in the clear implication that UCC catholicity has institutional expression which predates its own organization. "Historic continuities and traditions," of course, are institutionalized in various ways. In the Evangelical and Reformed Church, historic continuities were institutionalized primarily in its confessional statements, thus emphasizing *order* in preference to polity. In Congregational Christian Churches the reverse was true, as I have shown in chapters 2 and 3 especially. Historic continuities and traditions in that communion were inherently polity-framed. I have traced earlier also the historical-conditioning factors that are responsible for those differences. What is important to draw from paragraph 11 is the responsibility the UCC has today for those continuities and traditions. Their reappropriation for the facing of new responsibilities under a new model of organization is as much a requirement for fulfillment of the obligations of catholicity as it is of self-understanding and identity. Much of the "unfinished business" of our UCC experience relates to the exploration of the contemporary meaning of these "continuities and traditions."

Inasmuch as paragraphs 12 and 13 are largely of a procedural character, the purposes of this discussion of the local church are better served by turning to paragraphs 14 through 16. My frequent reference to the problems that paragraph 15 have created for the UCC in its ecumenical relationships suggests the need for careful consideration of this section. In pointing to the social contract character of the language in that paragraph as the core of the problem the UCC must face in seeking to realize its ecumenical vision, I have suggested the possibility that the Constitution is fatally flawed. Such a sharp judgment would be unwarranted if so much were not at stake.

It is important to recognize that in a covenantal context the intention of paragraph 15 is to *confirm the responsibility of the local church to govern itself.* No one person and no other organization in the UCC has that responsibility. By "its own action," of course, it can seek assistance in fulfillment of that responsibility. Likewise, in covenantal intention, the paragraph affirms that the communion of which Christ is the head is based on mutual trust and respect; therefore, no part, or agency, of that communion—whether the General Synod, Conferences or Associations—will violate that trust and respect by interfering with the local church's responsibility for self-government (or, to use the words of the paragraph, "the management of its own affairs"). When viewed, then, in convenantal terms, the details of that responsibility, as listed in the remaining lines of the paragraph, are clearly derivative from the acknowledged headship of Christ over the entire communion, whether in local or universal manifestations. In the faith community, where the responsibility of a shared "priesthood" (to be to one another as Christ is to me) under Christ is the focal aspect of its life, all relationships are *ministerial* rather than *magisterial,* even as is Christ's headship in the Body.

The covenantal interpretation of the autonomy of the local church stands in sharp contrast to the concepts implied in the contractual language used in paragraph 15 as it stands. On the one hand, the covenant assures mutual care, respect, and trust in which the spirit of reconciliation and wholeness—always the gifts of the Christ—nurture the capabilities for self-government in the organization. On the other hand, the contract assumes an adversarial attitude, engenders distrust and suspicion, and builds defensive lines that divide and alienate. The covenant assumes and affirms the redemption and transformation of human nature, and gives opportunity for its fulfillment in *koinonia*. The contract assumes that in any organized form of community the base, unredeemed elements of human nature must be restrained by law (contract). Paragraph 14, of course, implies the covenant throughout, but in the prevailing individualistic ethos of American church life, paragraph 15 gains wider recognition. Both paragraphs 14 and 16 are regarded as advisory.

When allowed to stand in its "social contract garb," the affirmation of the autonomy of the local church becomes a "red flag" in ecumenical relationships. Where is the church—as Christ's *koinonia*—in the so-called United Church of Christ? *Because it does not take autonomy seriously in a covenantal mode,* the UCC undercuts the creative potential its ecclesial model has in this ecumenical age. That creative potential surely lies in the dimensions of responsibility assigned to the local church in the UCC organization. The UCC model claims that it is in the local church that the gospel is to be known in its fullness, where issues of justice and power must be adjudicated in reconciling fellowship, where the sharp edges of the church's mission are to be known among and with the poor, the oppressed, and the violated in every community.

The *genius,* if I may risk what may seem an immodest claim, *of the UCC model does lie in the concept of local church autonomy.* But it will never be realized, and the significance of its contributions to the church universal will never be known, as long as the covenant of grace God has called us to accept is obscured and neglected by a frame of mind caught in eighteenth- and nineteenth-century social models. The implications of the covenantal mode of ecclesial formation have not been explored either theologically or politically for this time in the church's mission. It is urgent that the UCC bend itself to that task. The obsolescence of denominationalism, and its institutionalizing of privatistic religion,* both being the most restrictive forces working against all that the gospel

---

*The reader is referred again to Frederick Herzog, *Justice Church,* chapter 6 especially; Ehrenstrom and Muelder, *Institutionalism and Church Unity,* chapter 1; and J. Lesslie Newbigin, "Can the West be Converted?" in the *Princeton Seminary Bulletin,* vol. VI, no. 1, 1985, in which the limitations of denominationalism are helpfully analyzed.

of God proclaims, underline the special opportunity given in this time to develop models of ecclesial life that will overcome the damaging effects of those forces. When the union was consummated in 1957, that was a "star-bright" hope; but the development of the Constitution was hampered by the circumstances of legal threats and the stipulations attached to the *Basis of Union,* and the resulting document did not become explicit in the use of the covenant. The consequence was, as described above, a flawed document. That flaw need not be fatal. The UCC agenda for the future can overcome it with utmost devotion to the vision.

It is important to conclude this discussion of the local church in the model of ecclesial life by reminding ourselves of the "historic continuities and traditions" that bear upon this subject. The Reformed tradition, especially in its Puritan expression, provides some of the most important indicators of the potential of the covenant concept. It is especially important to reach back of the Lockean and Hobbesian distortions of that tradition in Enlightenment times to recover some foundational thinking about the covenant model. Some lines from Robin W. Lovin will serve to underline a few of the salient features of Puritan thought that support points I have made in this and earlier chapters.

Lovin, writing about "Covenantal Relationships and Political Legitimacy" in American social history, makes points that apply equally to the ecclesial covenant:

> Life among those who share in the covenant is marked by *communication,* by *earnest conversation,* and *where necessary by mutual correction.* . . . The Puritan society was profoundly convinced that the full reality of human freedom could never be achieved by one person alone. *The communal discipline which the covenant entails is the structure of accountability which balances the structure of freedom in covenant relationship.*[12]

"Mutual correction" and "structures of accountability" are the crucial concepts for UCC ecclesial life. We shy away from both because we think in Enlightenment terms rather than gospel terms, where responsibility is always framed by reconciliation and forgiveness. Here again we see the covenant paradigm, in Walter Brueggemann's terms, as "subversive" of our usual organizational and community life.

In his further development of this, Lovin identifies two basic requirements of covenantal life: "equality among the persons who make up the community" and "participation."[13] Both requirements have been taken seriously, although certainly not perfectly, in UCC organizational life. However, participation continues to be a serious problem, particularly in the local church where privatistic religiosity prevails. Nevertheless, Lovin's points need continued attention. It is clear that ecclesial organization in covenantal mode is not simply an expression of "democracy" in religious garb. Covenant life, as intimated above, involves relationships grounded in Divine forgiveness and reconciliation. In that life, the coercive consequences of majority rule are intentionally countered and ameliorated for the sake of the community's unity and the individual's well-being. Learning covenant life moves beyond the democratic models of human organization to the ministerial (servant) model of life in the *koinonia.* Ideally, the local church is the nurturing community for that covenantal style of life.

An examination of Article V on "The Ministry" yields further perceptions of the distinctive features of the UCC covenantal model of ecclesial life. Here again the distinctions between *order* and *polity* can be helpful, bringing into sharp focus both potentialities and unresolved issues in the Constitution and Bylaws.

The first paragraph (#17) of this article applies the polity principle of "mutual accountability of persons and groups who acknowledge Christ as head"* to the definition of ministry. The church, which is created by God's call in Christ—this is the principle of *order*—exists for the purpose of extending Christ's ministry. "The whole church and every member" has this responsibility. In mutual accountability—this is the *polity* principle—the UCC "seeks to undergird the ministry of its members by nurturing faith, calling forth gifts, and equipping members for Christian service." The accent of both principles, then, is on the mutuality and wholeness, the *koinonia,* of the community of faith in Christ.

The application of this polity principle in subsequent paragraphs of the article on "The Ministry" is confined to "various forms of ministry in and on behalf of the church for which *eccle-*

---

*See the discussion of this principle on page 162.

siastical authorization is required." These are identified as: ordained, commissioned, and licensed; as well as the granting of ministerial standing to persons already ordained. Although not explicitly asserted, the meaning of "ecclesiastical authorization" is to be inferred from the principle of order in the first paragraph: the church under Christ acting to undergird and nurture its members for ministry. It is, to repeat a point I have made before, the constitutional principle of all Protestant communions that the congregation of the faithful* *(congregatio fidelium)* is *the* authority for ecclesiastical action. The community of faith acts—whether as local church or a group of local churches—under and for Christ the head in all matters that are essential to the fulfillment of the church's ministry. It is Christ's ministry in which the church is engaged. It is the exercise of contingent authority.

Amendments to this article on "The Ministry" adopted in 1983–84 gave clearer expression to the polity principle of mutual accountability. The term covenantal was introduced to define the relationship, not just between the minister and the local church, but *among* the several parties and individuals involved in establishing either a pastoral or some other form of ministry. Mutual accountability is a multiway relationship that accentuates respect, trust, care, and mutual correction, thus manifesting the contingent authority derived from the headship of Christ and fulfilling covenantal principles. In that way, the relationships that make up the structures of the church's ministry are ministerial rather than magisterial.

The UCC constitutional provisions for "The Ministry" reflect the influence not only of major tenets of Reformed ecclesiology but also of at least two ecumenical accents: the ministry of the whole people of God, and the conciliar principle of authority. Reformed ecclesiology, stressing the Divine action in Christ that *creates* and *governs* the church, has found wider expression in those ecumenical accents. However, the UCC understanding of ministry reflects influences that tend to inhibit fulfillment of the ecumenical vocation to be a united and uniting church. Reference was made to two of these in chapter 6, where the focus of the discussion was on the

---

*"Congregation of the faithful" denotes the community of faith under Christ in the universal as well as the particular (local church) manifestation.

possibility of a consensus on ministry in the Consultation on Church Union. The two influences cited were: (1) a long-time neglect of the catholic tradition in which the unity and continuity of the church in Jesus Christ is conveyed in the creeds, sacraments, and *ministry;* and (2) the failure to acknowledge the persistent distortions of an understanding of the ministry resulting from the anti-ecclesial bias inherited from the Enlightenment. These influences, deeply embedded in large segments of American Protestantism, have left their mark on the UCC as well. The results can be identified at two important points.

First, the omission of reference to the ministry in the Preamble paragraph that sets forth the principles of *order,* suggests that the framers of the Constitution were sensitive to the anti-ecclesial (therefore also the anticlerical) bias in at least a significant segment of the UCC. Recognition of the authority of the "Word of God in the Scriptures" and the traditional place of the sacraments in the church is couched in language that avoids identifying these as "institutions" of order; the complete lack of reference to ministry suggests indifference to the catholic tradition. A surprisingly narrow historical perspective is evident therefore—surprising in view of the ecumenical vision expressed in the *Basis of Union.* It is important to remember, however, that the Constitution was framed in an acute awareness of the diverse perspectives on the nature of the church in the newly united constituency of the UCC. The result is a "looseness" of language that is confusing for many, and "starkly ambivalent"[14] for others. In such circumstances an anti-ecclesial bias easily links up with a prevailing Protestant indifference to the institutional marks of the church in their universal (catholic) significance.

Second, the same influences would seem to be responsible for the somewhat imprecise language of Article IV, paragraph 11, which offers the assurance that "Congregational Christian Churches and the Evangelical and Reformed Church unite . . . without break in their respective historic continuities and traditions." That paragraph, of course, had an "inclusive purpose"—to insure that no local church would be excluded from the UCC by any failure to conform to a single way of achieving membership. At the same time, the wording of the paragraph is an assurance of respect and fulfillment of "historic continuities and traditions." But what continuities and traditions are meant? Surely only those that do not violate the unity of the UCC. But what are they? Without guidance here the UCC either neglects those continuities and traditions altogether, or becomes selective in ways that do violate unity.

At this point, as much as at any other, the conciliar mandate of the covenantal model of ecclesial life could be very helpful in removing serious misinterpretation of those continuities. The UCC understanding of, and provision for, "ministry" is a prime example. As Article V now stands, it exhibits a view of ministry that needs ecumenical elaboration to overcome the two influences cited above. By a felicitous use of UCC historic continuities and traditions concerning the ministry, anchored in its predecessor bodies, that ecumenical elaboration could be achieved. Not least of these would be the supportive complementarity of two perspectives on ministry that Barbara Brown Zikmund has identified.[15] *Empowerment* and *embodiment,* historically, are ways of characterizing the patterns of creating and recognizing the leadership of the church. Empowerment is given by the community of faith for the meeting of its needs. It is a functional perspective. Embodiment characterizes a ministry based on God's call in which divine gifts are provided for ministering, that is, for "building up the body of Christ. [Eph. 4:12]." Both patterns belong to UCC traditions, for a theology of empowerment and a theology of embodiment can be traced in our historic traditions. Developing a polity that can express both is a UCC challenge. Dr. Zikmund, acknowledging that "our polity seeks to sustain a covenant system which honors all of these . . . ," goes on to say:

> I am concerned that we are undoing the balance *by overemphasizing empowerment.* . . . [We] have problems in our polity when it comes to more universal and eschatological convictions about the church. . . *When we move into issues of ministry beyond the local church* . . . the balance between empowerment and embodiment begins to collapse.[16]

The "issues of ministry beyond the local church," that is, those that affect ecumenical responsibilities, are of crucial significance in terms of the UCC ecumenical vocation. This is not to disregard the negative effects of imbalance within the UCC community itself where the "particularity of the office of ministry is unclear."[17] The problems are interrelated, and resolution of the one would apply to the other as well. Certainly as a church committed to the ecumenical vocation the UCC is in an especially favorable position to garner help and counsel from the intensive efforts under way in two major efforts to redefine "ministry"— the *Baptism, Eucharist and Ministry* project of the World Council of Churches, and the *Consensus* and *Convenanting* proposals of the Consultation on Church Union.[18] The covenant model of UCC ecclesial life is uniquely qualified to be fully engaged in such efforts. That engagement, however, calls for a willingness to be "open to the leading of the Spirit," and an equal readiness to acknowledge the distortions of UCC understandings of ministry by historical circumstance. In that process, older terminology, now freighted with emotional significance that obscures essential truths, can take on new and relevant meaning for this age. Many terms grounded in our historic continuities and traditions are neither meaningless nor inappropriate; they simply need to be freshly perceived and employed.

The relationships among the several units of UCC organizational life, as stated earlier, are *delineated* but *not regulated* by the Constitution and Bylaws. In this section of our examination of that covenantal instrument I want to employ again the principle of differentiation between *order* and *polity*. The covenantal model stands in sharp contrast to our experience in most social organization. It requires different perceptions of the exercise of authority and power for which, then, the distinctions between order and polity are critical. In covenantal relationships there are units, not levels, of organization. Superiority and inferiority are not implied by unit designation as they would be by designation of levels. Authority and power are exercised ministerially, not magisterially.

The principle of order in the UCC covenantal system precludes the pyramidal image of relationships in the community of faith by its singular affirmation of Jesus Christ as head of the church (his body), whose authority is *immediate* to every part. The relationships are binding in and through Christ, not by independent choice or decision. Once Jesus Christ is confessed, the relationships to other parts of the body are binding through him. Thus authority for the relationship rests with Christ, whose call and claim have elicited the confession. Although this is rather elementary and is easily understood when applied to the local church, it is not as easily perceived when applied to Associations, Conferences, and the General Synod. Our common experience in most social organization tends to place these in relationships suggesting subordination. The UCC principle of order subordinates each *only to Christ*. Each is responsible to Christ.

The polity principle for these units—mutual accountability—flows from that principle of order, for all are one in Christ and responsible for one another. This requires each unit to make its own decisions in fulfillment of that responsibility. Thus each unit develops its own constitution and bylaws. The contingent authority guiding such organizational development is not grounded in self-interest (as in most social organization) but in Christ's claim and call to participate in God's mission. This provides flexibility in meeting the diverse requirements for mission in different circumstances while at the same time acknowledging responsbility to other units in their special needs.

UCC experience with this model over three decades has been mixed. Old habits prevail, especially when circumstances seem to call for preservation rather than creative effort. Examples are hardly necessary, but if such experiences have been discouraging, particularly for lack of uniformity and consensus, we should be reminded that the conciliar mode of living in covenant requires continual learning. It is true that our inclinations for independence and accountability-to-self-only give the impression of the UCC as a loosely organized conglomerate of churches and regional bodies. But we confess that we are *one* in Christ.

It is in this connection that the General Synod's importance in the UCC system takes on special meaning. It is the General Synod, comprised of representatives of local churches who are chosen as delegates by the Conferences, that symbolizes the organizational unity of the church. It is an organizational symbol whose power of government can be exercised only in relation to itself and to the bodies it creates or recognizes. But the *effective* power of the Synod for the whole church lies in the opportunities it provides for the exercise of the conciliar mode of organizational government. As a human organization it is itself a *learning* as well as a *teaching* convocation. It is the occasion for use of the conciliar method in relation to issues requiring wider perspectives than those ordinarily available to local and regional units. This contribution to the enrichment and strengthening of the local church and regional bodies is often overlooked, usually because of a falsely premised assumption that local units are in fact fully equipped to address any issue. Conciliarity is first of all an acknowledgment of the *need for one another* in fulfilling the God-given mission of the church. Certainly in the global village context of the church's mission, all units of the church's life—local, regional, and national—are in need of learning from one another.

Does the General Synod serve adequately on the national level? Can it? Those questions elicit diverse responses, of course. Along the way the Synod often has been an exclusively political body, responding to the pressures of particular interest groups and struggling for the survival of the denominational machinery.[19] At the same time, its procedures and agenda again and again have generated new perspectives on the church's responsibility, and have given encouragement in much needed efforts for faithful witness. Providentiality, and under the guidance of the Holy Spirit, the Synod is often the conciliar body, working in covenantal consciousness, where the elements of Robin W. Lovin's characterization of covenant life are demonstrated: "communication, earnest conversation, and mutual correction."[20] Associations and Conferences have equal opportunity, and even more occasions, for such learning/teaching demonstrations.

In the foregoing sections of this chapter I have sought to give an example of a method that can be helpful in a disciplined and intentional examination of the UCC covenantal instrument—the Constitution and Bylaws. The example, limited in scope as it is, can suffice, I believe, to indicate the way both the potentialities and the weaknesses of that instrument can be uncovered. In offering the example, I am affirming both my own confidence in the Spirit that formed the UCC and my deep conviction that the covenantal instrument we have devised, despite all its limitations, has the potential of continually shaping a new form of the church for God's mission. I hope the urgency of the need to do this has been illustrated as well. That urgency now needs some reiteration in the concluding section of this chapter.

175

The implications of the disciplined examination discussed earlier for the UCC ecumenical vocation can be drawn out almost endlessly. However, both this chapter and this book can be brought to a conclusion consistent with the theme—the meaning of an ecclesial journey—by referring once more to the indissoluble link between unity and mission. That link, although clearly expressed in the chartering documents of UCC formation, and repeatedly reaffirmed at critical points in the ecclesial journey, nevertheless has seemed to some to have minimal influence in shaping our communion's ecclesial consciousness.

That negative conclusion, however, should not be allowed to obscure the essential point that the concern to develop a new ecclesial model issued from the conviction that formed and spurred the ecumenical movement from the beginning*—unity and mission can not be separated. The experience of the ecclesial journey of thirty years, marked by mind-boggling changes in the human condition, has not changed the crucial perception that the visible form of the church must embody its mission. That is grounded in the faith that "a salvation whose very essence is . . . the restoration of the broken harmony" between humanity and God and humanity and nature, "must be communicated in and by the actual development of a community which embodies, if only in a foretaste, the restored harmony of which it speaks. A gospel of reconciliation can be communicated only by a reconciled fellowship."[21] What *has changed* are the perceptions of the nature of the ecclesial form and of the dimensions and character of mission. I have discussed these in some depth and need not repeat them. It is important here, however, to ask: With these changing perceptions, how is it possible to inform and undergird our ecclesial consciousness in ways that will faithfully exhibit the wholeness of unity and mission? If the basic argument of this book is sound, two responses to the question suggest themselves.

First, the covenantal model of ecclesial organization, as it has been described, provides both the responsibility and the opportunity for continuous learning about unity and mission. The ecclesial

---

*This was traced in chapters 2 and 3.

journey continues to be a learning experience. Again, "commu/
tion, earnest conversation, and mutual correction" are the sr
aspects of covenant life that encourage the learning that is essentiai
to the realization of unity in mission and mission in unity.
   In covenant life, taken seriously, the experience of reconciliation and oneness is open to new understandings. It is the way of
living *toward* and *in* unity even in the midst of radical changes in the
context of mission. Such changes can engender divisions in the
community of faith that can be devastating to the church's witness.
But in covenant, where unity is the gift, calling for mutual accountability and responsibility, the power of reconciliation is experienced
by reliance on the presence and power of the Holy Spirit in fulfillment of God's covenant promise.
   A contemporary example of this reconciliation in covenantal life
is reflected in a statement produced at a UCC conference on
mission in which diverse groups, often in open conflict over theological issues, worked together to express today's mission perspective:

Statement of Mission

As people of the United Church of Christ, affirming our statement of
faith, we seek within the church universal to participate in God's
mission and to follow the way of the crucified and risen Christ.

Empowered by the Holy Spirit, we are called and commit ourselves . . .

   To praise God, confess our sin, and joyfully accept God's for-
        giveness;
   To proclaim the Gospel of Jesus Christ in our suffering world;
   To embody God's love for all people;
   To hear and give voice to creation's cry for justice and peace;
   To name and confront the powers of evil within and among us;
   To repent our silence and complicity with the forces of chaos and
        death;
   To preach and teach with the power of the Living Word;
   To join oppressed and troubled people in the struggle for libera-
        tion:
   To work for justice, healing, and wholeness of life;
   To embrace the unity of Christ's church;
   To discern and celebrate the present and coming reign of God.[22]

The mission concepts in this statement represent a fundamental shift—under way now for some years—that heretofore many have not found acceptable. The covenant paradigm *is* "subversive" of positions of fate and convenience too long cherished! Reconciliation in the community of faith is both a product of the church's mission and a power for reconciliation in the world.

Second, the covenantal model of ecclesial life requires the formative and nurturing power of liturgical discipline to exhibit the wholeness of unity and mission.[23] Liturgical life in the UCC, as in much of American Protestantism, represents the dominance of privatistic faith and therapeutic religious practice. But world conditions are forcing the opening of our "windows of worship" as ecumenical voices call for liturgical expression of the reality of unity (the reconciled community) and mission (the reconciling community). The introduction, for example, of *Baptism, Eucharist and Ministry* includes these words:

> We live in a crucial moment in the history of humankind. As the churches grow in unity, they are asking how their understandings and practices of baptism, eucharist and ministry relate to *their mission in and for the renewal of human community as they seek to promote justice, peace, and reconciliation.*[24]

How do UCC practices of the sacraments relate to the mission of reconciliation, peace, and justice? Here, too, we are in an important time of learning. Baptism, for generations understood *solely* in terms relating to personal salvation, must be seen in its corollary accents, given in the New Testament—the call to live the new life in Christ and to accept the ministry of reconciliation (Romans 6:4, 11; 2 Corinthians 5:18). As the sacrament of *vocation,* and of salvation, baptism is one of the two anchoring points of that liturgical discipline so necessary to unity and mission. Every baptismal act in the church's corporate worship signifies and seals (thus reiterating the sacramental meaning) to the believer the vocation God gives through participation in Christ's death and resurrection. The anchor of that vocation—marked in baptism—is Christ's own giving of self to death, and then rising to life. This is, then, the *measure* of the mission in which each believer shares—a mission defined by Christ, not by the believer's personal preference.

In the same way, the eucharist, or Holy Communion, is an

anchoring point for that liturgical discipline in which unity and mission are fully exhibited. When baptism is understood in terms of vocation, the eucharist is understood in terms of *discipleship*. The Holy Supper was first shared with disciples; and thus it must always be. It is not a holy rite of religious mysticism; it is the thankful act of the community of faith gathered by the Christ at the table. There Jesus Christ is host, where the broken bread and the poured wine define the life he gives to those who accept him. That life is a "spent" life—broken and poured out; but also a risen life—new and victorious. The life Jesus Christ gives to his *disciples* is defined by him in the symbols of his own self-giving.

In corporate worship, anchored in these sacraments and informed by the proclaimed Word, the church experiences the liturgical discipline that nurtures and actualizes the link between unity and mission. In this way corporate worship can serve to bind us in the "mutual accountability" that marks the covenant life.[25] And where that binding takes place, the vision and grasp of the mission of reconciliation, justice, and peace is given a Christ-dimension.

The UCC ecclesial journey is not ended; it continues by the mercy and grace of God, hearing always the mandate laid on those who first envisioned what this community of faith must be when they listened to the words of our Lord: "I do not pray for these only, but also for those who believe in me through their word, *that they may all be one;* even as thou art in me, and I in thee, that they may also be in us, *so that the world may believe* [John 17:20–21]."

179

───────── APPENDIX A ─────────

Ecumenical Partnership Between the United Church of Christ and the Christian Church (Disciples of Christ)

Declaration of Ecumenical Partnership

The General Synod of the United Church of Christ and the General Assembly of the Christian Church (Disciples of Christ), declare and celebrate a new ecumenical partnership between the United Church of Christ and the Christian Church (Disciples of Christ), and identify three primary marks of our ecumenical partnership beginning in 1985: (1) commitment to respond together to the mission God has entrusted to the church, (2) theological work to equip our churches as they grow toward full communion, and (3) common worship with frequent and intentional sharing in the Lord's Supper/Holy Communion.

This ecumenical partnership is to be set within the context of our churches' participation in the Consultation on Church Union. We see the partnership of our two churches as a positive contribution to COCU and its life, even as we receive gifts from the Consultation. Further, we affirm that, in both our participation in COCU and this ecumenical partnership, our ultimate goal is the oneness of the whole body of Christ.

Theological Affirmations for Our Life as Ecumenical Partners

As the basis for making this declaration of a new ecumenical partnership:

 1. We affirm that the God of Jesus Christ has given the unity of the Church, and that all who confess Jesus Christ as God and Saviour are members one of another in the one body of Christ.

───────────────

From the Minutes of General Synod XV, June 1985, pp. 58–60.

2. We affirm that all who have received the grace of new life in Christ are called to manifest the given unity of the Church for the sake of reconciliation in the Christian community, the reconciliation of humankind, and the fulfillment of God's mission.

3. We affirm that our two churches are kindred in Christ, members together of the one, undivided Church of Jesus Christ.

4. We affirm, with thanksgiving, that our two churches have been called by God and led by the Holy Spirit to be witnesses to the given unity of the Church, and to labor for the unity of all Christians. For our two churches the visible oneness of the whole body of Christ is the ultimate goal and overarching context in which this ecumenical partnership will evolve.

5. We affirm and rejoice in the long history of our partnership in the Gospel, and give thanks for the grace of God that has brought us, through conversation, covenanted studies and cooperation in mission to a new threshold in our life as partners in the one Church.

6. Affirming the mercies of God, we express deep sorrow and penitence that our two churches participate in the separations and divisions that violate the will of God for the one body, and that hinder the mission of God to bring wholeness and unity to the human family.

7. Affirming that "all are one in Christ Jesus," and that "Christ is our peace," we hear with urgency God's call to our two churches to claim together the signs of a fuller communion, namely, the recognition of one baptism and one eucharist, the mutual recognition of members, the recognition and reconciliation of ministries, the common commitment to confess the Gospel of Christ by proclamation and service to the world, and openness to common decision-making.

8. We affirm that God, who in the crucified and risen Christ acted to bring the world to wholeness, calls for our obedience and sacrifice from every center of pain and injustice, hunger and homelessness, violence and peril of war, and all wasted and endangered environments.

9. We affirm these essential elements in the common journey to be God's people: life in a worshipping community, the treasuring of scripture and the apostolic faith, and self-giving discipleship in and for the world. These, together with other graces from God, nourish members of the one Church and support God's saving mission to the whole creation.

10. We affirm that our brokenness is transcended at the Table of Christ Jesus where we are called to confess our sinfulness and receive the cup "poured out for many for the forgiveness of sins" (Matt. 26:28). There we discover our given unity in Christ, "for we all partake of the

one bread" (1 Cor. 10:17). There we are empowered by God's grace and witness to the saving acts and presence of the crucified and risen Christ.

Implementation of Our Ecumenical Partnership

In order to give concrete expression, meaning and direction to the ecumenical partnership:

· I. The General Assembly and the General Synod establish an Ecumenical Partnership Committee with responsibility to

A. Provide general guidelines to the Ecumenical Partnership in the following areas:

1. MISSION

Local churches, associations, regions and conferences, instrumentalities and general units, seminaries, and all other bodies in the two churches will be called upon to commit themselves, in all possible areas, to expressions of common mission, building on those that already exist and creating new initiatives. In particular, appropriate national and regional/conference bodies are called upon to begin, during the 1985–87 biennium, coordinated planning and, wherever possible, joint staffing in areas of mission such as: education, evangelism, peace with justice, economic justice and human equality.

Opportunities for the ecumenical expression of mission will also be encouraged with other Christian bodies, particularly those with whom we share in the Consultation on Church Union.

2. THEOLOGICAL WORK

The Ecumenical Partnership Committee will encourage in both churches the process of receiving and claiming the theological convergence of the World Council of Churches, *Baptism, Eucharist and Ministry,* and the theological consensus of the Consultation on Church Union, *In Quest of a Church of Christ Uniting,* as guides for understanding the theology of Christian unity. Building upon this work, the Ecumenical Partnership Committee is asked to develop recommendations for submission to the General Assembly and General Synod in 1989 regarding actions that would lead to full communion between our two churches, which includes mutual recognition of baptism, full eucharistic fellowship, the mutual recognition of members and ordained ministers, the common commitment to confess the gospel of Christ by proclamation and service to the word, and common decision-making.

183

3. WORSHIP

Recognizing the centrality of worship in the life and witness of the Church, a service of Word and Sacrament be prepared to celebrate the Ecumenical Partnership. This service will be used in national, conference/regional, area, and local celebrations beginning with the General Assembly and General Synod in 1987. The Ecumenical Partnership Committee is asked to assist in familiarizing the churches with each other's worship resources, to prepare and provide resources for education in worship, including the significance of the sacraments and worship resources from Christian traditions throughout the world.

Worship is a significant aspect of our growing relationship. Frequent shared worship will be encouraged so that congregations and the various plenary bodies and boards of our churches might build on this foundation. Wider ecumenical worship is to be encouraged, including a growing use of the worship resources of the Consultation on Church Union.

B. Listen and respond to the partnership experiences of people throughout the two churches, so that insights might be shared and deepened.

C. Encourage understanding of and participation in the Ecumenical Partnership in order that it may be claimed more fully throughout the two churches.

D. Formulate and make recommendations, at appropriate times, on further specific steps and activities between these two churches in the pursuit of full communion and visible unity.

II. The General Assembly and the General Synod authorize, respectively, the Administrative Committee of the Christian Church (Disciples of Christ) and the Executive Council of the United Church of Christ to elect ten persons to the membership of the Ecumenical Partnership Committee. The presidents of each church shall be included in the delegations. In addition, provision shall be made for the inclusion of two ecumenical members from other churches in the Consultation on Church Union. The Administrative Committee and the Executive Council shall develop common procedures for establishing the terms of office as well as the orderly replacement of members. The Ecumenical Partnership Committee shall report biennially to the General Assembly and the General Synod through the General Board and the Executive Council.

III. The General Assembly and General Synod authorize the Administrative Committee and Executive Council to negotiate with the appropriate bodies in the two churches for staff and funds to implement the work of the Ecumenical Partnership Committee. It is understood that in accomplishing its mandate the Ecumenical Partnership Committee will seek inclusive and collegial participation in the partnership endeavors.

IV. As part of our search for growing relatedness and as a concrete way to express common decision-making, the General Assembly and General Synod encourage all governing and decision-making bodies to explore the possibility of moving toward ecumenical membership, with voice and (where possible) vote, from the partner church.

Conclusion

The General Synod and General Assembly call upon all congregations, districts and areas, associations, regions and conferences, institutions and national bodies to encourage and implement this partnership. In shared mission, growing theological understanding, and worship, we look forward to the leadership of God's spirit in our midst.

In adopting this proposal, we celebrate and declare to each other and before the world a new Ecumenical Partnership which we pray God will bless, enrich, and use as together we seek to be more faithfully and fully the people God calls us to become.

APPENDIX B

Bibliographical Note

Readers who wish to trace in some detail the parallel journeys of the United Church of Christ and the Christian Church (Disciples of Christ) may be quickly overwhelmed by the volume of literature available. A selective approach is suggested by the fact that the most formative influences in the modern development of both communions stem from the nineteenth century heyday of denominational expansion. The mid-twentieth-century struggle with both the limitations and possibilities of the denominational form of the church, must take into account the nineteenth century story. In that story the parallel journeys of these two ecumenical partners were shaped.

The Christian Church (Disciples of Christ) story is unusually well-documented and interpreted. Although some attention should be given to founders' writings, it is of greater importance to see how twentieth-century scholars of that communion understand their history. Thus, while Thomas Campbell's *Declaration and Address* (1832) and Alexander Campbell's *The Christian System* (1835) are foundational, a modern perspective on their significance is especially helpful. For this purpose the reader will find a most helpful three-volume work prepared by a panel of scholars, with Ronald E. Osborn as general editor. These volumes, published in 1963 by Bethany Press (St. Louis), effectively show the theological ferment that led to the denominational restructuring of the late 1960s. Their titles suggest the focus of concern among the panel of scholars: *The Reformation of Tradition,* R.E. Osborn, ed.; *The Revival of the Churches,* Ralph G. Wilburn and W.B. Blakemore, eds.; *The Reconstruction of Theology,* Ralph G. Wilburn, ed.

Four additional volumes, published by Bethany Press (St. Louis), provide a wealth of supplementary interpretation, all of them published subsequent to the restructuring that gave the denomination its present name: The Christian Church (Disciples of Christ). They are: Loren E. Lair, *The Christian Church (Disciples of Christ) and the Future* (1971); George C. Beazley Jr., ed., *The Christian Church (Disciples of Christ): An Interpretative Examination in the Cultural Context* (1973); and Lester G.

McAllister, *Journey in Faith: A History of the Christian Church (Disciples of Christ)* (1975).

An exceptionally valuable resource is available in *Mid-Stream*, a publication of the Council on Christian Unity (Disciples), particularly those volumes dated from 1957 through the 1980s.

The United Church of Christ's story is in many ways more difficult to trace since it involves four uniting communions, three of which have much longer histories than do the Disciples of Christ. For example, one hundred and twenty-four titles are listed in the bibliography for Congregational history by Gaius Glenn Atkins and Frederick L. Fagley, *History of American Congregationalism* (Boston: The Pilgrim Press, 1942). Writings of the founders—William Ames, John Cotton, Cotton Mather, Richard Mather, John Wise, and others—are the basic resources for understanding the Puritan roots of Congregationalism. However, the late nineteenth-century shaping of Congregational churches into a denomination is of greater importance for UCC/Disciples relationships. In addition to the Atkins and Fagley volume, readers will want to rely on: Williston Walker's, *The Creeds and Platforms of Congregationalism* (New York: The Pilgrim Press, 1893 and 1960) and *A History of the Congregational Churches in America,* vol. III of *American Church History* (New York: Charles Scribner's Sons, 1916). The Congregational story is filled out by George J. Eisenach, *A History of the German Congregational Churches in the United States* (Yankton, SD: Pioneer Press, 1938). Three volumes are important to an understanding of the Christian part of the Congregational Christian segment of the UCC: Milo T. Morrill, *A History of the Christian Denomination in America* (Dayton: Christian Publishing Association, 1912), D.T. Stokes and William T. Scott, *A History of the Christian Church in the South* (Elon College, NC 1975), and J. Taylor Stanley, *A History of the Black Congregational Christian Churches of the South* (New York: United Church Press, 1978). For the Evangelical and Reformed Church story, three books will serve adequately: J.H. Dubbs, *Historic Manual of the Reformed Church in the United States* (Lancaster, PA, 1885), Carl E. Schneider, *The German Church on the American Frontier* (St. Louis: Eden Publishing House, 1939), and David Dunn, et al., *A History of the Evangelical and Reformed Church* (Philadelphia: The Christian Education Press, 1961). The latter is especially valuable in showing the significance of the difference between the eighteenth- and nineteenth-century immigration of the German people of the Reformed Church.

The relatively brief existence of the United Church of Christ is told in Douglas Horton, *The United Church of Christ* (New York: Thomas Nelson & Sons, 1962) and Louis H. Gunnemann, *The Shaping of the United Church of Christ* (New York: United Church Press, 1977). Barbara Brown

Zikmund, ed., *Hidden Histories in the United Church of Christ* (New York: United Church Press, 1984) is an especially important contribution to understanding UCC diversity.

Those who seek firsthand access to UCC ecumenical involvements must turn to the Minutes of the Commission on Christian Unity and Ecumenical Study and Service, 1961–1972, and Minutes of the Council for Ecumenism, 1975–1986, both available through the UCC Historical Archives at Lancaster, PA.

Ecumenical Stance of the UCC

It was
73-GS-71 VOTED: The General Synod adopts the alternative I statement on Ecumenical Stance of the United Church of Christ as amended.

I. Theological Affirmation and Call

Humanity is broken and divided yet one. The Church of Jesus Christ is broken and divided yet one. The ecumenical commitment of the Church to mission and unity is to symbolize through its worship, its communal and structural life, and its work in the world the Christian union which points toward the larger union of creation. Its task is to work in effective mission to heal dehumanizing divisions and to realize more fully the universal human community which is proclaimed in the reality and the hope of the Kingdom of God.

The ultimate personal identity of each individual is that of a human being, created and loved by God, and part of His universal family. Our identities as individual members and as churches in the corporate life of the United Church of Christ are fragmental identities, necessary but provisional. The task our Lord Jesus Christ sets before us is to realize more fully in our churchly symbols, common life, ecclesiastical structures, and mission the ultimate union of creation, to point with gratitude and to participate where possible in those places where God's spirit is at work in the world making life whole. To the end that the union and wholeness of God's creation may be affirmed, we believe the effective union and wholeness of Christ's Church is intended.

We affirm, therefore, the description of the nature and shape of unity recommended to the Churches by the Third Assembly in New Delhi of the World Council of Churches:

> We believe that the unity which is both God's will and his gift to his Church is being made visible as all in each place who are baptized into Jesus Christ and confess him as Lord and Savior are brought by

From the Minutes of General Synod IX, June 1973, pp. 58–59.

the Holy Spirit into ONE fully committed fellowship, holding the one apostolic faith, preaching the one Gospel, breaking the one bread, joining in common prayer, and having a corporate life reaching out in witness and service to all, and who at the same time are united with the whole Christian fellowship in all places and all ages in such wise that ministry and members are accepted by all, and that all can act and speak together as occasion requires for the tasks to which God calls his people.

We call the whole Church and the communion to which we belong to the task of giving full witness to the continuing process of uniting in ways known and to be made known to us.

Ecumenical commitment and involvement, even as all Christian life, involve costs of time, energy, and fundamental risk. Nevertheless, ecumenicity is not an option for us; rather it is a mandate that prohibits a restrictive view that would separate mission from unity, or unity from mission. Whenever we view ecumenicity as mainly cooperative planning and action rather than as the name for those active steps toward the goal of church union for the union of all humankind, we trap ourselves in the false dichotomy of mission vs. unity or unity vs. mission. The goal is the *union* of the church and the *union* of creation, and mission and unity are the processes to be followed in reaching the goal. We affirm that these belong irrevocably together in God's order.

We confess our need to understand more fully the demands of the gospel in a world of conflicting demands. We need to *clarify* those demands, particularly as they relate to church union and the union of all creation. We need to provide guidelines, in light of the gospel imperatives for mission and unity, for choosing among the various ecumenical models according to their functions.

We believe that such policy and clarity are built on theological foundations.

II. Actions

In the light of the above theological affirmation and call, the Ninth General Synod adopts the following policies and processes for use as they apply throughout the fellowship of the United Church of Christ.

1. The Ninth General Synod declares its *recognition of members and ministers* of other Christian Churches as members and ministers of the Church of Jesus Christ, and particularly those who are related to communions involved in the Consultation on Church Union. Conferences, Associations and churches of the United Church of Christ are requested to make this recognition tangible.

190

2. The Ninth General Synod pledges itself to strengthen the mission and witness of *the conciliar movement* as expressing the wholeness of Christ's Church.

A. The Ninth General Synod urges Instrumentalities throughout the Church to commit their resources and staffs to the work of the National Council of the Churches of Christ, particularly so that the recently adopted structures of the Council may have a fair chance to succeed;

B. The Ninth General Synod supports the allocation of the *minimum askings* for the central budgets of the World Council of Churches and the National Council of the Churches of Christ for 1974 and 1975;

C. The Ninth General Synod declares that conciliar groups must be encouraged by responsible judicatory leaders at all levels to become representative of the widest possible range of judicatory structures to become recognized vehicles for the theological, structural, and experimental efforts in the process of growing together recommended by the Consultation on Church Union and to be arenas for planning, strategy, and judicatory decision-making.

3. The Ninth General Synod looks with favor on the possibility of *Roman Catholic membership* in conciliar ecumenism everywhere, and encourages all parts of the United Church of Christ to engage in dialogue and cooperative action with the Roman Catholic Church.

4. The Ninth General Synod declares its support for *coalitions, consortia, and clusters* as appropriate vehicles for specific inter-church programs and projects and conciliar organizations.

5. The Ninth General Synod declares its commitment to the process of growing together represented in the *Consultation on Church Union* and is determined to press forward with vigor in deeply involved cooperation with those churches of COCU to experience increased cooperation and unity, and to gain clearer and fuller insights through worship, study, fellowship, and action, so that there will be steady and determined progress toward full union. The Executive Council is directed, in consultation with the UCC delegates to COCU and with the Commission on Christian Unity, to seek to mobilize full support throughout our communion for the COCU process, particularly as it seeks new directions in experimental processes of growing together.

6. The Ninth General Synod declares that *regional and local ecumenism* are basic and fundamental ingredients of the life of the Church and affirms that theological sensitivity and competence are needed ingredients in the ecumenical life of all churches everywhere. The Ninth General Synod urges that United Church of Christ members and agencies participate fully in regional and local ecumenical expressions so that all of our members may have local experiences of the ecumenical movements.

7. The Ninth General Synod values its association with the member churches of the *World Alliance of Reformed Churches (Presbyterian and Congregational),* and appreciates the opportunities for study and deepening friendships which membership offers. As the time of financial stringency continues, and as other ecumenical needs seem more pressing, our financial commitment to the WARC must rank lower than our commitment to the Consultation on Church Union, the World Council of Churches, and the National Council of the Churches of Christ.

NOTES

Prologue

1. Arnold J. Toynbee, *A Study of History* (New York: Oxford University Press, 1947), p. 1.
2. See, e.g., issues of *New Conversations, Prism, United Church News.*
3. James E. Andrews and Joseph A. Burgess, eds., *An Invitation to Action: The Lutheran-Reformed Dialogue, Series III, 1981–83* (Philadelphia: Fortress Press, 1984), p. 90.
4. For example, see John R. Fry, *The Trivialization of the Presbyterian Church* (New York: Harper & Row, 1975); Richard B. Wilke, *Are We Yet Alive? The Future of the United Methodist Church* (Nashville: Abingdon Press, 1985).
5. Mark Horst, "The Problem of Theological Pluralism," *The Christian Century,* Nov. 5, 1986, vol. 103, no. 33, p. 973.
6. See Christopher Lasch, *The Culture of Narcissism* (New York: W.W. Norton, 1978), p. xiv.
7. See the perceptive comments of Gabriel Fackre, Lori A. Buehler, and Richard L. Floyd in *New Conversations,* vol. 8, no. 1, Spring 1985, pp. 33–38.
8. See Frederick Herzog and Susan Thistlethwaite, "Response: the Theologians Appeal" for identification of these issues. Ibid. pp. 26–29.
9. Gordon Harland, *The Thought of Reinhold Niebuhr* (New York: Oxford University Press, 1960), p. 91.

Chapter 1
Introduction to a Journey Undertaken

1. Robert W. Spike, "The United Church of Christ: In Search of a Special Calling" in *What's Ahead for the Churches?* Martin Marty, Kyle Haselden, eds. (New York: Sheed and Ward, 1964), p. 54. Italics added.
2. United Church people have often referred to themselves as a pilgrim people, thus echoing one of the important strands of the biblical heritage, and especially of the Puritan era. A helpful imaging of the pilgrim journey motif is in Gabriel Fackre's "Theology and Forms of Confession in the UCC," *Encounter,* vol. 41, no. 1, Winter 1980, p. 39.

3. See Rooks' article of that title in *New Conversations,* vol. II, no. 1, Spring 1977, p. 4.

4. The roster of prominent leaders in the worldwide ecumenical movement included many of the chief architects of the United Church of Christ: George W. Richards, Douglas Horton, H. Richard Niebuhr, Reinhold Niebuhr, Truman Douglass, Samuel D. Press, James E. Wagner, and many others.

5. This is discussed at length in my book *The Shaping of the United Church of Christ* (New York: United Church Press, 1977), ch. 4.

6. Paul S. Minear, *Images of the Church in the New Testament* (Philadelphia: Westminster Press, 1960), p. 24.

7. Although the Minutes of the General Synod do not often reveal the temper of the debates, a careful reading of parliamentary rulings and maneuvers, as well as of reports, yields strong hints of deep feelings. Minority reports especially exhibit the rising alienation and partisan spirit of the times.

8. See Minutes of General Synod IX, June 22–26, 1973, pp. 58–60, for this and the following quotations. President Moss's message is found on pp. 98–101. The resolution included specific recommendations designed to give the UCC more effective ecumenical leadership. Most of those recommendations, referred to the Executive Council, were actually attempts to overcome structural inconsistencies in United Church of Christ organization.

9. Ibid., p. 59.

10. Minutes of General Synod X, 1975, p. 36.

11. This is discussed more fully in chapters 7 and 8 of this book.

12. See, for example: Peter Berger, et al, *The Homeless Mind* (New York: Random House, 1973); and other books of this genre.

13. See Gabriel Fackre, "Theological Soul-Searching in the United Church of Christ," *TSF Bulletin,* Nov.–Dec. 1984, p. 5; and Clyde J. Steckel, "Theology in the United Church of Christ," *Theological Markings,* Spring 1982, p. 5.

14. See Barbara Brown Zikmund, "Theology in the United Church of Christ: A Documentary Trail," *Prism,* Intro. Issue, Fall 1985, for a helpful record.

15. In a letter of Reuben A. Sheares II, executive director of the Office for Church Life and Leadership, dated July 1978.

16. The report *Toward the Task of Sound Teaching in the United Church of Christ* is included as an appendix in Frederick Herzog, *Justice Church* (Maryknoll: Orbis Books, 1980).

17. The special reasons for the attention given this report in 1982–83 are discussed in chapter 3.

18. Charles Shelby Rooks, "Between Memory and Hope," *New Conversations,* vol. 2, no. 1, Spring 1977, p. 7.

19. See ibid., p. 3, "Identity and Covenant."

20. See Marty's review of *The Shaping of the United Church of Christ,* in *Theological Markings,* vol. 7, no. 1, Winter 1977, p. 35.

21. This was not a matter of "liberalism versus conservatism" as implied in Dean Kelley's *Why Conservative Churches Are Growing* (New York: Harper & Row, 1972, 1977). Those terms have diverse meanings and cannot identify in any helpful way the malaise of many churches.

22. Quoted from *The Shaping of the United Church of Christ,* op. cit., p. 16.

23. See Paul Minear, op. cit., p. 24.

24. William McKinney gathered the first four of these in one issue of *New Conversations,* vol. 8, no. 1, Spring 1985, as a "Conversation Piece: Toward Theological Self-understanding in the United Church of Christ."

25. Organized initially by Frederick R. Trost, then pastor of St. Paul's Church in Chicago, for the 100th Anniversary of the Evangelical Synod of North America, this informal group has provided an ongoing effort to explore United Church of Christ tradition in depth.

26. Minutes of General Synod, XIII, 1981, pp. 61–63.

Chapter 2
The Context of the Journey

1. A survey of book titles in the period between 1927 and 1965 illustrates the intensive focus on ecclesiology. A shift from a theological (ecclesiological) to a sociological understanding of the church came to prominence from the mid-'60s.

2. A phrase used by President Avery D. Post in an effort to interpret the United Church of Christ experience of spiritual and theological malaise in the '80s.

3. The origins of the Life and Work Movement are a fascinating and important story. They lie in the merging of social concern and activity in the churches with the growing international peace efforts among the churches of Europe and America beginning in the late 19th century and developing powerfully in the 20th.

4. See Nils Ehrenstrom's "Movements for International Friendship and Life and Work" in Ruth Rouse and Stephen Neill, eds., *A History of the Ecumenical Movement, 1517–1948* (Philadelphia: Westminster Press, 1967), pp. 572ff.

5. Ehrenstrom, op. cit., especially p. 572.

6. This was the motto of the 1925 Stockholm Conference on Life and Work.

7. The one major exception to this was the Mercersburg Theology (or Movement) in the Reformed Church in the United States in the early 19th century.

8. See my discussion of this in *The Shaping of the United Church of Christ* (New York: United Church Press, 1977), pp. 13–14.

9. *The Constitution and Bylaws of the United Church of Christ,* 1984 edition.

10. See *The Shaping of the United Church of Christ,* op. cit., ch. 1, for a discussion of the role of these in pre-union debates.

11. Hanns Peter Keiling, *Die Entstehung der "United Church of Christ"* (Berlin: Lettner-Verlag, 1969). The sub-title, *Fallstudie einer Kirchenunion unter Berucksichtigung des Problems der Ortgemeinde,* indicates the focus of the study on the issues of the relation of the local church to the larger church.

12. See my discussion of this in "Unity and Church Union in the Antecedent Communions of the United Church of Christ," *Historical Intelligencer,* vol. I, no. 1, Fall 1980.

13. George W. Richards in R. Newton Flew, ed., *The Nature of the Church* (London: SCM Press, 1952), p. 262.

14. Ibid., p. 255.

15. Louis W. Goebel files, 55 (1), folder 48-6, Archives, Eden Theological Seminary.

16. Ibid.

17. See William K. Newman, "A Crisis of Experience" in *New Conversations,* vol. II, no. 1, Spring 1977, p. 8.

18. See Colin W. Williams, *The Church,* vol. IV in *New Directions in Theology Today,* William Hordern, ed. (Philadelphia: Westminster Press, 1968). But see also Meredith B. Handspicker, "Faith and Order 1948–1968" in Harold Fey, ed., *A History of the Ecumenical Movement,* vol. 2, 1948–1968 (Philadelphia: Westminster Press, 1970).

19. Williams, ibid., p. 14.

20. See Flew, op. cit. This set of papers from the 1937 Faith and Order Conference preparatory work illustrates the approach of comparative ecclesiology.

21. Examples of this position: Paul S. Minear, *Images of the Church in the New Testament* (Philadelphia: Westminster Press, 1960); and J. Lesslie Newbigin, *The Household of God* (New York: Friendship Press, 1953).

22. See my *The Shaping of the United Church of Christ,* op.cit., p. 46.

23. *The Church for Others* (Geneva: World Council of Churches, 1967).

24. Karl Barth's emphasis on the church as "event" was of major importance.

25. J.C. Hoekendijk, *The Church Inside Out* (Philadelphia: Westminster Press, 1966).

26. See Newman, op. cit., p. 9.

27. See, for example, Colin W. Williams, *Where in the World,* and *What in the World* (New York: National Council of Churches, 1963 and 1964); also George W. Webber, *The Congregation in Mission* (New York: Abingdon, 1964).

28. Jurgen Moltmann, *The Church in the Power of the Spirit* (New York: Harper & Row, 1977), pp. 5–6.

29. For example: Juan Luis Segundo, *Our Idea of God* (Maryknoll: Orbis Books, 1974); Gustavo Gutierrez, *A Theology of Liberation* (Maryknoll: Orbis Books, 1974).

30. Frederick Herzog, *Liberation Theology* (New York: Seabury Press, 1972).

31. Frederick Herzog, *Justice Church* (Maryknoll: Orbis Books, 1980). This penetrating discussion has special significance for the United Church of Christ.

32. Ibid., p. 9. Italics added.

33. Geoffrey Wainwright, *The Ecumenical Moment* (Grand Rapids: Eerdmans, 1983), p. 190.

34. *Baptism, Eucharist and Ministry,* Faith and Order Paper, No. 111 (Geneva: World Council of Churches, 1982).

35. Ibid. This and the following quotations in this paragraph are taken from the Preface.

36. See Minutes of General Synod XV, UCC, 1985, pp. 159–64.

37. Ibid., p. 160.

38. See Charles Hambrick-Stowe, "The Nature of the Ministry: The United Church of Christ and *Baptism, Eucharist and Ministry,*" in *Prism,* Intro. Issue, Fall 1985, p. 26ff.; and Thomas E. Dipko, "Baptism in the United Church of Christ, from the Perspective of *Baptism, Eucharist and Ministry*"; David L. Beebe, "Baptism in the Congregational Christian Tradition"; Harry G. Royer, "Baptism in the Evangelical and Reformed Tradition," in *Prism,* vol. I, no. 1, Spring 1986; Gabriel Fackre, "BEM on the Eucharist: A United Church of Christ Perspective"; Theodore L. Trost, "The Eucharist in the Evangelical and Reformed Tradition"; and Horton Davies, "The Lord's Supper in the Congregational Christian Tradition," in *Prism,* vol. I, no. 2, Fall 1986.

39. This project, undertaken in 1978, had produced several study documents through 1985, including especially Faith and Order Paper No. 119,

The Roots of Our Common Faith; and No. 124, *Apostolic Faith Today: a Handbook for Study* (Geneva: World Council of Churches, 1985).

Chapter 3
Christian Unity and Church Union

1. See Meredith B. Handspicker, "Faith and Order 1948–1968" in Harold Fey, ed., *A History of the Ecumenical Movement,* vol. 2, 1948–1968 (Philadelphia: Westminster Press, 1970), pp. 143 ff.; as well as reports of World Council of Churches assemblies from 1961 to the present. Also see Michael Kinnamon, ed. *Unity in Each Place, in All Places: United Churches and the Christian World Communions,* Faith and Order Paper No. 118. (Geneva: World Council of Churches, 1982), p. 1.

2. *Constitution of World Council of Churches* (Geneva, 1972).

3. Reports of these consultations—Bossey 1967, Limuru 1970, Toronto 1975, and Colombo 1981—are available from the World Council of Churches.

4. "Notes from the Limuru Discussion," *Mid-Stream,* Conference on Church Union negotiations, vol. IX, nos. 2–3, April 1970, p. 22.

5. In this connection see Handspicker's discussion, op. cit., pp. 162–64.

6. See Roger L. Shinn, "Doctrinal Freedom and Responsibility," in *Prism,* Intro. Issue, Fall 1985, pp. 45–56.

7. Ibid. See specifically pp. 45–47.

8. "Called to Witness to Christ's Cross and Glory"—A Message from the Toronto Consultation of United Churches and Committees on Union, June 2–9, 1976, in *Mid-Stream,* vol. XIV, no. 4, Oct. 1975, p. 546.

9. Article IV, paragraph 219 of the Bylaws. In the 1961 edition of the Constitution this responsibility belonged to the Theological Commission.

10. Article V, paragraph 228 of the Bylaws.

11. These include the World Council of Churches, National Council of Churches, World Alliance of Reformed Churches, Consultation on Church Union, and all interconfessional dialogues as well as union conversations.

12. Frederick Herzog, *Justice Church* (Maryknoll: Orbis Books, 1980), p. 121. Italics added.

13. Paul Minear, *Images of the Church in the New Testament* (Philadelphia: Westminster Press, 1960), p. 24.

14. See Daniel K. Elazar and John Kincaid, "Covenant and Polity," in *New Conversations,* vol. 4, no. 2, Fall 1979, pp. 4–8. Also Harris Joachim Kraus, "God's Covenant: Old and New Testament," and Fred H. Klooster, "Covenant, Church and Kingdom of God in the New Testament," in Allen O. Miller, *A Covenant Challenge to Our Broken World,* Caribbean and

North American Area Council, World Alliance of Reformed Churches, 1982.

15. *The Christian Century,* no. 12, 1980, pp. 1094ff.

16. Ibid., p. 1097.

17. Ruth Rouse and Stephen Neill, eds., *A History of the Ecumenical Movement, 1517–1948* (Philadelphia: Westminster Press, 1957), p. 495.

18. *Foundations for Ecumenical Commitment* (New York: National Council of Churches, 1980), p. 19.

19. See also Roger L. Shinn, *Unity and Diversity in the United Church of Christ* (Royal Oak, MI: Cathedral Publications, 1972); and especially his "Doctrinal Freedom and Responsibility," op. cit., pp. 45ff.

20. See Ted Peters, "Pluralism as a Theological Problem," *The Christian Century,* Sept. 28, 1982, pp. 843ff.

21. *Mid-Stream,* April 1970, op. cit., p. 14. Italics added.

22. David G. Colwell, "Church Union" in *Reform and Renewal* (Philadelphia: United Church Press, 1966), p. 104.

23. This, unfortunately, was the implication of assurance given in the addition of the "Interpretations" to the *Basis of Union.* See *The Shaping of the United Church of Christ,* pp. 30–37.

24. Rouse and Neill, op. cit., p. 491.

25. *Growing Toward Consensus and Commitment,* Report of the Fourth Consultation of United and Uniting Churches, 1981. Taken from Faith and Order Paper No. 118, *Unity in Each Place, in All Places,* Michal Kinnamon, ed. (Geneva: World Council of Churches, 1983), p. 121.

26. For United Church of Christ awareness of these questions, see Minutes of the Commission for Christian Unity and Ecumenical Study and Service, especially Feb. 19–21, 1962, pp. 2–3 (United Church of Christ Archives, Lancaster, PA).

27. Organized in 1970 by a union of the World Alliance of Reformed Churches Holding the Presbyterian System, and the International Council of Congregational Churches.

28. *An Invitation to Action: The Lutheran-Reformed Dialogue Series III, 1981–1983,* James E. Andrews and Joseph A. Burgess, eds. (Philadelphia: Fortress Press, 1984). See pp. 4–6 for action recommendation.

29. The United Church of Christ reception and action on this report was in the hands of the Council for Ecumenism at this writing.

30. *Report of the Third Assembly of the World Council of Churches, 1961, at New Delhi* (Geneva: World Council of Churches, 1961).

31. Minutes of General Synod XV, June 27 to July 2, 1985, p. 58. Italics added.

32. David Johnson, ed., *Uppsala to Nairobi* (Geneva: World Council of Churches, 1975), p. 79.

33. Brian Tierney, *Foundations of the Conciliar Theory* (Cambridge: Cambridge University Press, 1955).

34. Ibid., pp. 239–40.

35. Ibid., p. 5.

36. John McNeill, *Unitive Protestantism* (Richmond: John Knox Press, 1964), p. 129. Italics added.

37. Ibid., p. 9; see also chapters 1, 2, and 3.

38. See the New Delhi statement of the nature of unity.

39. I am grateful to Paul A. Crow Jr. for this way of characterizing conciliarity. See his *Christian Unity: Matrix and Mission* (New York: Friendship Press, 1982), esp. pp. 109–10.

40. See, for example, David Nelson Beach, *Conciliar Congregationalism in the United States* (New Haven: Whaples-Bullis, 1957).

Chapter 4
The Ecumenical Vocation: Full Communion

1. See the report as quoted in chapter 3, p. 56.

2. A discussion of the meaning of "conciliar fellowship" is included in chapter 3, pp. 55–58.

3. See Appendix 6, pp. 59–71 of the Minutes of General Synod II, July 5–9, 1959.

4. Ibid., p. 71.

5. Ibid., pp. 58–60. The importance of this was discussed in chapter 1.

6. See Minutes of the General Council of Congregational Christian Churches, June 1942, Durham, NH. Later, this work was related also to the Congregational Christian Service Committee, which was given responsibility for relief and reconstruction.

7. For the above information and parts of the subsequent sessions I am indebted to Howard F. Schomer, Harold H. Wilke, and Peter J. Meister who provided personal interviews and many documents; to Robert B. Starbuck for a clarifying letter; and to Kenneth R. Ziebell, Europe Secretary of the UCBWM, for access to pertinent files. Additional information was gleaned from the official Minutes of the General Synod.

8. A notable example, which actually predated the formation of the UCC by two months, involved English Congregationalism in a relationship of full communion with the United Evangelical Protestant Church of the Palatinate in the upper Rhineland of West Germany. In April of 1957 an agreement on "unrestricted communion of Pulpit and Lord's Table" between churches of the Palatinate and the International Council of Congregational Churches was celebrated at the cathedral in Speyer (West Germany). Douglas Horton and Howard Schomer represented American

Congregationalists as observers. In this case also, it was the reaching out of the EKU that led to a momentous celebration of reconciliation.

9. In this matter see Minutes of the EKU/UCC Consultation, June 2–9, 1980 in East Berlin, in the Archives, Eden Theological Seminary, St. Louis, MO.

10. "Called to Witness to Christ's Cross and Glory," *A Message from the Toronto Consultation of United Churches and Committees on Union*, June 2–9, 1975, in *Mid-Stream,* vol. XIV, no. 4, October 1975, p. 546.

11. Ibid., p. 549.

12. Ibid., pp. 547–49.

13. Moss had further talks with EKU delegates at Toronto, especially with Dr. Friedrich Winter of the EKU East and Dr. Reinhard Groscurth of the EKU West.

14. The EKU East delegates included Bishop Horst Gienke, the Rev. Ursula Radke and Dr. Erwin Hinz. Also present was a delegation from the EKU West: Mr. Hans Eissler and Pastors Peter Kraske, Juergen Schroer, and Horst Wiegand.

15. In a memorandum from Howard Schomer to David Stowe and Robert Moss, dated Sept. 3, 1975 (from the files of the UCBWM).

16. Ibid., p. 2.

17. This hope was forstalled when the government of the German Democratic Republic refused approval. The GDR was highly suspicious of any approaches from churches of the West at the very time it was exerting every effort to shape the EKU East into the patterns of life in a socialist state.

18. This information is drawn from correspondence among Meeks, Stackhouse, Schomer, Meister, of the UCC; and Ernst-Eugen Meckel of the EKU East. Copies are in the files of the UCBWM and the Archives, Eden Theological Seminary, St. Louis.

19. *Report on the Establishment of the UCC/EKU Working Group,* Nov. 1976, Archives, Eden Theological Seminary, and the UCBWM files.

20. See Minutes of the UCC/EKU Working Group, March 15–17, 1979, Eden Archives.

21. Minutes of the UCC/EKU Working Group, June 6–12, 1980. The resolution in full appeared in *A.D.,* May 1981, p. 35.

22. Ibid., p. 2.

23. Ibid., p. 1. Italics added.

24. Reference was made to the "Sound Teaching" report in chapters 1 and 2.

25. Op. cit., p. 2.

26. Ibid., p. 5.

27. The substance of this and the implementing actions (including quotations) is taken from the Minutes of General Synod XIII, June 27–July 1, 1981, pp. 61–62.

28. See the discussion of socio-moral ecumenicity in chapter 2 where that is seen as "life and work" ecumenicity.

29. Minutes of UCC/EKU Working Group, Oct. 15–17, 1981, p. 2. Eden Archives. Italics added.

30. The issues implied in the "full communion" action had received full discussion in the Working Group, the most helpful being recorded in the Minutes of Sept. 25–27, 1980, just three months after the EKU Synods had voted. The discussions underline the *unfinished* character of the whole matter.

31. The *UCC/EKU Newsletter,* published about twice each year, was a medium of communication with persons in the Instrumentalities, Conferences and various Agencies.

32. As quoted in Minutes of the EKU/UCC Consultation in East Berlin, June 6–12, 1980. Eden Seminary Archives.

33. From a letter of Prof. Lothar Schreiner to Prof. Frederick Herzog, quoted in the *EKU/UCC Newsletter,* vol. II, no. 1, April 1981, p. 3.

34. See ibid., vol. II, no. 2, Aug. 1981, p. 2.

35. Ibid., p. 3. Italics added.

36. Minutes of General Synod XIII, 1981, pp. 61–62.

Chapter 5
The Ecumenical Vocation: Ecumenical Partnership

1. See Minutes of General Synod XV, June 27–July 2, 1985, pp. 58–60.

2. See the discussion of conciliarity in the concluding section of chapter 3.

3. See David Johnson, ed., *Uppsala to Nairobi* (Geneva: World Council of Churches, 1975), p. 79. Italics added.

4. Minutes of the General Synod XII, 1979, p. 72.

5. See "Report and Recommendations of the Steering Committee on the Covenant Between the United Church of Christ and the Christian Church (Disciples of Christ)." Minutes of General Synod XV, 1985, p. 171.

6. Ibid., p. 167. Italics added.

7. Ibid., p. 168.

8. Ibid., p. 169.

9. Ibid., p. 170.

10. Ibid., Italics added.

11. Ibid.

12. Ibid., 1985, p. 171. Italics added.

13. Guidelines for the implementation of partnership in these areas are the responsibility of an Ecumenical Partnership Committee, the appoint-

ment of which rested with the Christian Church General Assembly and the United Church of Christ General Synod.

14. Minutes of General Synod XV, 1985, p. 171.

15. See Appendix A. Italics added.

16. See Appendix B for a bibliographic note concerning pertinent historical materials.

17. Characterizing the Disciples of Christ "an American religious movement" is common among their own writers. See, for example, George G. Beazley Jr., ed., *The Christian Church (Disciples of Christ): An Interpretative Examination in the Cultural Context* (St. Louis: Bethany Press, 1973), p. 16.

18. See, for example, David Dunn, et al., *A History of the Evangelical and Reformed Church* (Philadelphia: The Christian Education Press, 1961).

19. This is an observation made by Dietrich Bonhoeffer on his first American visit when commenting on the issue of the unity of the church in relation to denominations. See his *No Rusty Swords, Letters, Lectures, Notes, 1928-36,* from his Collected Works, vol. 1, ed. & trans., by E.H. Robertson and John Bowden (New York: Harper & Row, 1965), pp. 94-101.

20. See Beazley, op. cit., chaps. I and XIII; also Ronald E. Osborn, ed., *The Reformation of Tradition* (St. Louis: Bethany Press, 1963), pt. I.

21. Although there are excellent special studies of each of these founders, the general reader will find exceptionally helpful interpretations in Beazley, op. cit., and Osborn, op. cit. In addition, see Ralph G. Wilburn, ed., *The Reconstruction of Theology* (St. Louis: Bethany Press, 1963).

22. In this matter, see especially the three-volume work by a panel of scholars, edited by R.E. Osborn, op. cit., especially R.G. Wilburn and W.B. Blakemore, eds., *The Revival of the Churches* (St. Louis: Bethany Press, 1963).

23. See Beazley, op. cit., p. 24; but especially Dwight E. Stevenson, *Walter Scott: Voice of the Golden Oracle* (St. Louis: Christian Board of Publication, 1946).

24. See Wilburn, op. cit., pp. 315-16.

25. See, for example: the *Evangelical Catechism* of the Evangelical Synod of North America, which affirms that "faith is complete trust in God and willing acceptance of his grace through Jesus Christ." (Question and Answer #80) (St. Louis: Eden Publishing House, 1929); and the *Heidelberg Catechism* of the Reformed Church in the U.S., which affirms that faith "is not only a certain knowledge by which I accept as true all that God has revealed to us in his Word, but also a wholehearted trust which the Holy Spirit creates in me through the gospel, that, not only to others, but

to me also, God has given the forgiveness of sins, everlasting righteousness and salvation, out of sheer grace solely, for the sake of Christ's saving work." (Question and Answer #21) (New York: United Church Press, 1962).

26. In this connection see David D. Hall, *The Faithful Shepherd: A History of the New England Ministry in the Seventeenth Century* (New York: W.W. Norton & Co., 1972), ch. 2. The literature on Puritan life is voluminous, but Hall's book serves to set the issue of the authority of the Bible in relation to the Puritan understanding of the ministry.

27. Robert Richardson, quoted in Osborn, *The Reformation of Tradition*, op. cit., p. 34.

28. Beazley, *op. cit.*, p. 87.

29. Elmer J.F. Arndt, *The Faith We Proclaim* (Philadelphia: The Christian Education Press, 1960).

30. Ibid., pp. 5-6.

31. Thomas Campbell, *Declaration and Address* (St. Louis: Bethany Press, 1955).

32. Alexander Campbell, *The Christian System* (St. Louis: Bethany Press, 1955).

33. Barton W. Stone, *Last Will and Testament of the Springfield Presbytery* (St. Louis: Bethany Press, 1955).

34. John Locke, *The Reasonableness of Christianity* (London: Adam and Ch. Black, 1958).

35. Williston Walker, *The Creeds and Platforms of Congregationalism* (New York: The Pilgrim Press, 1960).

36. Ibid. In this matter see Douglas Horton's "Introduction."

37. Ralph G. Wilburn's discussion is especially revealing. See Osborn, op. cit., ch. 11.

38. Ibid., pp. 230–31. Italics added.

39. See Ronald E. Osborn's "Crisis and Reformation" in *The Reformation of Tradition* op. cit., pp. 23ff.

40. Quoted in Beazley, op. cit., pp. 21–22, from Thomas Campbell's *Declaration and Address.*

41. See Osborn, *The Reformation of Tradition,* op. cit., p. 27.

42. In Wilburn and Blakemore, *The Revival of the Churches,* op. cit., p. 97.

43. See Minutes of the Commission on Christian Unity and Ecumenical Study and Service, 1960–1973, Archives, Lancaster Theological Seminary. The ecumenical roles, respectively, of the Commission, the President, and the Executive Council were continuing subjects of discussion and debate.

44. Ibid. See especially the Minutes of Nov. 4–6, 1964 and Nov. 10–15, 1965.

45. See Minutes of General Synod XV, 1985, p. 171. Italics added.

Chapter 6
The Ecumenical Vocation: Consensus and Covenanting

1. The COCU proposal set forth in *Covenanting Toward Unity* and *The COCU Consensus* was received by the United Church of Christ in 1985. The Council for Ecumenism set up a reception process that anticipated General Synod action in 1987. See Minutes of the Council for Ecumenism, Sept. 22–24, 1985.

2. The stages of this growing thrust of the ecumenical movement are shown in the themes of the first three assemblies of the World Council of Churches: Amsterdam in 1948—"Man's Disorder and God's Design"; Evanston in 1954—"Christ the Hope of the World"; New Delhi in 1961—"Jesus Christ the Saviour of the World."

3. See "Response" by Eugene Carson Blake, in *Digest of the Proceedings of the Fourteenth Meeting of the Consultation on Church Union,* vol. XIV, Jan. 22–24, 1980, p. 8.

4. Co-presidents Fred Hoskins and James Wagner were among other UCC delegates present at the triennial meeting of the National Council of Churches, at Grace Episcopal Cathedral in San Francisco, December 1960, when Eugene Carson Blake, Stated Clerk of the United Presbyterian Church, gave the sermon—"Toward the Reunion of Christ's Church"—in which he proposed that the United Presbyterian Church, the Episcopal Church, the Methodist Church, and the United Church of Christ, gather to form a "plan of union." David Colwell represented the UCC at a planning meeting in Washington in October 1961. In March 1962 the Consultation on Church Union was born.

5. From Blake sermon, ibid. Italics added.

6. This formulation is known as the *Chicago-Lambeth Quadrilateral,* a series of agreements required by the Episcopal Church in its conversations with the Presbyterians in 1886–1888.

7. Stephen C. Rose, "Councils, Consortia, and COCU," in *Church Union at Midpoint,* Paul A. Crow Jr., and William Jerry Boney, eds. (New York: Association Press, 1972), p. 160. Italics added.

8. Paul A. Crow Jr., "Living Our Way Toward Union: COCU's Vital Signs," in *Mid-Stream,* vol. XIV, no. 2, 1975, p. 211.

9. Ibid., pp. 212–13. Italics added.

10. Ironically, many persons saw the abandonment of a design for union as a defeat and the possible death of the Consultation. The new model had no basis in most church union experiences up to that time.

11. John Deschner, "The Theological Agenda of the Consultation on Church Union," *Mid-Stream,* op. cit., p. 275. Italics added.

12. Albert Outler, "The Mingling of Ministries," *Digest of the Proceed-*

ings of the Eighth Meeting of the Consultation on Church Union, March 17–20, 1969, vol. VIII, p. 107.

13. See J. Lesslie Newbigbin, "Can the West Be Converted?" *Princeton Seminary Bulletin,* vol. VI, no. 1, 1985, p. 36.

14. Ibid. See also in this connection Robert Bellah, et al., *Habits of the Heart* (Berkeley: University of California Press, 1985).

15. Canon Burgess Carr, "Liberation, Solidarity and Promise," *Mid-Stream,* vol. XVI, no. 1, Jan. 1977, pp. 4–5.

16. *Digest of the Proceedings of the Fifteenth Annual Meeting of the Consultation on Church Union,* March 9–12, 1982, vol XV, p. 255ff.

17. Ibid.

18. Ibid., p. 256. Italics added.

19. Ibid., p. 194. Italics added.

20. A helpful discussion of the catholicity of the Reformed tradition is given in M. Eugene Osterhaven, *The Spirit of the Reformed Tradition* (Grand Rapids: Eerdmans, 1971), pp. 39–43.

21. See John T. McNeill, *Unitive Protestantism* (Richmond: John Knox Press, 1964), ch. II.

22. *Digest of the Proceedings,* 1982, op. cit., p. 259. Italics added.

23. Other churches raised questions too. For example, a Presbyterian response was: "Save us from bishops and a hierarchy of command; we thought we got away from Rome. . . . We need a bishop like we need another head." See *Digest,* ibid., p. 240.

24. Paul M. Harrison, *Authority and Power in the Free Church Tradition* (Princeton: Princeton University Press, 1959), pp. 21–22. Italics added.

25. Ibid., p. 24.

26. *The COCU Consensus: In Quest of a Church of Christ Uniting* (Princeton: Consultation on Church Union, 1985), pp. 40–45.

27. Roger Hazelton, "Consensus Theology: Reflections on the COCU Experience," *Andover Newton Quarterly,* vol. 12, no. 1, p. 10. Italics added.

28. *The COCU Consensus,* op. cit., p. v.

29. Ibid., p. 2.

30. Ibid., p. 3. Italics added.

31. *Uppsala to Nairobi* (Geneva: World Council of Churches, 1975), p. 79.

32. *Covenanting Toward Unity: From Consensus to Communion* (Princeton: Consultation on Church Union, 1985), p. 7.

33. Ibid., p. 5. Italics added.

34. Ibid., p. 6.

35. Evidence of this is the extremely limited budget provided for ecu-

menical responsibility—a factor that has been noted by other church bodies.

Chapter 7
Learnings from the Ecclesial Journey

1. See my "Order and Identity in the United Church of Christ," *New Conversations,* vol. 4, no. 2, Fall 1979, p. 9.

2. See Reuben A. Sheares II, "Perspectives on the Polity of the UCC," a paper prepared for the Office for Church Life and Leadership and included in part in *The Manual on Ministry,* 1986 edition; also James E. Andrews and Joseph A. Burgess, eds., *An Invitation to Action: The Lutheran-Reformed Dialogue, Series III, 1981–83* (Philadelphia: Fortress Press, 1984), p. 90.

3. Sheares, ibid., pp. 4–7.

4. The Church of South India is an outstanding example. However, the example of the United Church of Christ and its influence in the new directions of the Consultation on Church Union is also obvious.

5. J. Lesslie Newbigin, *Reunion of the Church* (London: SCM Press, 1948), p. 184. Italics added. Bishop Newbigin was the preacher at the Uniting General Synod on June 27, 1957 when the UCC was born. See also Michael Kinnamon, ed., *Unity in Each Place, in All Places: United Churches and the Christian World Communions,* Faith and Order Paper No. 118 (Geneva: World Council of Churches, 1983).

6. Newbigin, ibid., p. 185.

7. See the Preambles of both the *Basis of Union* and the UCC Constitution and Bylaws.

8. Much of the material in this section is drawn from my essay "Order and Identity in the United Church of Christ," *New Conversations,* op. cit., pp. 9–16. Used by permission.

9. John T. McNeill, *Unitive Protestantism* (Richmond: John Knox Press, 1964), p. 129. See also the discussion of this in chapter 3 above.

10. See the discussions of this in *The Shaping of the United Church of Christ,* chapter 4.

11. See Williston Walker, *The Creeds and Platforms of Congregationalism,* Introduction by Douglas Horton (New York: The Pilgrim Press, 1960), p. viii.

12. See Minutes of General Synod XV, 1985, p. 58; also Minutes of General Synod XIII, 1981, p. 62.

13. See "Toward an Understanding of Local Autonomy," published in 1969 by the Executive Council. The Faith Exploration process, authorized

in 1971 and implemented by the Council for Lay Life and Work, had its primary focus on issues of personal faith. Ecclesiological questions were tangential.

14. Available from the Office for Church Life and Leadership, but also included as an appendix in Frederick Herzog, *Justice Church* (Maryknoll: Orbis Books, 1980), pp. 140ff.

15. See Herzog, ibid., p. 140.

16. The message of the "thirty-nine" was entitled: "A Most Difficult and Urgent Time," and was printed in *New Conversations,* vol. 8, no. 1, Spring 1985, pp. 2–4.

17. In "Response: the Craigville Colloquy," by Gabriel Fackre, Lori Buehler, Richard L. Floyd in *New Conversations,* vol. 8, no. 1, Spring 1985, p. 33.

18. Frederick H. Herzog and Susan B. Thistlethwaite, *New Conversations,* ibid., p. 5.

19. See Minutes of General Synod XIII, p. 62.

20. See the discussion of organizational anomalies of the UCC in chapter 4.

21. In correspondence about the full communion covenant with the EKU, Frederick Herzog raised with me the question of UCC capability for that covenant.

22. Oral reports from Frederick Herzog and Frederick Trost are the basis of this discussion. These representatives of the UCC had the responsibility of interpreting UCC ecclesiological and doctrinal traditions.

23. The traditional tension between Life and Work/Faith and Order has been at the very heart of many of the inconsistencies in UCC ecumenical responsibilities.

24. See Minutes of General Synod XIII, 1981, p. 62. Italics added.

25. James E. Andrews and Joseph A. Burgess, eds. (Philadelphia: Fortress Press, 1984).

26. Ibid., p. 90.

27. Ibid., p. xvii.

28. See Todd W. Nichol, "An Invitation to Action: Dialogue, Debate, and Decision" in *Dialogue,* Summer 1986, pp. 217–18 especially.

29. Minutes of General Synod IX, 1973, p. 58. Italics added.

30. Ibid., p. 59. Italics added.

31. Ibid., p. 59. The statement includes actions recommended for implementation of this "ecumenical stance," all of which specifically relate the UCC effort to the wider bodies of the church universal.

32. Ibid., p. 60. Italics added.

33. In this connection see again J. Lesslie Newbigin, "Can the West be

Converted?" in *The Princeton Seminary Bulletin,* vol. VI, no. 1, 1985, p. 36.

34. *The Christian Century,* no. 12, 1980, pp. 1094ff. Italics added.

35. In "Consensus Theology: Reflections on the COCU Experience," *Andover Newton Quarterly,* vol. 12, no. 1, p. 10. Italics added.

36. See the discussion of this in chapter 2.

37. See Question and Answer #54, *Heidelberg Catechism.*

38. Frederick S. Carney, in D. B. Robertson, ed., *Voluntary Associations: A Study of Groups in Free Societies* (Richmond: John Knox Press, 1966), pp. 49–50.

39. For a good discussion of this see Karl Hertz, "The Nature of Voluntary Associations," in Robertson, ibid., pp. 17–35.

40. See James M. Gustafson, "The Voluntary Church: a Moral Appraisal," in Robertson, ibid., p. 313.

Chapter 8
The UCC Ecclesial Model

1. Minutes of General Synod VI, June 22–29, 1967, p. 175.

2. E.g., see the 1984 edition, Constitution and Bylaws, Art. V, paragraph 22.

3. Ehrenstrom and Muelder, *Institutionalism and Church Unity* (New York: Association Press, 1963), pp. 29–30.

4. Ehrenstrom and Muelder, ibid., p. 33.

5. In this connection see Robert N. Bellah, et al, *Habits of the Heart: Individualism and Commitment in American Life* (Berkeley: University of California Press, 1985), especially chapters 6 and 9.

6. Hans Dombois, "The Church as Koinonia and Institution," in Ehrenstrom and Muelder, op. cit., p. 119.

7. See Frederick Herzog's excellent discussion of the relationship, for example, between worship and polity, in Herzog and Thistlethwaite, *New Conversations,* vol. 8, no. 1, Spring 1985, p. 27.

8. John Calvin, *Institutes of the Christian Religion* (Philadelphia: Presbyterian Board of Christian Education, 1930), vol. II, bk. III, ch. 7, paragraph 1. Italics added.

9. See my discussion of this in "Order and Identity in the United Church of Christ" in *New Conversations,* vol. IV, no. 2, Fall 1979, p. 14.

10. John T. McNeill, *Unitive Protestantism,* (Richmond: John Knox Press, 1964), p. 129. Italics added.

11. Roger L. Shinn, "Doctrinal Freedom and Responsibility" *Prism,* Intro. Issue, Fall 1985, p. 46.

12. Robin W. Lovin in *The Journal of Religion*, vol. 60, no. 1, Jan. 1980, pp. 8–9. Italics added.

13. Ibid., pp. 11–12.

14. See Roger L. Shinn in *Prism*, Intro. Issue, Fall 1985, p. 46.

15. See Zikmund's perceptive discussion of this in "Minister and Ministry in a Covenant System," *New Conversations*, vol. 4, no. 2, Fall 1979, pp. 23–28.

16. Ibid., p. 26. Italics added.

17. *Manual on Ministry* (New York: Office for Church Life and Leadership, 1977), p. 5.

18. In this connection see Charles Hambrick-Stowe, "The Nature of the Ministry: The United Church of Christ and Baptism, Eucharist and Ministry," *Prism*, Intro. Issue, Fall 1985, pp. 26–44, in which the complementary understandings of the ministry in early Congregationalism and early Reformed practice are indicated.

19. Susan Brooks Thistlethwaite has properly lamented the growing tendency to use the politically-conceived caucus method of doing theology that has accompanied the confrontation and caucus tactics frequently employed in General Synod. See "The Vision That Has Formed the United Church of Christ: Authority and Accountability" in *On the Way*, Occasional Papers of the Wisconsin Conference of the UCC, vol. 3, no. 2, Winter 1985–86, p. 7.

20. Lovin, op. cit., p. 9.

21. J. Lesslie Newbigin, *The Household of God* (New York: Friendship Press, 1953), p. 161.

22. Produced by the UCC Conference on Mission, Jan. 9–12, 1987, and used by permission of the Stewardship Council of the United Church of Christ.

23. I have discussed this in two lectures published in *On the Way*, vol. 3, no. 2, Winter 1985–86, pp. 12–27: "Baptism, the Sacrament of Christian Vocation" and "The Eucharist, Sacrament of Discipleship." It is a subject that will receive major attention throughout the Christian community of faith in the next few years.

24. Faith and Order Paper No. 111, Geneva: World Council of Churches, 1982, pp. vii–ix. Italics added.

25. In this connection see the points made by Frederick Herzog concerning the structures of worship in *New Conversations*, vol. 8, no. 3, Spring 1985, p. 27.

Index

Freedom 153-54, 159
Fry, John L. 193
Full Communion 22, 60-62, 65, 69-84,
89-90, 109, 143-46

German Congregational churches/people
28, 62-63
German Evangelicals 95
German Reformed Church 95, 124
Gienke, Horst 201
Goebel, Louis W. 31, 196
Grauer, Gerhard 114
Great Awakening 94, 124
Grengel, Christa 70
Groscurth, Reinhard 70, 201
Gustafson, James M. 209
Gutierrez, Gustavo 197

Hall, David A. 204
Hambrick-Stowe, Charles 197, 210
Hammelmann, Howard K. 64
Hammer, Paul L. 70
Handspicker, Meredith J. 196, 198
Harder, Gunther 61, 64
Harland, Gordon 193
Harrison, Paul M. 124, 206
Hazelton, Roger 61, 114, 151, 206
Held, Heinrich 60
Herbster, Ben M. 64, 114
Hertz, Karl 209
Herzog, Frederick 35, 37, 70-71, 81,
144-45, 193-94, 197-98, 202, 208-10
Hinz, Erwin 201
Historical consciousness 59, 81, 123
Hobbes, Thomas 47, 168
Hoekendijk, J. C. 35, 197
Hordern, William B. 196
Horst, Mark 193
Horton, Douglas 31, 140, 200, 207
Hoskins, Fred 60, 205
Huenemann, Ruben H. 35
Hume, Theodore C. 62

Idealism (German) 96
Iserlohn 78, 81, 83

Johnson, David 199, 202
Justice 73-74, 77-78, 81, 83

Keiling, Hanns Peter 28-31, 196
Kelley, Dean 195
Kincaid, John 198
Kinnamon, Michael 198-99, 207
Kirchengemeinschaft 71, 73-74, 79, 81-82
Klooster, Fred H. 198
Koch, Henry 64
Koinonia 66
Kraske, Peter 201
Kraus, Harris J. 198

Lasch, Christopher 193
Ledbetter, Theodore A. 32
Lee, Carlton 63
Libbey, Scott 35, 106
Liberation theology 37
Life and work ecumenicity 75
Life and Work Movement 12, 25
Lima Consultation 54
Liturgies/liturgical 128-29, 178
Locke, John 47, 95, 97, 103, 105, 168, 204
Lovin, Robin H. 168-69, 175, 210
Luther, Martin 57, 99
Lutheran churches 147-48
Lutheran tradition 79
Lutheran World Federation 147
Lutheran-Reformed dialogue 53, 55,
147-48

McKinney, William 195
McNeill, John 56-57, 139-40, 163, 200,
206, 209
Marty, Martin 11, 193, 195
Meckel, Ernst-Eugen 68, 201
Meeks, M. Douglas 35, 68-69, 201
Meister, Peter J. 35, 42, 63, 65, 68-69,
200-201
Mercersburg Theology 124, 196
Miller, Allen O. 198
Minear, Paul S. 12, 194-96, 198
Ministry 77, 119-22, 169-72
Mission
and unity 176-78
statement (UCC) 177

213

Minear, Paul

images &
church of NT

fly '98 —
reference